D0795166

HUMAN RELATIONSHIP SKILLS

Also by Richard Nelson-Jones and published by Cassell:

Practical Counselling and Helping Skills
The Theory and Practice of Counselling Psychology
Effective Thinking Skills: Preventing and Managing Personal
Problems

To be published in 1991:

Group Leadership: A Lifeskills Approach

HUMAN RELATIONSHIP SKILLS:
TRAINING AND SELF-HELP
SECOND EDITION

RICHARD NELSON-JONES

CASSELL

First published in 1990 by
Cassell Educational Limited
Villiers House, 41/47 Strand, London WC2N 5JE

© Richard Nelson-Jones 1986, 1990

First published 1986
Reprinted 1989
Second edition 1990

British Library Cataloguing in Publication Data
Nelson-Jones, Richard *1936*–
 Human relationship skills: training and self-help.
 2nd. ed.
 1. Interpersonal relationships. Psychological aspects
 I. Title II. Nelson-Jones, Richard *1936*–. Human
 relationship skills
 158.2

ISBN 0-304-31962-7

Designed by Vaughan Allen
Typset by Colset Private Limited, Singapore
Printed and bound in Great Britain by
Biddles Ltd., Guildford and King's Lynn

CONTENTS

EXERCISES

EXPERIMENTS

PREFACE

*T*his book represents a development of my earlier book, *Human Relationship Skills*. It explores the practical, day-to-day realities of striving to be a loving person. Love is viewed as more than a sentiment, be it affectionate nurturing, romantic or erotic. Love entails using relationship skills that affirm and support yourself and others. The skills of loving are the skills of effective relationships. They are skills that are applicable not just to close personal relationships, but to all dealings with other humans, for instance, in schools and workplaces.

Paradoxically, despite the centrality of relationships in all our lives, few children are systematically trained in the skills of relating. Consequently, all too often, people bring to their later relationships significant gaps in information and skills. This book is intended to provide a resource for relationship skills courses in a wide variety of settings inside and outside education: schools, colleges, teacher training institutions, marriage guidance councils, parent education centres, youth centres, social work agencies, hospitals, businesses, industrial organizations, the civil service, prisons, career services, religious institutions and voluntary agencies. Furthermore, the book may be used by clients working on relationship problems in counselling and psychotherapy. Additionally, it may be used for self-help by those neither on courses nor in therapy. In particular, I hope this book reaches out to and strikes a respondent chord in young people.

I do not advocate a 'pill' mentality. Loving or relationship skills are difficult both to acquire and to use on a daily basis. How many truly loving people have you come across in your life? Relationships are all too often disfigured by inner ignorance, fears and anxieties that translate into outer unhelpful behaviours. Relationship skills are viewed as series of choices that may be either well or poorly made. Ideally, people should be systematically prepared for loving relationships, especially before making major commitments such as marriage and parenthood. Even then, relationships require constant attention to the skills that keep them healthy rather than in pain.

Three main sets of values permeate this book. The first is pragmatic existentialism. Despite the givens of their existences, people are personally responsible for making their lives through the quality of their choices. The second value reflects Christian ethics. Loving relationships involve not just asking what others can do for you, an emphasis on being loved, but asking what you can do for others, an emphasis on expressing caring and love. This book offers a 'kinder, gentler' approach than that found in many psychology books on relating. The third value is that of applied social science. Much of this book is based on research evidence as well as on my professional experience as a counselling psychologist and counsellor educator.

This book differs from its predecessor in a number of ways. Greater emphasis is placed on people working together for me, you and us rather than for me alone. New chapters have been included on what you bring to relationships, choosing relationships and deepening relationships. Existing chapters have been rewritten, updated and expanded. In addition to the exercises throughout the book, readers are now invited to conduct a series of personal experiments, which challenge them to try out and evaluate the use of their changed skills in everyday life. Also, a much fuller listing of references is provided in the bibliography at the end of the book. Works likely to be of special interest to the non-professional reader are indicated with an asterisk.

Appreciations are due to: Naomi Roth and the editorial and production team at Cassell for their work in preparing the book; Dawn Butcher, who typed the manuscript; the undergraduates and postgraduates in my relationship skills and helping skills classes who have been a constant challenge to communicate clearly; and all those writers and researchers whose ideas are incorporated into the book.

I hope that you enjoy your time with the book. Also I hope that, even if only in some small way, the book helps put you more in touch with your potential as a loving person and enriches your relationships both now and in future.

Richard Nelson-Jones
Melbourne, Australia
September 1989

— 1 —

The challenge of loving relationships

Hatred paralyses life; love releases it.
Hatred confuses life; love harmonizes it.
Hatred darkens life; love illuminates it.

Martin Luther King

I love mankind – it's people I can't stand.

Charles M. Schultz

*T*his book explores what it means to be a loving person in your relationships. You are born and die alone. In between you are confronted with your existential isolation, solitariness and, sometimes, loneliness. Human beings hunger to break out of their isolation through connectedness with fellow humans. You seek to affirm your existence by reaching out and making contact with others. Your connections with others are your relationships.

The quality of how you relate is important. Ideally in relationships people strive to enhance each other through the giving, receiving and sharing of affection. However, in reality, perfect relationships are as much an illusion as perfect love. Loving relationships do not just involve sharing your strengths. They involve trying to confront and satisfactorily manage your own and others' vulnerabilities and anxieties. There can be strength in this too.

THE NATURE OF LOVE

Defining love

Dictionary definitions of love emphasize a warm or strong affection or liking for another person. This may or may not have a sexual component. However, such definitions of love are centred on the person feeling the love. They fail to indicate whether and how the love is expressed. They say nothing about the degree of commitment to the well-being of the beloved. Additionally, they beg the question of whether the expression of this love would affirm rather than upset its object or objects.

Popular definitions of love emphasize romantic love and erotic love. Romantic love focuses on the experience of falling in love. You meet a stranger and have the experience of strong mutual attraction and sudden intimacy. Romantic love is without effort on your part. You explore and experience each other in the best of circumstances and live happily ever after. In romantic love there is more an emphasis on being loved rather than on loving. It is the stuff on which illusions and false expectations are built. Such illusions may be enjoyable and risk free so long as they are not confused with reality.

Another popular fallacy is to confuse copulation with love. Sexual coupling can be an important manifestation of the fusion of two separate beings who are committed in their tender and affectionate feelings for each other. However, sexual coupling can also be one of the loneliest acts available to humans. People can claw at each other's bodies hoping for a temporary escape from the meaninglessness of their existence. The experience of 'making love' in these circumstances does not remove the pain of their emptiness. Above I have stated the two extremes: sex in a committed relationship and casual sex. Much sexual activity falls between these extremes. Though sexual intercourse may be a fundamental expression of love, copulation in itself is not.

What is the definition of love used in this book? When the Viennese psychiatrist Alfred Adler heard that an egocentric person had fallen in love, he said: 'Against whom?' The emphasis here is on the giving rather than on the receiving of love. Love is defined as *making choices that affirm both yourself and others in your relationships*. This giving of your yourself may entail receiving another's love. However, my main focus is on the messages you send rather than on those that you receive. Such love is expressed in your daily choices with a range of people and not just in your intimate relationships. To the extent that your thoughts, feelings and actions affirm rather than hurt others you are a loving person.

The targets of love

The major focus of this book is on starting, developing and maintaining close personal relationships with a partner and with friends. However, in your daily life there are many other possibilities for loving relationships. Below I list some of the possible targets for your loving behaviour. This list is intended to be illustrative rather than exhaustive.

- *Self-love.* In his play *An Ideal Husband* Oscar Wilde had a character say: 'To love oneself is the beginning of a life-long romance'. The extent to which you are able to care for and nurture yourself influences the energy and attention that you have available for loving others. There is a difference between self-love and selfishness. Self-love means having the personal security, knowledge and skills to be able to affirm your existence. Self-love is based on sufficiency, not deficiency. Your capacity to realize your full humanness is sufficiently intact so that you are capable of forming loving relationships with others. In Maslow's (1962) terms you are motived towards growth rather than towards defence and safety. Your growth entails the affirmation of others along with yourself.

    Selfishness, on the other hand, is a deficiency disease. You are fixated by your own unmet needs to the point where you relate to others as objects to be manipulated rather than as persons to be loved. Your preoccupation with yourself blocks you from transcending your ego-centricity to experience others as unique and separate individuals. Fromm (1956) observes: 'Selfishness and self-love, far from being identical, are actually opposites. The selfish person does not love himself too much but too little; in fact he hates himself' (p. 51).

- *Love for a partner.* Humans appear to have a need for a primary relationship in which they give and receive love from a special person with whom they live. Such relationships form the basis for procreating and rearing children. Ideally, these relationships are between partners who possess not only self-love but also the skills of loving relationships. Another way of viewing this is that, in most cultures, humans seek out one especially intimate relationship. Such intimacy has connotations of depth, privacy, physical closeness and psychological and sexual familiarity. The quality of such relationships is influenced by the extent to which partners are able to penetrate, prize and develop the core of personhood in each other.

• *Love of friends.* People also affirm themselves and each other in their friendships. Friends give an added sense of belonging. They provide opportunities for shared communication and activities. Additionally, they can provide psychological support, for instance cushioning the effects of a bereavement, and physical assistance, for instance help with tasks such as transportation and home decorating. Friends help you out of your solitude. Along with their positive benefits they can help you avoid the emotional ill-effects of prolonged isolation and loneliness. Furthermore, friends can support your view of the world and help keep your self-esteem intact (Duck, 1983).

• *Love for the young.* In his review of the theoretical and research literature on the effects of maternal deprivation in children's early years, Rutter (1972) observes that the chief bond need be neither with a biological parent nor with a female. He states: 'A less exclusive focus on the mother is required. Children also have fathers!' (p. 125). The issue of sex differences or the extent to which males and females differ by nature rather than by nurture is a theme that will be revisited at many points in this book. Rutter's observation supports the notion of a parenting instinct amongst humans that is relatively independent of biological sex. Additionally, it does not require that the children be your own. It is a more general love for the young which involves a mixture of nurturing them and helping them acquire the skills to take their place in the world. Fromm's (1956) division of these functions into motherly love and fatherly love appears erroneous. To be loved is every child's birthright. Unfortunately, many parents have difficulty adequately showing their love because their partner relationships are distressed. Rutter (1972) comments: 'Discord, tension and lack of affection in the home all appear to increase the likelihood of children showing disorders of conduct' (p. 125).

• *Love of neighbour.* In this context love of neighbour refers to the way you treat people with whom you come into contact outside your family and friends. One such group of people is literally your neighbours. To what extent do you show them affection, indifference or outright hostility? Would you and their life be richer if you chose to alter the nature of your contact? Most often you do not choose your neighbours and you may wish to preserve your privacy. Nevertheless, your neighbours provide a possibility for you to affirm each other's existence. Another opportunity is provided when you go to work. Many work settings are full of discord and dirty politics. To what extent do you help or hurt yourself and your colleagues? To what extent do you deal fairly with your clients? Still a further opportunity for affirming yourself or others comes in briefer contacts with people you meet in the street, at bus stops and in the shops.

- *Love of enemies.* This is a particularly difficult area for non-Christians and Christians alike. Also, it is not independent of the other targets of love. At times you may feel that your partner, friends, children and colleagues act in ways that are hostile to your interests. On other occasions, you may feel you are being discriminated against on account of your ethnic background, race, sex, age or some other distinguishing attribute. You and the groups to which you belong may be subject to unwarranted and unacceptable provocations. Loving your enemy cuts to the core of your own feelings of self-love and personal adequacy. It does not mean giving way to injustice. It does mean having the inner strength to be assertive rather than aggressive, working for reconciliation, and developing the capacity for forgiveness and understanding of your own and others' human fallibility. There is ample evidence that in personal as well as international relations hateful actions beget hateful actions. The urge for revenge and getting even can be strong. Concerning the need to avoid hatred in the American civil rights movement, Martin Luther King (1963) wrote: 'One day we shall win freedom, but not only for ourselves. We shall so appeal to your heart and conscience that we shall win *you* in the process, and our victory will be a double victory' (p. 55). King's message has relevance to striving for less hatred in personal relations.

- *Love of the human species.* This form of love is based on a deep identification with the human species. Its basic premise is that all people are brothers and sisters in the human family. What divides people is superficial, what unites them is their common humanity. This love is expressed by the Greek word *agape* meaning a selfless concern for all humans. Christians see *agape* as God's overflowing love operating in the human heart. However, such love is not restricted to people of specific religious faiths. It is a characteristic of all highly developed humans regardless of race, colour or creed. Maslow (1970) observed that his self-actualizing subjects possessed a deep affection, sympathy and identification with human beings in general, despite their manifest failings. He added: 'Because of this they have a genuine desire to help the human race. It is as if they were all members of a single family' (p. 165). Genuine concern for the human species involves acting on their behalf. Good intentions and warm feelings are insufficient.

You may be able to think of other targets of love not mentioned above; for instance, love of parents. Each of you is confronted with numerous everyday opportunities to affirm yourself and others in your relationships. The skills described in this book are focused on your immediate contacts. Nevertheless, they may have some relevance for how you relate to the wider human community.

WHAT ARE THE SKILLS OF LOVING?

Reasons for and against viewing loving in skills terms

There are a number of reasons why some of you may resist the notion that loving involves skills. You may focus on infatuation and falling in love where feelings are paramount. However, my focus is on the everyday skills of being a loving person. You may consider a skills approach unnatural. You have been born with a style of relating and you do not wish to have this interfered with by acquiring artificial skills. Also, you may find it hard to accept how much of your behaviour is learned habit.

You may consider a skills approach superficial in that it may help you to describe rather than to change your behaviour. You may consider it mechanistic in that people can go through the motions of having skills without engaging in genuine contact. Also, you may think a skills approach is manipulative in that it teaches people to get what they want without necessarily caring for others.

The above reservations indicate some of the dangers in viewing loving in skills terms. However, they are dangers connected with the inappropriate application of the concept of loving skills rather than with the concept itself. For instance, while clumsy application of skills may interfere with spontaneity in loving, use of good skills should enhance it.

There are also dangers in *not* viewing loving in skills terms. Relationships are perhaps the major source of human pleasure and pain. As documented later in·this chapter, there is ample evidence that problems of sustaining loving relationships are widespread in Britain and elsewhere. Paradoxically, despite their importance, little systematic attempt is made to train you in the skills of loving. Instead you are expected to 'pick them up' informally in your homes, schools, workplaces and communities. What tends to happen is that you learn many unhelpful along with helpful habits.

A systematic attempt to train you in the skills of loving means that these skills need to be identified and clearly stated. A major advantage of viewing loving in skills terms is that it encourages such specificity. Advice and admonitions to be more loving do not tell you how to go about it. You lack the 'handles' to work on your behaviour. When the skills of loving are clearly stated a number of important consequences follow. First, you can assess the degree to which you possess these skills. Second, either by yourself or with a trainer, you can work and practise to improve skills you have identified as deficient. Third, you are in a better position to maintain your loving behaviour because you know the component skills of which it is made up. Loving behaviour has been removed from the realms of romance and magic to specific skills. It is now something that you can strive to bring under your control.

What are skills?

The meanings of the word *skill* include proficiency, competence and expertness in some activity. However, the essential element of any skill is the ability to make and implement an effective sequence of choices so as to achieve a desired objective. For instance, if you are to be a good listener you have to make and implement the choices involved in good listening.

The concept of skill is best viewed not as an either/or matter in which you either possess or do not possess a skill. Rather it is preferable to think of yourself as possessing *skills strengths* and *weaknesses* or a mixture of the two. If you make good choices in a skills area, for instance either in listening or in talking about yourself, this is a skills strength. If you make poor choices in a skills area, this is a skills weakness. In all the skills areas of being a loving person you are likely to possess both strengths and weaknesses in varying degrees. For instance, in the skills area of listening, you may be good at understanding talkers but poor at showing them that you actually have understood. The object of working on your skills is, in one or more areas, to help you shift the balance of your strengths and weaknesses more in the direction of strengths. Put another way, it is to help you affirm yourself and others more by becoming a *better chooser*.

Defining the skills of loving

In your various relationships you need to use a *repertoire of skills*. Some of you may not have a particular skill in your repertoire: for instance, the ability to say no to an unreasonable request. Others of you may want to strengthen a skill in your repertoire: for instance, by being able to say no less aggressively.

Below is a definition of the skills of loving.

The skills of loving are sequences of choices that enable you to affirm yourself and others in your relationships. These sequences of choices involve thoughts, feelings and actions. Your repertoire of loving skills comprises your strengths and weaknesses in each skills area.

Identifying the skills of loving

The skills of loving involve you in being an authentic person. In other than casual contacts you are encouraged to avoid a superficial niceness in which you inhibit communicating what you really think and feel. However, one of the main themes of this book is that loving others requires self-awareness and self-discipline. Though you are real, this is not unnecessarily at others' expense.

At this stage it is only possible to identify the skills of loving in an introductory way. Further elaboration must be left to the remaining chapters. Exercise 1 encourages you to explore how you currently relate in a number of different skills areas. The meaning of some of the skills may not be altogether clear to you so early in the book. Nevertheless, the identification of the skills has been made into an exercise to encourage your active participation in assessing and working on your skills. Remember that you are viewed as having good skills if you make good choices and poor skills if you make poor choices.

EXERCISE
—1—

Assessing my skills of loving

The questionnaire below lists a number of the skills of loving relationships in thirteen broad areas. Rate how satisfied you are with your skills using the rating scale below:

3 *Much* need for improvement
2 *Moderate* need for improvement
1 *Slight* need for improvement
0 *No* need for improvement

Put a question mark (?) rather than a rating by any skill whose meaning is not clear to you at this stage of the book. Take as much time as you need.

Awareness of what I bring to my relationships

MY
RATING   SKILLS

	Awareness of my current skills strengths and weaknesses
	Assuming responsibility for my thoughts, feelings and actions in relationships

☐ Understanding the influence of my upbringing

☐ Ability to listen to my feelings

☐ Absence of debilitating fears

☐ Acknowledging and being comfortable with my sexuality

☐ Sensitivity to sex-role issues in relationships

☐ Sensitivity to social and cultural issues

Communicating myself

☐ Using words well

☐ Communicating well with my voice messages

☐ Communicating well with by body messages

☐ Using touch sensitively

☐ Ability to make 'I' statements

☐ Sharing personal information

☐ Expressing my feelings appropriately

Good listening

☐ Knowing the difference between my own and another's internal viewpoint

☐ Demonstrating interest and attention

☐ Ability to decode what another says

☐ Awareness of my barriers to listening

Helpful responding

☐ Showing accurate understanding of words

☐ Showing accurate understanding of feelings

☐ Showing accurate understanding of feelings and their reasons

☐ Being safe to talk to

☐ Using helpful questions

Confronting

☐ Knowing when to confront

☐ Confronting inconsistencies

☐ Confronting distortions of reality

Overcoming shyness and making initial contact

☐ Accurately attributing cause for my shyness

☐ Using coping self-talk

☐ Possessing realistic personal rules regarding rejection

☐ Not jumping to unwarranted perceptual conclusions

☐ Predicting reward as well as risk

☐ Conversation skills

☐ Making a date skills

Choosing relationships

☐ Avoiding impulsiveness

☐ Avoiding narrow-mindedness

☐ Picking up cues of interest

☐ Identifying another's values

☐ Identifying another's personal rules

☐ Assessing another's skills of loving

Developing relationships

☐ Progressively deepening and matching the intimacy level of disclosing

☐ Being trustworthy

☐ Confronting issues in the relationship

☐ Using touch constructively

☐ Integrating sexuality

Asserting myself

☐ Overcoming mental barriers to assertion

☐ Expressing wants and wishes

☐ Taking sex-role-free initiatives

☐ Acting positively towards others

☐ Standing up to negative behaviour

☐ Not letting others define me on their terms

☐ Ending relationships assertively

Perceiving in relationships

☐ Avoiding labelling myself negatively

☐ Owning my strengths

☐ Letting go of defensiveness

☐ Acknowledging another's strengths

☐ Explaining another's behaviour accurately

Managing anger and hatred

☐ Awareness of my anger

☐ Expressing anger constructively

☐ Using thinking skills to regulate angry feelings

☐ Handling criticism constructively

☐ Handling hatred constructively

☐ Forgiving and letting go of resentments

Managing conflict

	Possessing a collaborative orientation towards conflict
	Being prepared to increase rewarding behaviours
	Confronting conflicts constructively
	Understanding another's position
	Stating my own position clearly
	Defining problems constructively with another
	Searching for and evaluating alternative solutions with another
	Agreeing upon and making a clear 'contract' to implement the best solution

The strength to love

	Monitoring my skills of loving
	Maintaining my skills of loving
	Developing my skills of loving
	Possessing the inner strength and courage to keep loving

Conclude the exercise by summarizing your skills of loving. This statement should avoid generalities and specifically indicate:

1 my skills of loving strengths,
2 my skills of loving weaknesses, and
3 my goals for change.

PERSONAL RESPONSIBILITY FOR SKILLS OF LOVING

The basic assumption of this book is that ultimately you are personally responsible for your survival, happiness and fulfilment (Nelson-Jones, 1984). To use President Truman's expression: 'The buck stops here'. Now what does this stark existential truth mean? Here are some considerations.

Defining personal responsibility

When you are being personally responsible you are in the process of making the choices that maximize your happiness and fulfilment. Personal responsibility is a positive concept whereby you are responsible *for* your well-being and making your *own* choices. It contrasts with a common meaning of responsibility, namely that of responsibility *to* others, including living up to their standards. Though the process of personal responsibility can be far from easy, adopting it as a basic attitude toward living liberates you to concentrate on how you can be most effective. It entails neither focusing on other people's faults nor feeling that you need say 'my fault' all the time.

Are you always responsible for your choices? The answer is 'yes', but with qualifications. The first qualification is that there was a maturational lag in that your capacity for reasoning when a child developed later than your need to make some of the choices that would help you live most effectively. Consequently, one way in which you acquired skills weaknesses was through not having the early reasoning power to make good choices. Your bad initial choices may then have developed into bad loving skills habits. A second and related qualification is that an attitude of personal responsibility and the ability to make effective choices are learned. If your learning from the consequences provided for your behaviour and from observing others' examples has been deficient, that may well have diminished your effectiveness. Additionally, if your environment continues to be deficient in providing corrective learning opportunities, this may further contribute to maintaining your loving skills weaknesses. Third, many social factors may work against your assuming personal responsibility. Adverse conditions like poor housing, urban overcrowding, unemployment, poverty, racial discrimination, and poor educational opportunities each may make it difficult for you to learn to make and to keep making the choices that serve you best.

Assuming responsibility for the skills of loving

Earlier the skills of loving were defined as 'sequences of choices that enable you to affirm yourself and others in your relationships'. There are a number of aspects relevant to your assuming responsibility for your skills of loving. It is fruitless to blame yourself or others if your relationship skills are not as good as you would like. The important thing is to become aware of your present strengths and weaknesses and to work to shift the balance more in the direction of strengths. On the subject of blaming, the ancient philosopher Epictetus had the following to say:

> It is the act of an ill-instructed man to blame others for his own bad condition; it is the act of one who has begun to be instructed, to lay the blame on himself; and of one whose instruction has been completed, neither to blame another, nor himself.

All the skills mentioned in Exercise 1 involve choices for which you probably could assume more effective responsibility. Changing your skills weaknesses involves you in acknowledging responsibility for sustaining them. As this book progresses you will, I hope, gain a greater awareness of your present pattern of relating. If so, you are also likely to become more aware of the range of loving skills choices open to you. Then it becomes a matter of whether you wish to make the change choice or stay with the 'stick in the mud' choice.

actions. Assuming responsibility for these skills also involves this triple focus. For example, responsibility for feelings can involve both the capacity to be in touch with your feelings and to regulate them where appropriate. Responsibility for thinking emphasizes avoiding self-defeating thinking: for example, thinking skills weaknesses that contribute to anxiety, depression, anger and blaming. Responsibility for acting entails communicating yourself to others in ways that affirm rather than disconfirm.

Below is a sample of self-talk (what you can say to yourself) that may help you understand this section.

> I am personally responsible for the way I think, feel and act in my relationships. Adverse past and present circumstances may make it more difficult for me to be an effective chooser. Nevertheless, I am still responsible for making my life through the quality of my choices. For the sake of my future happiness and fulfilment I have much to gain for working hard to acquire, maintain and develop the skills of loving.

PAIN IN RELATIONSHIPS

The course of true love never did run smooth.

William Shakespeare

Human relationships can be a celebration of life for their participants. On the other hand they can cause much psychological pain and despair. The world is full of beauty and hate. Below I present some data indicating that the course of true love does not always run smooth.

Marital breakdown and distress

The rate of divorce in the USA is the highest in the Western world. In the early 1980s the divorce rate for first marriages was 49 per cent (Glick, 1984). Though not at the level of the United States, the number of divorces in England and Wales more than doubled in the period 1971 to 1985: from 75,000 to 154,000 (Office of Population Census and Surveys, 1987). Along with the increase in divorce, there has also been an increase in remarriage. In England and Wales, the proportion of marriages involving a divorced partner grew from 2 per cent in 1940 to 33 per cent in 1985. Population projections by marital status indicate that, between 1985 and 2000, the number of divorced people in England and Wales is expected to rise by 64 per cent, from 1.9 million to 3.2 million (Haskey, 1988).

In Australia, the percentage of marriages ending in divorce increased from 14 per cent in 1971 to 35 per cent in 1986. In 1971, in 14 per cent of marriages, one or both partners was remarrying: by 1986, this figure had more than doubled, to 33 per cent. Divorce rates were a little higher for remarriages of divorced persons than for persons in their first marriage (McDonald, 1988). In New Zealand, the divorce rate has more than doubled from 35.2 per 10,000 currently married women in 1968 to 87.0 in 1980 (Carmichael, 1985).

In Britain, Australia and New Zealand, the divorce figures underestimate the extent of marital breakdown. If figures for the separated population were added to those of the divorced population to form a 'dissolution index', the statistics for marital breakdown would be considerably higher. Additionally, for numerous reasons—such as cultural norms, concern for children, religious beliefs, financial insecurity and fear of loneliness—many couples remain neither separated nor divorced, but unhappy. Add these people to the 'dissolution index' and more marriages may end up unhappy than happy.

Marital breakdown and distress involve children. In 1986, in England and Wales, 152,000 children under 16 were affected by divorce (Office of Population Census and Surveys, 1987). Haskey (1986) estimated that, at the current levels of divorce, 20 per cent of children would experience a divorce in their family before reaching the age of 16. The situation in Australia is similar. McDonald (1988) writes: 'Based on 1986 experience, about 16 percent of children can expect to experience the divorce of their parents before they reach their 16th birthday' (p. 41). Unhappy parents are likely to have less positive energy to direct towards their children. Also, the risk is ever-present of children being used as unwitting soldiers in their parents' war games.

Divorce also leads to single-parent families. In 1984, there were approximately 940,000 such families in Great Britain, an increase of 12 per cent over 1979 (Haskey, 1986). Ninety-one per cent of these families were headed by lone mothers. In July 1983, there were 295,300 families characterized by the Australian Bureau of Statistics as 'other families' with dependent children present. Most of these were single-parent families headed by females (Australian Institute of Family Studies, 1985).

Rising to the challenge of loving relationships

Despite the above disquieting statistics, undoubtedly there are good as well as bad times in families that break up. Also, the position relative to the past seems worse than it is because divorce is now both easier to get and less socially stigmatized. Nevertheless, the amount of family breakdown, separation and distress suggested above is staggering. Tens of millions of people are hurting, hurting others and getting hurt through difficulties in sustaining loving relationships. The figures indicate how fragile human relationships can be, even when entered into with the best of intentions. They suggest all too many shattered dreams and broken promises.

The challenge of loving relationships is that they are extremely difficult. You are constantly faced with your own and others' weaknesses and required to rise above them. Each of you has a huge capacity for affection and kindness. You are challenged by life to develop the skills and make the choices that allow you to express this capacity. You have many strengths already. I hope that this book helps you to build on these strengths.

CONCLUDING SELF-TALK

This and subsequent chapters ends with a segment of self-talk that you can tell yourself to remind you of the chapter's main points.

To be a loving person I need to make choices that affirm both myself and others in my relationships. There is ample evidence that many people have distressed rather than fulfilled relationships. To relate well I need to develop and use a repertoire of loving skills. Each skill represents a sequence of choices made in an area. If I make good choices, I exhibit skills strengths. If I make poor choices, I exhibit skills weaknesses. The skills of loving are too important to be left to chance. I need to assess my skills strengths and weaknesses and to identify those skills requiring improvement. If I rise to the challenge of loving relationships by improving my skills I shall benefit both myself and others. I CAN BE A MORE LOVING PERSON!

— 2 —

What you bring to relationships

If you'd be loved, be worthy to be loved.

Ovid

He who conquers others is strong;
He who conquers himself is mighty.

Laotse

*T*his chapter aims to raise your awareness of the importance of what you bring into your relationships and of social and cultural factors affecting them. Each of you brings a personal history into your relationships. For instance, in England and Wales in 1987 the average at first marriage was 24 for brides and 26 for grooms (Office of Population Census and Surveys, 1988). Consequently, the average female and male brought 24 and 26 years of previous living into their marriages. They would need to be 48 and 52 before they had lived as much time within their marriage as outside it. If the trend toward later marrying continues then partners will bring even more years of previous living into their marriages. Just as people bring their personal histories into their marriages, so they bring them into all their other relationships, whatever the degree of intimacy. Additionally, relationships always take place in cultural and social contexts. These influence the previous personal histories of participants as well as how they behave together in the present and future.

This chapter looks at what you bring to your relationships in seven somewhat overlapping areas: how you learned your loving skills; your thinking skills; your capacity to feel; your sense of worth and anxieties; your sexuality; your sex-role identity and expectations; and your culture, race and social class.

HOW YOU LEARNED YOUR LOVING SKILLS

Unlike other animals whose behaviour is programmed by instincts, most human behaviour is learned. Humans tend to have instinct remnants rather than strong instincts (Maslow, 1970). The human animal is also distinguished from other animals by its capacity for self-awareness and conscious thought. Consequently, not only is human behaviour learned in the first place but then humans keep regulating it by the way they think.

Acquiring and maintaining loving skills

A useful distinction is that between *acquiring* skills and *maintaining* them. In a sense each one of you has at least two learning histories for every skill: acquiring the skill in the first place, which is the traditional definition of learning, and then improving, diminishing or maintaining your initial level of skill. It is an important distinction because changing or improving a skill entails changing what is *maintaining* the skill at a lower level than desirable in the present and future. It is impossible to go back and change how a skills weakness was first *acquired*.

For example, Jill, 17, initially learned to be shy because her parents had a 'children should be seen and not heard' rule. She maintained her shyness throughout her childhood and adolescence partly because her parents continued not to encourage her to talk about herself. At this stage she cannot change how she became shy. Also, it is uncertain whether her parents' behaviour, which plays an important part in maintaining her shyness, can be changed. However, Jill can work to acquire the self-help skills of being more outgoing. Also, if necessary, she can seek professional help, such as from a school or college counsellor, designed to provide her with learning experiences enabling her to become less shy. Thus, she can create for herself a third learning history by making new choices to overcome skills weaknesses that have previously been acquired and also maintained. A further reason why a distinction between acquisition and maintenance is desirable is that, even when you possess good skills of loving, you still have to work to maintain them. There is no concept of cure, just a daily struggle.

Sources of influence

From the moment of birth numerous people give you messages that influence the development of your skills of loving. Some of these messages help you to relate more effectively whereas others weaken your effectiveness. Sometimes these messages are consistent and at other times they may be contradictory, not just to the extent of different messages from different people but also from the same person. Children especially are influenced in acquiring good and bad skills of loving. They are physically and emotionally dependent on others and also intellectually immature.

Let us now look at the kinds of people who may have influenced and may still influence the choices you make in the relationships. Such people include:

- *Parents.* These include step-parents and other substitute parents.

- *Brothers and sisters.* They may be influential especially if older, but not too old to be out of frequent contact.

- *Grandparents.* Your grandparents brought up your parents, and consequently their influence lives on through others as well as through themselves, if alive.

- *Aunts and uncles.* Like grandparents, aunts and uncles may be important. However, greater geographic mobility than previously within families may sometimes lessen their importance.

- *Older friends.* Friends of the family who visit fairly frequently.

- *Community leaders.* People in church, medical, sporting and other visible positions.

- *Peer groups.* People of roughly your own age, outside your immediate family, with whom you play and study.

- *Teachers*. Contact with teachers may be either in class or in extracurricular activities, for instance games, music.

- *Famous people*. Such people may be well-known sports or entertainment personalities. Some may be historical and religious leaders.

- *Fictional people*. Characters portrayed in books, on TV and in movies.

- *Advertising*. People behaving in specific ways with the purpose of influencing purchasing decisions.

Learning from example

'Monkey see, monkey do' is one way of viewing learning from example. However, frequently people do not just imitate behaviour blindly but they think about what they have seen. Albert Bandura (1977) is a psychologist who has done much research into learning from example. He considers that the observer is more likely to adopt another's example if the behaviour demonstrated is valued by the observer and brings rewards to the person being observed. The other main way of learning, learning from consequences, gets discussed in the next section. In reality, learning from consequences and from example overlap.

The behaviour that you learn from example includes feelings, thoughts and actions. Below are some illustrations.

Charles's mother had a stroke when he was 17. As a result she was unable to dress herself and had much less energy than previously. He saw his father support her both practically, for instance helping her get dressed, and emotionally. His father never said 'What a great guy I am', but just quietly went about showing his care and concern.

Alice, 15, and Bruce, 10, live in a family where both parents find it very hard to express their emotions. There is virtually no touching between parents and children apart from a brief goodnight kiss. When Alice and Bruce do things that please their parents, this is seldom commented on. However, the children's 'faults' are painstakingly explained to them.

The style of managing conflict in the Morgan family is

one of competitive combat. Each parent has to be right, has 'legitimate' reasons for anger, and shouts and finger points. They do not listen to each other. Blame is the name of the game. The three children, aged 4, 7 and 9, get very upset when their parents fight.

A number of points are implicit in the above illustrations. First, demonstrating behaviour may be unintentional as well as intentional. Second, it often involves deficient rather than good skills of loving. Third, the observers may remain unaware that they are learning from example. In families, it is all to easy for children to adopt their parents' behaviour without conscious choice. They learn loving skills strengths and weaknesses along with eating their breakfast cereal. A consequence of this is that each of you may not only have absorbed some deficient loving skills, but you may have the added barrier of remaining unaware that you have done so.

You acquired and are influenced to maintain your loving skills strengths and weaknesses through messages received from many categories of people. The most important is usually your parents. You were exposed to them first, in a very intense way, when you were dependent on them at an age when your critical powers were still in process of development. Exercise 2 is designed to help you explore the loving skills behaviours (feelings, thoughts, actions) that your parents demonstrated and may still demonstrate. These include both strengths and weaknesses.

EXERCISE
——2——

Learning loving skills from the examples set by my parents

INSTRUCTIONS

1. What were the examples set by your parents in each of the following loving skills areas? In most instances 'parents' refers to your biological parents. However, if a step-parent or surrogate parent has been more important to you, answer in respect of him or her.

Sender skills	*Your mother*	*Your father*
Talking about their experiences		
Showing their feelings		
Standing up for themselves		

Receiver skills	*Your mother*	*Your father*
Being a good listener		
Understanding what others say		
Responding helpfully to others		

Managing anger & conflict skills	*Your mother*	*Your father*
Managing anger constructively		
Accepting responsibility for their behaviour		
Working for rational solutions		

2. Summarize what you consider the effects of your parents' examples have been on your current skills of loving in each of the following areas:

- sending information
- receiving information
- managing anger and conflict

Learning from consequences

When as a child you were naughty, your parents may well have said 'bad girl' or 'bad boy'. When you behaved well, your parents were more likely to say 'good girl' or 'good boy'. In each instance, your parents were granting or withholding the reward of their approval. As a child you not only learned from the consequences of your behaviour provided by others but also from the consequences or feedback given you by your feelings. For instance, if teasing one of your friends was pleasurable, this was likely to increase the probability of future teasing of that person. The main set of internal consequences provided by your feelings was whether your actions produced pleasure or pain for you.

Sometimes a conflict may have occurred in that behaviours that were pleasurable for you were disapproved by your parents. If your parents' reaction was very strong you may have buried your true feelings and owned your parents' feelings *as if* they were your own. People tend to talk about themselves as though they have access to their own feelings without distortion. However, frequently their feelings are the result of their parents' examples and rewards rather than what they would truly feel given a more accepting upbringing. Below is an example.

> When Frank was a child he would cry easily both when he got into fights with other children and when he saw something sad on television. When Frank cried during a fight, other children were quick to put him down as a 'sissy' and a 'cry baby'. His father, who was afraid his son might become a homosexual, told him how wet he was to cry watching television and that he was behaving more like a girl. After a time, Frank began to think of crying in boys and men as a sign of weakness.

Many people provided positive and negative consequences for your loving skills behaviour as you grew up. Both your strengths and your weaknesses may have been *either* rewarded, *or* discouraged and possibly punished, *or* ignored.

The basic idea is that behaviour that has resulted in positive consequences for you has a higher probability of being repeated than that resulting in negative consequences. Exercise 3 is designed to help you further understand how you came to learn your current loving skills behaviour. Though others too may have provided important consequences, the exercise focuses on the consequences provided by your parents.

EXERCISE
—3—

The consequences provided by my parents for my loving skills behaviour

INSTRUCTIONS

1. Indicate the extent to which you were rewarded by your parents for each of the following behaviours, by putting an M in the box that best describes your mother's reaction and an F in the box that best describes your father's reaction. Also, try to give one or two specific examples of their behaviour. If answering in terms of a biological parent is inappropriate, answer for a step-parent or surrogate parent.

Your behaviour	Reward from parents			
	Much	*Little*	*None*	*Punished*
Expressing affection to him/her				
Expressing anger to him/her				
Expressing your opinions on current affairs				
Expressing negative feelings about yourself (e.g. depression)				

Reward from parents

Your behaviour	Much	Little	None	Punished
Expressing positive feelings about yourself (e.g. happiness)				
Saying you wish to be left out of parental disagreements				
Being prepared to listen to him/her				
Responding helpfully to him/her				
Requesting participation in decisions involving you				
Wanting to discuss a conflict between you				
Stating your position in the conflict				
Trying to understand his/her position				
Placating and giving in to him/her				
Working for a rational solution to a conflict with him/her				

2. Summarize what you consider to be the effects of the consequences for your behaviour provided by your parents on your current loving skills strengths and weaknesses.

In this section I have focused more on how you initially acquired your loving skills, what others did to you, rather than in how you maintain them, what you do to yourself. You bring to your relationship your loving skills strengths and weaknesses. Though change can be difficult, you can choose not to stay with skills that do not work for you.

YOUR THINKING SKILLS

Since wars begin in the minds of men, it is in the minds of men that the defences of peace must be constructed.

UNESCO Constitution

When you relate to another, other than in casual contact, you think about what happens before, during and after you see them. Consequently, the skills of loving include your thinking skills. Your thinking skills are the choices that you make in various skill areas. A few of these skills are described below, but for a further discussion you are referred both elsewhere (Nelson-Jones, 1989) and to later chapters in this book. You can either support or oppress yourself and others by your thinking choices. In turn these choices lead to helpful or hurtful actions towards yourself and them.

You bring your thinking skills strengths and weaknesses into your relationships. A major theme of this book is that if you are to exercise the strength to love you must work hard to overcome the thinking skills weaknesses that are conducive to hatred. Effective thinking involves dealing with yourself and others on the basis of reality. You are open to all significant incoming information, appraise it rationally and then act appropriately. Ineffective thinking is characterized by rigidity, defensiveness and insufficient attention to the available facts. Since you deny and distort significant information you do not have an adequate data base for relating to others as both you and they are.

Thinking skills that are important in relating to others include the following. Each skill is mentioned briefly now and elaborated in later chapters.

- *Use of self-talk.*
    You can talk to yourself in ways that calm you down, keep you focused on what you want to achieve and help

you to emphasize positive rather than negative aspects of yourself and others. Alternatively, you can talk to yourself in ways that heighten negative feelings like hatred, depression, anxiety and jealousy.

- *Choosing realistic personal rules.*
    Each person has an inner rule book of personal rules for living. Your personal rules are the standards by which you live. Your rules can either blight your relationships through their rigidity and irrationality or provide you with realistic and flexible guidelines for your own and others' behaviour. The skill of choosing realistic personal rules includes becoming aware of when your rules may be oppressing rather than supporting you. In such instances, you need either to discard the unrealistic rules altogether or to reformulate them into more rational standards for your own and others' behaviour.
    Here are some examples of traditional personal rules in the areas of dating, sex, marriage and family.

Dating. People should act politely on dates and not reveal too much of their inner thoughts and feelings.

Sex. Sex before marriage, even in a steady relationship, is wrong.

Marriage. In marriage, each partner must meet all the intellectual, emotional, social and sexual needs of the other.

Family. The worst thing that can happen is for a family to break up, however unhappy everyone may be.

In a time when traditional rules and values are being challenged, there is more pressure on you to choose your own personal rules. You may have acquired many of your rules from others and be maintaining them without having thought them through for yourself. When your rules are life-enhancing, this may not matter. However, some rules may be destructive to your capacity to love, and they consequently require attention.

- *Perceiving yourself and others accurately.*
    Two people in a relationship do not just relate to each other. Instead, they relate to their perceptions of

themselves, each other and their relationship. These perceptions may be of varying degrees of accuracy. Another way of saying this is that in a relationship each person develops a *personification* of themselves and of the other person. These personifications – literally meaning making up or fabricating a person – are the mental maps that guide their relationship journeys.

You bring into your relationships your skills of perceiving yourself and others accurately. Central to this is the ability to distinguish fact from inference. Your perceptions are your subjective facts, but they are not necessarily objective facts. They may contain many inferences of varying degrees of realism in terms of the available facts.

There are other thinking skills that are important for your relationships. Fundamental is the skill of assuming responsibility for acquiring, maintaining and developing your skills of loving. Related to this you need a conceptual framework that allows you to think about relating in skills terms and identifies which skills are important. The challenge to work on your skills of loving requires specifying them. Other thinking skills important for your relationships include: how you attribute cause or offer explanations for your own and others' behaviour; how you make decisions, including major decisions about marriage and parenthood; and how you manage your problems and conflicts.

Adopting a sporting analogy, the skills of loving involve an inner game, coming to grips with your thinking, as well as an outer game, how you act towards others. If you play a good inner game, you increase your probability of acting in loving ways, preventing avoidable unhappiness, and working constructively to resolve conflicts.

YOUR CAPACITY TO FEEL

Seeing's believing, but feeling's the truth.
Thomas Fuller

You bring to your relationships your capacity to experience your feelings. Carl Rogers, in particular, stressed that a feature of modern life was that all people, in varying degrees, were out of touch with their inner valuing process (Rogers, 1961, 1980). Your capacity to experience your own feelings indicates both the degree to which you are able to love yourself and also how open you are to others' feelings.

There are many reasons why it is important to you to be responsive to the flow of your feelings when starting, maintaining and, if necessary, ending your relationships. These include: acknowledging liking and attraction, being spontaneous, being sensual and being rational. It may seem surprising also to include rationality. However, when you are truly in touch with what *you* feel about situations, you are less likely to react unthinkingly on the basis of your previous conditioning.

If you are out of touch with your feelings you are alienated from the core of your personhood. Relationships are most satisfactory when each of you has a secure sense of your own identity as separate individuals as well as an identity you possess in relation to each other. People who think and feel 'I don't really know who I am' or 'I know who I am and am not going to change under any circumstances' both exhibit their underlying feelings of insecurity regarding their identity. Your capacity to feel and, hence, your sense of identity have almost certainly been inhibited and distorted by your conditioning as a female or a male. This point is developed later in the chapter.

What are your feelings?

Dictionary definitions of feelings tend to use words like 'physical sensation', 'emotions' and 'awareness'. All three of these words illustrate a dimension of feelings. Feelings as *physical sensations* represent your underlying animal nature. People are animals first, persons second. As such you need to learn to value and live with your underlying animal nature. Also, to get it working for rather than against you. The word *emotions* implies movement. Feelings are processes. You are subject to a continuous flow of biological experiencing. *Awareness* implies that you can be conscious of your feelings. However, you may also deny and distort them. Furthermore, you may have learned some unexamined personal rules with their related feelings from your parents and others. Thus some of your feelings may be based more on *their* standards rather than on *your own* valuing process.

Listening to your feelings

In your relationships you are constantly required to listen to your feelings. This does not mean that you ignore others' feelings. Being sensitively attuned to your own feelings gives you an excellent basis for tuning into theirs. Listening to your feelings ideally means that these feelings are appropriate to the 'here-and-now' rather than residual feelings from your childhood or other relationships. Listening to past feelings in a present context lessens the relevant information available for you to meet your needs now.

As you read the above paragraph you may have thought, 'What, me? It surely applies only to others that, often without realizing it, they drag their past agendas and feelings inappropriately into the present'. If so, the news is that it probably applies to you, to a greater or lesser degree, as well. Most humans are subject to *illusions* of *autonomy* and *rationality*. They consider that they act independently and rationally most of the time without distracting interference from the residues of childhood and other learning experiences. Such illusions may block you from working to alter your thinking so that you can release your full capacity to feel.

YOUR SENSE OF WORTH AND ANXIETIES

No one can make you feel inferior without your consent.

Eleanor Roosevelt

You bring into your relationships your feelings of security or insecurity and your fears and anxieties. Vulnerability can be an attractive quality. It helps others feel that you and they are part of the human race. It provides the opportunity for caring and being cared for. You can share your own and your partner's vulnerability in ways that enhance and deepen your relationship. Mutual sympathy and liking develop from sensitive understanding of each other's vulnerabilities as much as from appreciation of strengths. Also, if you are unable to acknowledge your own fears and anxieties you are likely to lack responsiveness to other people's.

Your sense of worth

Insecurities and fears, if not confronted and managed, can be the breeding ground for hatred and distress in relationships. Nobody's upbringing is perfect. In varying degrees you have learned to feel 'Not OK' as well as 'OK', even though these 'Not OK' feelings may be difficult for you to acknowledge. Robert Carkhuff (1983) categorizes families into two broad groupings: facilitative and retarding. The members of facilitative families help each other become persons. The members of retarding families are in process of becoming non-persons. In facilitative families, parents are likely to have a secure sense of their own worth which is transmitted to their children. In retarding families, either or both parents feel insecure. Lacking a true sense of their own worth, they send messages that undermine the sense of worth of their children.

Intentionally or unintentionally, when people communicate they send two broad categories of messages. One set is specific, having to do with the ostensible purpose of the communication. The other set of messages may be more general and less intentional. These give the receivers messages pertaining to their worth as persons as well as revealing how high or low the senders value themselves. Children need the security of positive messages about their unique lovableness. Unfortunately, many parents fail to realize that they often send messages that undermine the tender self-esteem of those they love. Sometimes this can have devastating results. This is especially if parents compound their initial communication error by not hearing and understanding the pain their children suffer. Life can be very unfair. Children whose parents mostly send retarding messages are less likely to be heard, even though their need for understanding may be much greater than that of children whose parents mostly send facilitative messages. Exercise 4 aims to help you explore how you learned to feel either worthwhile or worthless as a person and how this affects you now.

EXERCISE
—4—

Learning to feel worthwhile: helpful and harmful experiences

INSTRUCTIONS

Think back over what you saw and experienced when you were growing up that influences the degree of self-esteem that you bring to your current relationships. Some of these experiences were helpful and constructive whereas others were harmful and destructive.

1. Take a piece of paper and head it LEARNING MY SENSE OF WORTH. Draw a line down the centre underneath this heading. At the top of the left column write HELPFUL EXPERIENCES, at the top of the right column write HARMFUL EXPERIENCES.

2. List five experiences that you consider were *helpful* in developing your sense of worth and capacity to love and that you would like to *repeat* with your children.

3. List five experiences that you consider were *harmful* in developing your sense of worth and capacity to love and that you would like to *avoid* with your children.

4. Summarize how secure and confident a person you feel now and how this affects your capacity to relate to others as a loving person.

Your fears and anxieties

Where fear is, happiness is not.

Seneca

Definition of an adult: a child who looks grown up but often has difficulty feeling it.

The late American psychiatrist Harry Stack Sullivan reportedly said that ninety per cent of human communication was specifically designed not to communicate. Anxiety on the part of both senders and receivers distorts much communication. It can be a powerful enemy of love. Ultimately, the fear of death and of non-being is the underlying fear from which all other anxieties are derived. I prefer the term survival anxiety. Anxiety can be both helpful and harmful. It has a survival value in that it alerts you to realistic dangers to your existence. Unfortunately, all people suffer in varying degrees from anxiety that is higher than that required to cope specifically with life's challenges. As such it is disproportionate and debilitating rather than facilitating.

The words anxiety and fear are often used interchangeably. Anxiety may be defined as your fears about your capacity to cope adequately with the future. This may either be a general *trait* of yours or a *state* that applies mainly to specific situations. There is a close connection between your sense of worth and feelings of anxiety. Insecurity both manifests and engenders anxiety. People who feel worthwhile are relatively free from debilitating anxieties.

Adults are little children grown up. One way of looking at loving another person is that the intuitive little child in you feels comfortable with and cares for the little child inside the adult exterior of the person you love. However, children can also carry their psychological wounds and scars into adulthood, especially if they have not developed the skills to manage them. Adults are often full of fears and anxieties. Sometimes these are acknowledged and obvious to all concerned. On other occasions they may not be acknowledged and their insidious effects on communication go largely unrecognized.

Below is an illustrative list of just a few of the anxieties that people may bring into their relationships. These fears represent their subjective rather than objective reality. However, often they are exaggerated and result in self-defeating feelings and actions. Sometimes you may be more afraid of getting what you want than not getting it. Consequently, I group fears into three categories, fear of failure, success and change.

Fear of failure
Fear of rejection
Fears about the attractiveness of your body
Fears about sexual
    performance

Fears about making
  mistakes
Fears about being
  engulfed
Fear of loneliness
Fear of being unhappy
Fear of coping with the
  other sex
Fear of what others
  think

Fear of success
Fears about intimacy
Fear of not being able
  to maintain success
Fear of being happy
Fear of others' envy

Fear of change
Fear of the unknown
Fear of commitment and losing independence
Fear of practical changes: for example, buying a house

Along with your fears and anxieties, you also bring into your relationships skills strengths and weaknesses in coping with them. Also, you possess strengths and weaknesses in coping with others' insecurities and anxieties. Exercise 5 encourages you to look at the fears and anxieties that you may bring into your relationships.

EXERCISE
—5—

Exploring my fears and anxieties

INSTRUCTIONS

Answer the following questions.

1. What fears and anxieties do you bring into your relationships in each of the following areas (if they apply to you):
   - fear of failure,
   - fear of success, and
   - fear of change?

2. What fears and anxieties have you noticed other people bringing into their relationship with you?

3. What do you consider the effects of your own and others' anxieties have been on the quality of your relationships?

YOUR SEXUALITY

Passion, though a bad regulator, is a powerful spring.

Ralph Waldo Emerson

All humans are sexual from birth. However, you have a choice concerning how much of your sexuality you bring into your relationships. Sexuality is at once both simple and complex. On the one hand, nothing can feel simpler than being attracted to someone and wanting to hold them in your arms. On the other hand, your sexuality consists of a complex interplay of physiological, psychological, social and cultural forces.

Sex and love are often confused. Your sexuality can be a powerful force for bridging your separation from others by making and maintaining contact with them. However, you can love people, for instance parents and friends, without being sexually attracted to them. Also, given the ambiguity of human nature and your capacity for choice, you can have affectionate relationships with varying degrees of sexuality implicit in them.

Your sexual feelings

Despite the strength of their sexual urges, people differ in their capacity to experience themselves as sexual beings. This is partly because humans need to learn how to express their sexuality. You bring into your relationships the fruits of your sexual learnings, for good or ill. Hopefully your attitude toward your sexuality is healthy and loving. However, ignorance and poor thinking skills may interfere with your effectiveness. There is probably less ignorance about sex now than previously. Nevertheless, people enter into their relationships with skills weaknesses in respect to: knowledge about their own bodies, how to express tender feelings, and how to give and receive pleasure. Despite the so-called sexual revolution, children's opportunities to learn about integrating their sexuality into loving relationships often leave much to be desired. How many parents are open in talking about their sexuality to their children without imposing their views on them?

Faulty thinking can lead people to either underemphasize or overemphasize their sexuality. Children can pick up their parents' inhibitions about being sexual. A major area for therapists working with sexually dysfunctional couples is that of helping either or both partners work through thoughts interfering with performance, for instance 'sex is dirty' or 'sharing sexual fantasies is wrong'. Additionally, many people have counterproductive fears about their bodies: for instance that either their breasts or penises are too small. Especially for males, poor thinking skills may lead to an exaggerated emphasis on sexual performance. They may boast about their sexual conquests to their peers and treat women as objects rather than persons. Fears underlie both inhibited and exaggerated sexuality. These fears include: acknowledging the strength of sexual feelings; performance fears; and fears about being seen to be sufficiently 'masculine' or 'feminine'.

Sexual preference

You bring your sexual preference to your relationships. The world is not divided into heterosexuals and homosexuals. Pioneering studies on sexual behaviour were conducted in America in the late 1940s and early 1950s by Alfred Kinsey and his colleagues (Kinsey, Pomeroy & Martin, 1948; Kinsey, Pomeroy, Martin & Gebhard, 1953). They found that, in the large predominantly white middle-class population that they surveyed, 4 per cent of males and between 1 to 3 per cent of females were exclusively homosexual. However, by age 45, half the males and about a quarter of the females had responded homosexually by either arousal or orgasm, at some point during their lives. In short, while heterosexuality was very much the predominant sexual preference for both males and females and exclusive homosexuality very much the minority preference, there was a considerable amount of bisexuality.

The Kinsey studies are outdated. Also, they were based on an unrepresentative sample. Nevertheless, they indicate that many females and males are confronted with choices about how to handle homosexual feelings, whether to engage in homosexual sex, and whether to admit their homosexual feelings openly. Kinsey and his colleagues considered that, if social constraints and taboos had not been so strong, there would have been a much higher incidence of homosexual response.

People not only bring their sexual preference to their relationships, but they also bring their fears about their sexual preference. Heterosexuality as well as homosexuality may be repressed. For example, a young man who experiences homosexual attraction to another man may wrongly label himself homosexual rather than, say, a bisexual who is predominantly heterosexual. Especially among males, there is much anxiety about being homosexual. For some the exaggerated emphasis on heterosexual performance is an attempt to gain reassurance. I think it preferable that you acknowledge rather than deny any homosexual feelings. You can then make a conscious choice as to how to handle them.

EXERCISE
—6—

Exploring my sexuality

INSTRUCTIONS
Answer the following questions.

1. To what extent are you satisfied or dissatisfied with your capacity to experience and express your sexuality?

2. Think of your body image. To what extent are you satisfied or dissatisfied with your body from the viewpoint of sexual relating?

3. What is your sexual preference and how do you know? If you are bisexual, identify the extent to which you are heterosexual or homosexual.

4. Do you bring any fears and anxieties about your sexuality into relationship(s) where sex may form a part? If so, be as specific as possible in identifying them.

5. Take a piece of paper and at the top write HOW I LEARNED ABOUT MY SEXUALITY. At the top of the left-hand column write HELPFUL EXPERIENCES and at the top of the right-hand column write HARMFUL EXPERIENCES. List important experiences that have helped or harmed you to express your sexuality in a loving way.

YOUR SEX-ROLE IDENTITY AND EXPECTATIONS

There was, I think, never any reason to believe in any innate superiority of the male, except his superior muscle.

Bertrand Russell

A fundamental value of this book is that of equality between females and males. Equality between the sexes means that both females and males should have the same opportunity to develop and express their humanity. Apart from the realistic constraints of their biological differences, they should have the same opportunity to exercise choice in their lives. Equality between the sexes is an ideal towards which progress is being made in Western societies. In the past both females and males have related both to their own sex and to the other sex in traditional ways that needlessly constricted choice. You are in a transitional period now where perhaps females especially, but also many males, are challenging conventional wisdoms about sex-related attitudes and behaviours. This poses threats and risks as well as exciting opportunities for both sexes. Gender is now on the agenda in all but the most unaware of male–female relationships.

Defining terms

Below I stipulate some definitions of basic terms relevant to your exploring the sex-role expectations that you bring to your relationships.

- *Sex.* In this context sex refers to biological differences between males and females: for instance, differences in genitals, reproductive functions, bone structure and size.

- *Gender.* Gender refers to the social and cultural classification of attributes, attitudes and behaviours as 'feminine' or 'masculine'.

- *Sex-role identity.* Your sex-role identity is how you see yourself on the dimensions of 'masculinity' and 'femininity'.

- *Sex-role expectations.* These are your thoughts and feelings about how you and others should think, feel and behave on account of differences in your biological sex. They are your personal rules in this area.

- *Sexism. Individual* sexism relates to any feelings, thoughts and actions that assume the superiority of one sex over the other. *Institutional* sexism relates to institutional structures that discriminate and devalue a person on the grounds of sex.

Masculinity, femininity and androgyny

In Western societies, certain psychological characteristics have been traditionally viewed as either 'feminine' or 'masculine'. Feminine characteristics have included being: affectionate, gentle, sensitive to the needs of others, tender and warm. Masculine characteristics have included being: aggressive, ambitious, assertive, analytical and dominant (Bem, 1974). The predominant traditional roles of women have been those of the nurturer and social harmonizer within the home. Men's traditional roles have focused on being the breadwinner outside the home and the enforcer of discipline within the home.

Because of differing views about their psychological characteristics and the different emphases of their lives, males and
females have developed different loving skills strengths and
weaknesses. Argyle (1984) states that the research evidence
suggests that there are a number of areas where females may be
more socially competent than males. These include: being
better at sending and receiving body language; being more
rewarding and polite; and disclosing more and forming closer
friendships. However, he notes that being assertive is an area
where women appear to have more problems than men.

Underlying the 'femininity–masculinity' dimension is the
issue of nature versus nurture. The consensus among social
scientists seems increasingly to be that humans have weak
instinctual remnants toward either a male or a female sex-role
identity and that such biological predispositions may be easily
overwhelmed by the strength of their learning experience
(Oakley, 1972). Related to the importance of nurture over
nature has been the increasing popularity of the concept of
psychological androgyny. The androgynous male or female
'. . . is flexibly masculine or feminine as circumstances
warrant . . .' (Bem, 1981, p. 362). Thus, females and males
can be brought up with the capacity to express a range of
characteristics independently whether they have traditionally
been viewed as 'masculine' or 'feminine'. For instance, men
can be tender and women assertive.

So long as males and females increasingly adopt the
strengths rather than the weaknesses of the other sex's gender
characteristics, androgyny offers much promise for improving
and enriching people's skills of loving. This is true for same-sex
as well as other-sex relationships. Already there are many of
both sexes who, in varying degrees, are flexible in exhibiting
masculine and feminine characteristics. It is to be hoped that
there will be a continuing trend toward bringing up and
encouraging more people to express and share the full range of
their psychological characteristics. This is likely to lessen the
amount of loneliness and alienation in Western countries.
Also, in time, 'masculinity' and 'femininity' may become out-
moded concepts.

The ways in which you learned your sex-role identity were
many and varied. Rather than write about them, I have
designed Exercise 7 to tap your recollections of influences on
you to exhibit either 'feminine' or 'masculine' characteristics or
a mixture of the two.

EXERCISE
—7—

Learning my sex-role identity

INSTRUCTIONS

The way you think of yourself as 'masculine' or 'feminine' has been largely learned. Think back over your experiences as you were growing up and answer the following questions.

1. Did you get different toys on account of your sex? Illustrate with examples.

2. Did you get different clothes, including their colour, on account of your sex? Illustrate with examples.

3. What roles did your mother and father play in caring for you as a child?

4. Who did the following household tasks in your family?

    Vacuum cleaning
    Dusting
    Shopping for food
    Cooking meals
    Washing dishes
    Making beds
    Polishing furniture
    Washing clothes
    Ironing
    Mending clothes
    Changing a fuse
    Interior decoration
    Exterior decoration
    Mowing the lawn
    Looking after the car

5. Either in your home or amongst your friends were you ever called a 'sissy' or a 'tomboy'? If so, please give an example.

6. Which of the following psychological characteristics do you consider your parents either encouraged you or discouraged you to show?

being analytical
gentleness
ambition
dominance
showing feelings of vulnerability
concern with your clothes
competitiveness
being nurturing
career orientation
home orientation

7. Did the books and magazines you read when growing up show males and females as having different psychological characteristics, interests and activities? Please give examples.

8. Did the TV programmes you watched when growing up show males and females as having different psychological characteristics, interests and activities? Please give examples.

9. Did the advertising you saw when growing up show males and females as having different psychological characteristics, interests and activities? Please give examples.

10. Which of the following activities were you encouraged to participate in at primary school?

   Football
   Cricket
   Cooking
   Needlework

11. Did your primary school and secondary teachers treat girls and boys differently?

12. At secondary school do you think boys and girls were encouraged differently in relation to choosing the following subjects?

   Physics
   Home economics
   Computer studies

Languages
Mathematics

13. In your secondary school, assuming it was mixed, did boys and girls obtain (a) popularity and (b) high status from their peer group for the same or for different reasons? If different, please specify in what ways.

14. Do you consider that your choice of occupation either has been or is being influenced by your sex? If so, please specify how.

15. Summarize how you see your current gender identity. To what extent does it work either for or against you?

Changing patterns of sex-role expectations

The increasing emphasis on equality of choice, where possible, between the sexes is becoming manifest in changes in expectation regarding specific aspects of male–female relationships. Below are some possible *emerging* personal rules in the areas of dating, sex, marriage and family that treat the sexes more similarly than *traditional* rules. Ultimately, each individual and each couple has to choose the rules for themselves and for their relationship that works best for them.

> *Dating.* It's OK for either sex to initiate a relationship. The expenses of going out together are to be shared.
> *Sex.* Mutuality and sensitivity to each other's pleasure is important. It's OK for both females and males to want sex and to show enjoyment of it.
> *Marriage.* Marriage is a relationship between separate, equal and interdependent partners. The roles that males and females play within marriage are to be decided by agreement rather than by tradition.
> *Family.* Child care is the responsibility of both parents. Children are brought up with as few biological sex-related fears and inhibitions as possible.

One of the most important areas in which sex-role expectations are changing concerns the place of women in the world of work. In America, between 1948 and 1985, women's share of the labour force grew from 29 to 45 per cent. The participation rate of women grew from 33 to 55 per cent (Bloom, 1986). In 1985, 42 per cent of American families had two earners, with an additional 14 per cent having three or more earners (Russell and Exter, 1986). There were similar trends in Canada. During the 1970s the number of women in the Canadian labour force increased by 61 per cent compared with a 24 per cent increase for men. The labour force participation rate for married women increased from 37 per cent in 1971 to 52 per cent in 1981. By then, 63 per cent of women in the childbearing age of 15 to 44 were in the workforce (Pryor and Norris, 1983).

The role of women in the workforce is changing. In America, the proportion of managers who were women rose from 27 per cent in 1972 to 36 per cent in 1986. Additionally, more women are becoming entrepreneurs. In 1960, women started one in ten new businesses; in 1985, one in five; by 1995 it is projected to be one in two (Bloom, 1986). Though in the early 1980s the average woman earned only about 60 per cent of a man's earnings, there were 6 million American wives earning more than their husbands (Bianchi, 1984).

As women increase their choices in relation to work, there are likely to be more opportunities for men to make choices traditionally restricted to women. These choices include spending more time on homemaking and children. Furthermore, a second income allows some husbands to find more fulfilling, though lower-paid or part-time work. In 1981, over half of American husbands who were secondary family earners worked either part time or only part of the year compared to less than one-fifth of husbands who were primary earners in dual-earner couples (Bianchi, 1984).

The changing role of women in the workforce may be associated with the increase in divorce over the same period. The growing financial independence and willingness of women to seek fulfilment outside as well as inside the home may make many less willing to stay in unhappy marriages. Furthermore, the fact that about a third of all first marriages in Britain end in divorce may reinforce women in wanting to develop their own careers as an insurance policy for being on their own. If people are increasingly going to stay in marriages because they *want* to be in them and not because they *have* to be in them, this puts more pressure on both females and males to develop the skills of loving relationships. This is for their children's sakes as well.

Sex differences in communication

The area of sex differences in communication is a vast one. Differences, as well as similarities, are pervasive in the ways males and females communicate within their sex and with the other sex (Henley, 1977; Eakins and Eakins, 1978). The area of sex differences in communication cannot be adequately covered in a book such as this. However, at points in subsequent chapters I draw attention to some of the different loving skills strengths and weaknesses of males and females. This is not to imply that all males and all females possess the same strengths and weaknesses: individual differences are a fact of life.

Exercise 8 concludes this section on how you bring your sex-role identity and expectations to your relationship. It asks you to explore your views on various aspects of male–female relationships.

EXERCISE
—8—

Exploring my sex-role expectations

INSTRUCTIONS

Answer the following questions:

Part A: taking initiatives

Below are a number of areas in female–male relationships where either or both of you may take the initiative:

Asking for a date
Ordering a meal
Paying the bill after
    eating out
Arranging to go to a
    movie
Arranging a vacation
Driving
Expressing affection
Touching
Making love
Asking for support

1. To what extent are you prepared to take the initiative in each of the above areas?

2. To what extent do you have a double standard between yourself and the other sex in regard to taking initiatives in each of these areas?

Part B: female–male roles

1. What do you think about equality of the sexes in each of the following areas?

    Being responsible for earning the family income
    Being able to have a
       career
    Nurturing children
    Disciplining children
    Doing housework
    Looking after the
       garden
    Looking after the car(s)
    Sexual behaviours
    Explaining the facts of
       life to girls and boys
    Showing feelings
    Offering emotional
       support
    Being able to dress in
       many colours
    Getting custody of
       children after divorce
    Engaging in professional and managerial work
    Engaging in manual work, for example repairing roads
    Being conscripted into the forces in time of war

Part C: assessing my sex-role expectations

1. Make a summary statement of the sex-role expectations that you bring to female–male relationships with people roughly your own age.

2. Do you think your current sex-role expectations help you or harm you in being a loving person towards the other sex?

YOUR CULTURE, RACE AND SOCIAL CLASS

Human life is reduced to real suffering, to hell, only when two ages, two cultures and religions overlap.

Herman Hesse

You bring your cultural background, racial characteristics and social class into your relationships. Furthermore, you bring your degree of sensitivity to these characteristics in yourself and others.

Culture

Culture refers to the predominant patterns of behaviour of a given group during a given period. In Britain, there is a majority British culture, though there are many sub-cultures within it, as well as many ethnic minority groups. During the period 1984–86, the size of Britain's ethnic minority population was around 2.4 million, or 4.5 per cent of the total population of 54.2 million. South Asians—Indians, Pakistanis and Bangladeshis—were 52 per cent of the total ethnic minority population; West Indian and African groups, 26 per cent; the population of mixed origins, 10 per cent; Chinese, about 5 per cent; and Arabs, about 2½ per cent. Some 57 per cent of the ethnic minority population had been born outside the United Kingdom (Shaw, 1988). Thus, many people from ethnic minority groups feel the tension of adjusting to a different culture, while their locally born and educated children may feel caught between the culture of their parents and that of Britain. As Britain draws closer to Europe, numerous Britons are likely to have more exposure to European cultures. The huge increase in Britons taking holidays abroad also brings this about.

The Aboriginals were the first inhabitants of Australia. The 1986 census counted 228,000 persons who were either Aboriginal or Torres Strait Islanders, constituting about 1.4 per cent of the total Australian population. The Aboriginals possess one of the oldest cultures in the world. Though settler Australian culture has its origins in British culture, it is evolving a culture of its own, influenced by those of numerous ethnic minority groups. Up until World War II the vast majority of migrants came from the United Kingdom and Ireland, but times change. In 1988, 34 per cent of migrants were born in Asia, 19 per cent in the United Kingdom and Ireland, 16 per cent in other European countries, 15 per cent in New Zealand, 7 per cent in the Middle East, and 14 per cent in other countries (Australian Department of Immigration, Local Government and Ethnic Affairs, 1988).

Settler New Zealand culture also has its origins in British culture: in fact, New Zealanders are sometimes called 'the Poms of the Pacific'. However, there is a substantial ethnic minority group of Maoris, who constitute about 10 per cent of New Zealand's population of just over 3 million. The Maoris came to New Zealand in great waves of migration starting around 1350 AD. They tend to be very·mindful that they and their culture were in the country long before the Pakeha (European.)

The message from the above figures is simple. Though there are undoubtedly national characteristics common to most Britishers, Australians and New Zealanders, sensitivity to cultural differences and the ability to transcend them can be very important relationship skills. The above figures disguise the amount of cultural variation: for example, migrants from Vietnam and Hong Kong do not come from a single Asian culture. It is well beyond the scope of this book to pinpoint all the variations in the ways different cultures and sub-cultures conduct their relationships. In cross-cultural relationships, each of you can use your skills of giving and receiving information to learn about each other's cultures. This can be a mutually enriching experience.

Race

You can also bring your racial grouping to your relationships, for instance, whether you are white, black, Asian or Polynesian. Additionally, you bring your attitudes towards race. In Britain, approximately 95 per cent of the population is white. While, currently, the vast majority of Australians are white, the proportion of Asians is steadily increasing with immigration. This increase points to the possibility of a Eurasian future. New Zealanders are also predominantly white, but the Maoris are Polynesians.

Social class

Every society throughout the world has its pecking order or
status system. These are open to various degrees of vertical
mobility. Many people migrated to the Antipodes to get away
from what they perceived as the stultifying, traditional social
class systems of Europe, based on old money, landed estates,
titles, what school you went to and how you spoke, in which
they were made to feel NQOCD, 'not quite our class, dear'.
Income, educational attainment and occupational status are
currently three of the main measures of social class in Britain,
Australia and New Zealand. In all three countries the social
class into which you are born and raised is likely to influence
your chances of surviving at birth, your educational and
occupational opportunities, whom you are likely to meet and
marry, how much money you are likely to make, how well
your health is looked after, and the quality of your funeral.

Social class can be an important consideration in starting
and maintaining personal relationships. People from different
social classes have different patterns of behaviour. Those born
on opposite sides of the tracks can feel awkward about going
out with or marrying one another. Additionally, families often
exert pressure on children to relate only to people within their
social class.

EXERCISE

——9——

Exploring my culture, race and social class

INSTRUCTIONS

Answer the following questions:

Part A: culture

1. Other than your national culture, from which ancestral culture are you?

2. What behaviours and expectations do you possess that are related to your ancestral culture(s)?

3. What are the main problems that you experience in your relationships with people from different cultures?

Part B: race

1. From which race are you?

2. What behaviours and expectations have you learned that are related to your race?

3. What are the main problems that you experience in your relationships with people from different races?

Part C: social class

1. To what social class do you belong?

2. What behaviours and expectations do you possess that you related to your social class?

3. What are the main problems that you experience in your relationships with people from different social classes?

———————————

CONCLUDING SELF-TALK

I bring many things, for good or ill, into my relationships. As I grew up I learned skills strengths and weaknesses from the examples and consequences provided by others. I now sustain my loving skills weaknesses as well as my strengths. I bring the quality of my thinking into my relationships, for example my personal rules and how I perceive. I bring my capacity to be aware of my feelings which, in turn, is related to how responsive I can be to others' feelings. I bring my sense of worth and my fears and anxieties. I can use my vulnerability to deepen or to destroy my relationships. I can choose how much of my sexuality I bring into my relationships. I also have many sex-role thoughts, feelings and behaviours that reflect more my upbringing than my sex. These can interfere with equality in female–male relationships. Furthermore, I can help or damage my relationships through how I handle cultural, racial and social class differences in them.

— 3 —

Disclosing yourself

Man is nothing but what he makes of himself.
Such is the first principle of existentialism.

Jean-Paul Sartre

They do not love that do not show their love.

William Shakespeare

This chapter focuses on how you send messages, sometimes intentional and sometimes unintentional, to others. In loving relationships, being an effective sender of messages can have at least four important functions. First, it is a means by which you create and define yourself. Second, you influence how others respond to you. Third, you may help others to be more themselves. Fourth, you reduce the chances of misunderstanding and increase the chances of working through genuine differences.

All relationship messages are encoded by a sender and then decoded by a receiver (Argyle, 1983).

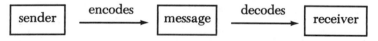

Mistakes can be made at both ends. Senders may not send the messages they wish to send. Much human communication is either poor or unintentional. Also, senders sometimes intentionally seek to deceive. At the receiving end even the clearest of messages may be decoded wrongly. However, the likelihood of this is much greater if you send unclear messages.

In this chapter I look at five important ways that you send messages.

- *Body messages.* Sometimes called body language, those are the messages that you send with your face and with other parts of your body.

- *Touch messages.* Touch is a special kind of body message involving physical contact with another.

- *Voice messages.* These messages relate to *how* you talk, for example either loudly or softly.

- *Verbal messages.* These are messages expressed in words, for example, what you say and how you express your feelings.

- *Action messages.* Action messages are what you *do* as contrasted with what you *say* or how you *say* it.

Since humans can send messages in so many different ways, the issue of *genuineness* becomes important. The question was asked concerning a prominent politician: 'How you can tell when he's lying?' The response was: 'When his lips move'. How do you know when someone is being real or phoney, sincere or insincere? A simple answer is that you use your decoding abilities to look for congruence between *what* is said and *how* it is said. The same will be true for decoding judgements made about your messages. If you send messages 'loud and clear' your voice and body messages match your words. Also, if relevant, so do your touch and action messages.

The notion of social *rules* is important for both how you encode and decode messages. Every group, however large or small, establishes rules for the expected behaviour of its members. Thus all your relationship behaviour – be it friend-ship, dating, copulating, being married, raising a family, working, pursuing leisure interests – is likely to be influenced by a network of social rules and expectations. In Britain and Ireland, some rules apply to everyone: for example, saying 'hello' on meeting someone. Other rules differ according to your sex: for instance, it is more OK for women to wear skirts than men and it may be more OK for men to interrupt than women. Still others vary according to your culture: for example, the greater emphasis both on face-saving and also on respect shown to older people in Asian cultures. In your relationships you have a choice as to whether you stick to the rules or, if necessary, establish ones that work better for you. For instance, Alan, 23, did not care for the rule that men should not show 'feminine' feelings, like caring. Consequently, he decided to become very emotionally literate regarding expressing, where appropriate, the full range of his feelings.

BODY MESSAGES

It ain't what you say, but how you say it.

Anon

Man is the only animal that blushes. Or needs to.

Mark Twain

When talking about yourself, your communications consist of verbal messages and voice and body *framing* messages which may or may not match the *literal* content of what you say. These framing messages are extremely important. The impact of your verbal messages can be heightened, lessened or completely countermanded by your voice and body framing messages. For instance, Joanne may be saying 'Everything is all right in my relationship with Darren', but at the same time look very unhappy, talk with a choked voice, and fight back tears. Here, it does not take an expert decoder to surmise that everything is not all right. Before going into an examination Paul says 'I'm feeling pretty confident', but laughs and smiles nervously, paces up and down, and breathes in a shallow and rapid way. Again, *how* Paul is speaks louder than *what* he says.

As you grew up you may have learned to mask many of your thoughts and feelings by choosing not to express them with either your words, or your body or your voice. However, sometimes you deceive yourself more than others since the meaning of your words points in one direction and your body and voice messages point in another. Professional actresses and actors consciously try to control the body and voice messages of the characters they play to suspend your disbelief. People like Maggie Smith and Michael Caine are experts in sending body and voice messages.

Below are some of the main forms of body messages.

- *Facial expression.* Facial expressions are perhaps the main vehicle for sending body messages. Ekman, Friesen and Ellsworth (1972) have found that there are seven main facial expressions of emotion:

  happiness
  interest
  surprise

fear
sadness
anger
disgust or contempt

Much of the information in these facial expressions is carried through the mouth and the eyebrows: for instance, 'down in the mouth' and 'raised my eyebrows'. There are display rules which indicate which facial expressions can be shown when: for instance, at funerals downturned mouths are more appropriate than upturned ones, even for people who are only at the funeral to make sure that the corpse is really dead!

- *Gaze and eye contact.* As Humphrey Bogart said: 'Here's looking at you, kid'. Gaze, or looking at other people in the area of their faces, is both a way of showing interest and also a way of collecting facial information. Women are more visually attentive than men in all measures of gaze (Henley, 1977; Argyle, 1983). Additionally, there are cultural differences in gaze. In the 'contact cultures', of the Arab world, Latin America and Southern Europe, the amount of gaze is high. Too little gaze is seen as impolite and insincere. However, in 'non-contact' cultures like North America, Northern Europe and Asia, too much gaze is perceived as threatening (Watson, 1972). In fact, the Japanese when conversing gaze at the neck rather than at the face (Pease, 1981).

   Eye contact is a more direct way of sending messages, be they of interest, anger or sexual attraction. Seeing 'eye to eye' is better than having 'shifty eyes'. The dilation of pupils is another source of eye messages: dilated pupils can indicate 'bedroom eyes' or sexual attraction, while undilated pupils may get decoded as 'beady little eyes'.

- *Gesture.* Gestures can take the place of words: for example, nodding your head either up-and-down or sideways are substitutes for saying 'yes' or 'no', respectively. However, gestures have different meanings in different cultures. In Greece, people toss their heads back to say 'no'. The 'A-Okay' sign in North America of thumb-and-forefinger-in-a-circle means in France and Belgium, 'You're worth nothing', and in Southern Italy either 'You asshole' or signifies that you desire anal sex (Ekman, Friesen and Bear, 1984).

Gestures can also frame or illustrate words. They may be physical acts that help explain what is being said, but have no meaning on their own. Argyle (1983) suggests four functions of gestures that accompany speech: displaying the structure of the utterance by enumerating elements or showing how they are grouped; pointing to people or objects; providing emphasis: and giving illustrations of shapes, sizes or movements, particularly when these are difficult to describe in words. An example of a gesture used to show an emotion, with or without words, is the clenched fist for aggression. Your gestures may also vary according to your sex. Eakins and Eakins (1978) suggest that men's gestures are larger, more sweeping and forceful, while women's gestures are smaller and more inhibited.

• *Body posture.* Various messages may be conveyed by your body posture. People who are confident and assertive 'walk tall'. Less confident people may not stand so erect, put their chest out, or square their shoulders. Height tends to be associated with status: for instance, you 'talk down to' or 'talk up to' someone. This may put children and women at a disadvantage unless another's body posture is changed, say by either crouching to be at the same level as children or sitting down. Turning your body towards someone is more encouraging than turning away from them. Also, whether you lean forwards or backwards may indicate interest or disinterest. Your body posture may also communicate how anxious you are: for instance, sitting with your arms and legs tightly crossed suggests that you are emotionally as well as literally uptight. However, especially if you are female, you may appear too relaxed: for instance uncrossed and open legs may be perceived as a sign of sexual availability whether the women wears a skirt, trousers or jeans. This is the double standard at work in how people perceive body messages.

• *Physical distance.* The degree of physical proximity that is comfortable for North Americans, British and Australians is generally the same (Hall, 1966; Pease, 1981). The zones vary according to the nature of the relationship.

   1. *Intimate zone* (between 6 and 18 inches). Here it is easy to touch and be touched. This zone is reserved for spouses, lovers, close friends and relatives.

2. *Personal zone* (between 18 and 48 inches). This zone is appropriate for less close friends and for parties and other social gatherings.
3. *Social zone* (between 4 and 12 feet). This zone is comfortable with shopkeepers, tradespeople and for people not known at all well.
4. *Public zone* (over 12 feet). This is the distance for addressing public gatherings.

People stand or sit closer to those whom they like. Men may be readier to enter a woman's space than the reverse and women more ready to move out of the way (Eakins and Eakins, 1978). There are also large cross-cultural differences: for instance, Arabs and Latin Americans stand very close. Physical distance is also used in starting and ending conversations: for instance, you go up to someone to start and edge away as a signal to finish.

- *Clothing and grooming.* If clothes do not make the woman, man or child, they certainly send many messages about them. These messages include: social and occupational standing, sex-role identity, ethnicity, conformity to peer group norms, rebelliousness, how outgoing you are, and your sexuality. People dress for effect. They wish to influence others by engaging in impression management. A young man who goes to a party in a sober blue suit and tie projects a very different definition of himself than one who dresses in tight jeans that outline his genitals, a colourful open-neck shirt showing some of his hairy chest, and a gold chain around his neck. Children, also, are quick to decode clothing cues. In one study of fourth- and sixth-grade children, they attributed different personalities to other children depending upon what jeans they wore; the options being a designer brand, a medium-price traditional brand, and an inexpensive Sears Roebuck brand (Solomon, 1986). Your personal grooming also provides important information about how well you take care of yourself and how you wish to be seen by others. For instance, you may be clean or dirty, tidy or untidy, and smelly or fresh. Additionally, the length, styling and care of your hair sends messages about you.

EXERCISE
—10—

Sending messages with my body

INSTRUCTIONS

1. Make out a worksheet for yourself based on the following outline.

My body messages

Area	Skills strengths	Skills weaknesses
Facial expression		
Gaze and eye contact		
Gesture		
Body posture		
Physical distance		
Clothing and grooming		

2. Analyse your strengths and weaknesses in each of the six broad areas on your worksheet.

3. To what extent do you think your body messages are affected by your cultural and sex-role conditioning?

4. Where appropriate, set yourself goals for changing your body messages to make you a better communicator.

5. Practise changing your body messages in real life to attain your goals.

TOUCH MESSAGES

*Devils can be drawn out of the heart by the touch
of the hand on a hand, or a mouth on a mouth.*

Tennessee Williams

In touching another you are in their close intimate zone. Touch
connects humans in a most fundamental way. In parent–child
relationships it offers security, tenderness and affection. Touch
is a major way in which adults can demonstrate protection,
support and caring for each other.

Touch messages can be positive or negative. Positive touch
messages are those which the recipients appreciate. Affection
and tenderness may be expressed through: a light touch on the
hand, arm or shoulder; holding hands; walking arm in arm; an
arm over the shoulders; a caress on the side of the face; a semi-
embrace; a warm hug; and a kiss on the cheek or mouth, to
mention but some ways.

Negative touch messages are those which, with varying
degrees of severity, violate another's physical and psychological well-being. Women, men and children can be the
victims of negative touch messages. Though occasionally males
are raped by females (Timnick, 1983), the vast majority of
rapes are done by males. Sexual harassment is almost entirely a
problem for females being crudely and insensitively treated by
males. Most child sexual abuse, be it of girls or boys, is done by
males. Though wives sometimes may punch, scratch and
throw things at their husbands, acts of domestic physical
violence are mainly committed by males. Within their own
sex, males more than females are likely to send negative touch
messages by pushing, shoving and hitting. In short, blatant
negative touch messages are almost entirely a skills weakness of
males. However, there are other negative touch messages, like
hurtful and aggressive pushing away of affection, that are the
preserve of both females and males. Also, sometimes touch
messages can have both positive and negative elements in
them: accentuating the positive and eliminating the negative
can be an issue for both sexes.

A touch too little

An interesting question is whether people in Anglo-Saxon
cultures use positive touch too much or too little. Britain,

Australia and New Zealand are low-contact cultures. There are numerous social rules and taboos regarding who may touch, which parts of the body, when. Females may feel freer to touch other females than males to touch other males (Jourard, 1971b). In relating to their own sex, males more than females may need to be more assertive in risking positive touch messages. Then males can find out which messages lessen their isolation without getting them where they would rather not be. In relating to the other sex, possibly females could assert their equality by initiating and risking more positive touch.

VOICE MESSAGES

Below are some examples of people illustrating emotions with voice messages.

> Tina, 17, feels scared when she goes on dates and speaks very softly.

> Bernard, 26, is nervous when he meets new people and speaks very quickly.

> Jeff, 42, feels very depressed and speaks in a slow and monotonous voice.

> Angie, 22, is mad as hell with Nick, 22, and screams and shouts at him.

> Steve, 19, is getting bored with his relationship with Barbara, 18, and says 'I still love you' in a flat and mechanical way.

The way you use your voice can speak volumes about what you truly feel. Also, it can give a skilled observer insight into your capacity to experience your feelings. For instance, some people who are out of touch with their feelings often speak in a flat and monotonous way, even though the words they use express strong feelings. Others show their anxiety by coming on far too loud and strong.

Below are some dimensions of voice messages.

- *Volume.* How loud or quickly you speak. At the two extremes, whether you whisper or scream.

- *Emphasis.* The degree to which you emphasize certain phrases, words or syllables or speak monotonously.

- *Tone.* Are you high pitched or low pitched, shrill or deep?

- *Enunciation.* Do you speak clearly or is your speech mumbled or slurred?

- *Accent.* What rational, regional or social class variations are there in the way you speak?

- *Firmness.* The degree to which, when you need to, you speak in a firm and confident voice rather than in a weak and diffident one.

- *Use of pauses and silences.* The degree to which you intersperse your speech with brief pauses and longer silences.

If you can control your voice messages, you have acquired a very useful skill in dealing with others. Experiment 1 is the first of the personal experiments in this book. The idea is that you first change your behaviour in your daily life in some specific and desired way and then evaluate what happens. If the consequences of your changed behaviour are positive for you, and possibly others too, you may wish to retain the change.

EXPERIMENT
——1——

What happens when I change my voice messages?

INSTRUCTIONS

Part A: assessment

1. Assess your voice message strengths and weaknesses on the following dimensions. You may wish to cassette record and play back your speech for evidence.

My voice messages

Area	*Skills strengths*	*Skills weaknesses*
Volume		
Pace		
Emphasis		
Tone		
Enunciation		
Accent		
Firmness		
Use of pauses and silences		

2. Ask at least two people who know you well to give you feedback on how they find your voice and whether they think it could be improved.

3. Summarize your voice message strengths and weaknesses. Be specific about voice behaviours that you wish to change.

Part B: make an 'If . . . then . . .' statement

An 'If . . . then . . .' statement is in two parts:

1. In the 'If' part, state as specifically as possible the change or changes you wish to make in your voice messages. For instance: 'If I speak much more loudly . . .'.

2. The 'then' part of the statement indicates the specific consequences you predict will follow. For instance: '*If* I speak much more loudly, for 24 hours, *then* (a) during this period

I will think myself less of a wimp and (b) others will take more notice of what I say'. Now make your own 'If . . . then . . .' statement.

Part C: try out and evaluate your change of behaviour

Try out your changed behaviour. Then assess whether you gave it an adequate try out. Also assess whether it produced positive or negative consequences for yourself and others. Have your predictions been confirmed or disconfirmed? Is your changed behaviour worth maintaining or modifying?

VERBAL MESSAGES

The examples below show some of the implications for various people of their use of words.

> Bernadette, 16, is very shy. She finds it hard to accept that anyone might be interested in her. She talks little about herself and has few friends since people find she is too hard to get to know.

> Mel, 24, has trouble getting on with people. He has a bad habit of putting other people down. His colleagues feel that underneath he is too angry with himself and the world.

> Lorna, 63, found out that she had cancer in her uterus and that its spread had not been caught in time. She was able to talk about her situation and her fears to her family and close friends and was warmed by their support.

> Rachel, 18, has trouble making friends. She always seems to be promoting herself by stressing her accomplishments. Her acquaintances find this a turn-off.

> Don, 19, feels much closer to Moira, 20, after their last date. He was able to tell her how hurt he had been by the displaced negative comments his Mum made about him when she was really upset with his dad. Moira talked about growing up under the shadow of a handsome, successful and spoiled older brother. Don thinks that his relationship with Moira deepened as a result of their sharing.

Sending 'I' messages

Thomas Gordon (1970), in his book *Parent Effectiveness Training*, makes a useful distinction between 'You' messages and 'I' messages. 'You' messages focus on the other person and are judgemental: for example, 'You stop that now, do you hear me?' or 'You're getting on my nerves'. 'I' messages are centred in you as the sender: for example: 'I cannot rest when your stereo is so loud' or 'I don't feel like playing just after I've got home'. When sending an 'I' message you clearly *own* your message and talk for yourself.

You communicate more openly and honestly in relationships if you speak for yourself. A clear way of speaking for yourself is to send messages starting with the word 'I' when you choose to disclose your feelings, thoughts and actions. This can have a number of advantages. First, you can acknowledge that 'I' and 'You' are separate people and what I think or feel about you is my perception and not necessarily what you are. Second, you assume responsibility for your own thoughts, feelings and actions. Third, 'I' messages tend to cause less defensiveness than 'You' messages, with their connotations of blame. Fourth, positive statements such as 'I love you', sound much more as though coming from your heart rather than from your head.

Disclosing yourself entails talking for yourself. Ways in which you may avoid sending 'I' messages include starting messages with words like 'You', 'People', 'We', 'That' and 'It'. Below are some possible example of non-'I' messages:

> 'Would you like the salt?'
> 'It just happened that my girlfriend got pregnant.'
> 'Would you like us to buy that painting?'
> 'You do not love me any more.'
> 'Are you dumb?'
> 'You are the pits.'
> 'A lot of people find you attractive.'
> 'You made me drive too quickly.'
> 'We are not too happy with you as a teacher.'
> 'They want me to stand for public office.'

You can either send or fail to send 'I' in regard to your feelings, thoughts and actions. Here are some examples.

- Owning a feeling
  Ray and Cathy are having a row.

Ray's non-'I' message: 'You are the end.'
Ray's 'I' message: 'I feel hurt and angry.'

- Owning a thought:
  Betty and Richard go to a play which Betty enjoyed.
  Betty's non-'I' message: 'What did you think about the play?'
  Betty's 'I' message: 'I thought the play was excellent.'

- Owning an action:
  Julie has dropped a plate when her mother arrives.
  Julie's non-'I' message: 'It just broke.'
  Julie's 'I' message: 'Mum, I've just broken a plate. I'm sorry.'

A final word is that I do not suggest that you *never* start relationship statements with 'You' or 'They'. You need to be flexible. However, in general, when you wish to define yourself by sending messages about your feelings, thoughts and actions, you communicate more clearly when you start with the personal pronoun 'I'.

Disclosing personal information

*It is in our faults and failings, not in our virtues,
that we touch one another and find sympathy.*

J.K. Jerome

An important category of verbal messages is the personal information that you reveal about yourself. All humans in varying degrees lead secret lives. Sometimes, even in long-standing marriages partners know relatively little about each other. Humans are highly concealing as well as revealing. They often engage in deliberate lying, omissions of truth and partial truths. They are many reasons why good self-disclosure skills are fundamental to loving relationships. These include the following.

- *Defining yourself.* Disclosing personal information lets you be known to others. If you do not define yourself, misunderstandings are more likely to occur. Another person may define you anyway, on their own rather than on your terms.

- *Knowing yourself.* As you talk about yourself you can get deeper insights and understandings about the sort of person you are. Also, you give others the opportunity to provide feedback.

- *Making contact.* Talking about yourself, and letting others talk about themselves, gives each of you the chance to break out of your separateness and make contact. Each is given the opportunity to share and receive.

- *Developing intimacy.* A sharing of yourself is at the heart of intimacy. As you embark towards a deeper level of mutual disclosure: trust may be enhanced, misunderstandings cleared up, and each of you may become more comfortable about being open.

Appropriateness of disclosure

Underdisclosing and overdisclosing may each be a cause and a symptom of psychological maladjustment. People who exhibit either extreme put people off. By concealing, you are hard to get to know. By plunging in, people know too much about you too soon.

There are many considerations relevant to the *appropriateness* of sending personal information messages. Amongst these are the following.

- *Your goals.* Is revealing the information likely to help you or harm you in attaining your goals?

- *Sensitivity to the receiver.* You need to show respect and caring for the recipient of your disclosures at the same time as asserting your right to define yourself.

- *Amount.* The quantity of personal information you reveal.

- *Topic area.* The area or areas in which you reveal personal information. Taylor and Altman (1966) have suggested thirteen broad topic areas: religion; own marriage and family; love, dating and sex; parental family; physical condition and appearance; money and property; government, politics, current events and social issues; emotions and feelings; interests, hobbies and habits; relationships; attitude values, ethnics and self-evaluation; school and work; and biographical characteristics.

- *Breadth*. The range of topic areas in which you reveal personal information.

- *Depth*. The degree of intimacy of your revelations.

- *Timing*. When to reveal personal information in a relationship.

- *Body and voice messages*. How you frame your disclosures of personal information by body and voice messages.

- *Positiveness/negativeness*. Items of personal information you like and dislike about yourself.

- *Target person(s)*. The person or persons to whom you reveal.

- *Social context*. The occasion or social context, with its accompanying rules, in which you reveal information.

Fears about disclosure

There are both risks and gains to revealing personal information. I earlier suggested some gains. The risks, sometimes more imagined than real, include: being rejected; being misunderstood; lack of confidentiality; and disclosing too much too soon and having your disclosures used against you. You may also be afraid of the positive consequences of your disclosures: people may start liking you: you may be in a position of having to choose amongst girlfriends or boyfriends; and you might be entering your first intimate relationship and think: 'Help, how do I handle this?'

What items of personal information do people consider most negative. Stanley Strong and I asked 150 British undergraduates to rate 120 items on a positive/negative scale 'if this item were true for me' (Nelson-Jones and Strong, 1977). The 12 most negative rated items were:

I hate myself
I have attempted
  suicide
I am violent
I have suicidal thoughts
I am a homosexual/lesbian
I am dull

I often hurt people I
  care about
I am erotically attracted by some men (male question)/women
  (female question)
I pity myself
I am a hypocrite
I am generally
  uninteresting
I have a 'fear' of the
  opposite sex.

In general males and females evaluated these characteristics
much the same. There were, of course, individual differences
in how people responded. Furthermore, the fact that people
rate a characteristic of themselves very negatively does not
necessarily mean that they are going to be so hard on others
who disclose it to them.

The difference between what you think of your personal
characteristics and how others react to your disclosures may be
even more pronounced if you reveal what you like about yourself. Revealing positive characteristics risks being viewed as
self-promotion and boasting. It can threaten others. You run
less risk if you intermingle negative with positive disclosures
than if you consistently extol your virtues. Many people, with
some justification, have fears about revealing positive personal
information as well as fears about revealing negative
information.

Cultural and gender considerations

Many broader contextual considerations influence how much
and in what ways people reveal themselves. With about one-
third of British and Australasian first marriages ending in
divorce, people feel less inhibited in talking about their own or
their parents' divorces than previously. There are also
differences between cultures. For example, British female
undergraduate students have been found to disclose less than
their American counterparts (Jourard, 1971b). Furthermore,
differences have been found between the sexes, with women
tending to be more revealing than men (Cozby, 1973, Jourard,
1971b). This may partly be because there are dissimilar
expectations regarding the appropriateness of males' and
females' levels of disclosure. The 'strong silent' role may be perceived as more likeable for males, whereas females may be

more favourably evaluated when they are expressive and revealing (Chelune, 1976). Loneliness, through skills weaknesses in revealing personal information, appears to be more a problem for males than it is for females. However, females may also feel lonely if and when males fail to reciprocate the intimacy of their disclosures. Again, I stress that there are individual differences amongst both males and females. Any generalizations based on sex must be treated cautionsly.

EXPERIMENT
——2——

What happens when I reveal more personal information?

INSTRUCTIONS

Part A: assessment

1. Assess your skills strengths and weaknesses in revealing personal information.

2. Think of either a personal or a school/work relationship that you think could be improved by your deepening, by as much as you feel you can handle, the level of your disclosure.

3. Using the scale below, assess how threatening it would be for you in this relationship to reveal personal information in the areas listed.

   4   Impossible, much too threatening
   3   Very threatening
   2   Moderately threatening
   1   Slightly threatening
   0   Not threatening at all
   N/A Not applicable

   Rating   *Personal information areas*

Positive thoughts/feelings about my parents

☐ Negative thoughts/feeling about my parents

☐ Positive thoughts/feelings about the other person

☐ Negative thoughts/feelings about the other person

☐ Problem areas in our relationship

☐ Feelings of loneliness

☐ Feelings of inadequacy

☐ Feelings of depression

☐ Failures in my work

☐ Successes in my work

☐ Work habits

☐ Successes in my personal relationships

☐ Failures in my personal relationships

☐ Things I like about my body

☐ Things I dislike about my body

☐ Leisure interests

☐   Feelings about death

☐   Religious beliefs

☐   Political preferences

☐   Past sexual experiences

☐   Sexual fantasies

☐   Masturbatory behaviours

☐   Homosexual tendencies

☐   Intellectual ability

☐   Musical preferences

☐   Financial position

☐   Times I have lied/cheated

☐   Things that make me happy

☐   Things that make me miserable

☐   Things that make me angry

☐   Things that make me afraid

☐   My goals in life

☐   My central values

☐   How worthwhile I feel

☐   The people I love

☐   The people I hate

☐   My peak experiences in life

Part B: make an 'If . . . then . . .' statement

1. The 'If' part of your statement as specifically as possible states the change or changes you wish to make in how much you reveal in this relationship: For instance 'If I reveal (a), (b) and (c) to . . .'.

2. Then 'then' part of the statement indicates the specific consequences you predict will follow from the changes in your behaviour stated in the 'If' part of your 'If . . . then . . .' statement.

Part C: Try out and evaluate your changed behaviour

Try out your changed behaviour. Assess its positive and negative consequences for yourself and others. Have your predictions been confirmed or disconfirmed? Has the experiment taught you something about how you can strengthen your skills of sending personal information messages? If so, what?

Expressing your feelings

The finest people marry the two sexes in their own persons.

Ralph Waldo Emerson

In Chapter 2, I emphasized the importance of emotional self-awareness-tuning in to yourself. All your feelings are OK. They are a fundamental part of your humanness. However, your degree of skill at sending feelings messages can help or hinder others in tuning in to you. Here the focus is on appropriate ways of sending feelings messages. Though much of the emphasis is on verbal messages, voice and body messages are so important when you express your feelings that I include them as well. In later chapters I discuss how you can *regulate* your feelings, for instance shyness and anger, by regulating your thinking.

Expressing your feelings involves letting what is going on inside you be released and revealed outside. Thus it involves a translation of your inner sensations into outer expressions. Sometimes the translation process is immediate, like your startle reaction to a loud noise. On other occasions, expressing your feelings is less reflex. It can involve conscious choices both regarding how you label them and also regarding whether and how you reveal them.

Identifying and labelling your feelings

Labelling your feelings involves putting your physical sensations into words. Feelings as such have no words. You supply the words to describe them. The feelings you experience are related to your interpretation of situations. For instance, Alex asks Anne for a date and she politely but firmly refuses. There are a range of possible feelings Alex might have. These include hurt, anger, humiliation, inferiority, anxiety, tension, relief, resolution, confidence, cheerfulness and optimism. Each of these feelings involves an interpretation of Anne's refusal. For instance, Alex could choose to think either 'It's the worst thing that has ever happened to me', or 'That's her problem, how dare the stupid bitch turn me down', or 'She's perfectly entitled to her position, I'm an OK guy who can try elsewhere'. The first choice may contribute to feelings of anxiety and depression, the second to anger and the third to confidence.

Table 3.1 List of feelings words

accepted	free	responsible
adventurous	friendly	sad
affectionate	frightened	secure
aggressive	grieving	shy
ambitious	guilt-free	stressed
angry	guilty	strong
anxious	happy	superior
apathetic	humiliated	supported
appreciated	hurt	suspicious
assertive	indecisive	tense
attractive	independent	tired
bored	inferior	trusting
carefree	insecure	unambitious
cautious	interested	unappreciated
cheerful	involved	unassertive
competitive	irresponsible	unattractive
confident	jealous	underconfident
confused	joyful	uneasy
contented	lonely	unfit
cooperative	loved	unfree
daring	loving	unfriendly
decisive	optimistic	unloved
dependent	outgoing	unsupported
depressed	pessimistic	upwanted
discontented	powerful	uptight
embarrassed	powerless	vulnerable
energetic	rejected	wanted
envious	relaxed	weak
excitable	resentful	worried
fit		

If Alex were to think about his feelings or to try to describe them to a friend he would need to put them into words. There may be slippage between his feelings and their verbal description. For instance, he may find it difficult to admit that he is hurt and find it more comfortable to label his feeling as anger. He may have conflicting feelings which he does not fully admit. He may think about his feelings in black-and-white terms. Alex may acknowledge neither ambivalence nor nuances in the intensity of his feelings. Also, he may lack the vocabulary with which adequately to identify and to express his feelings.

To send good feelings messages, it may be useful if you build up a repertoire of words both to describe and also to catch the nuances of your own and others' feelings. Learning to become a skilled counsellor or psychotherapist involves building up a repertoire of feelings words to help clients feel accurately understood. You need to become a good counsellor to yourself and accurately identify and label your feelings. Table 3.1 is a list of some of the feelings words you may use.

EXERCISE
—11—

Identifying and labelling my feelings

INSTRUCTIONS

Complete the following sentences regarding your feelings in relationships. Focus on how you actually feel rather than on your thoughts about the other person. Indicate the strength of your feelings. If you have conflicting feelings, state what these are.

When someone ignores me I feel _____

_____

When someone cries I feel _____

When someone praises me I feel _____

_____

When someone talks about themselves all the time I feel _____

_____

When someone gets mad at me I feel _____

_____

When someone acts superior to me I feel _____

_____

When someone attracts me I feel _____

_____

When someone breaks a confidence I feel _____

_____

When someone is very late for an appointment I feel _____

_____

When I am in a group of strangers I feel _____

_____

When someone deeply understands me I feel _____

_____

How good are YOU at identifying and labelling your feelings in your relationships?

_____

Feelings difficult to express

In revealing your feelings you may put yourself 'very much on the line'. This is the real you that you share, not just your social mask. Opening up can be scary. Sometimes you may not like your own feelings. Also, you may be afraid of the consequences to you and others of expressing your feelings. However, there are risks to *not* sharing your feelings as well as to sharing them. You lose vitality if you continually sit on your feelings. Others do not get to know you and you do not get to know yourself. There may be unfinished business in your relationships. This can be a triple negative. First, the unfinished business or conflict does not get dealt with. Second, your upset feelings may 'come out sideways' in unhelpful activities like nit-picking, sarcasm and gossiping. Third, your not having worked through your negative feelings may interfere with your willingness to express positive and loving feelings.

Some feelings are difficult for most people to express, especially when they do not feel safe with another.

- Feelings of being worthless. 'If you really got to know me you would realize how empty and unlovable I am.'

- Feelings of incompetence. 'I'm dumb. No matter how hard I try I still end up at the bottom of the class.'

- Feelings of being unattractive. 'I'm a dull person and I don't like my looks. I wish I had another body.'

Some feelings may be more difficult for women to express, though some men may have difficulty expressing them too.

- Feelings of ambition. 'I badly want to get to the top in my field and enjoy the status and money that goes with it.'

- Feelings of leadership. 'I like power and having people working under me.'

- Feelings of assertion. 'I'm determined not to let myself get pushed around against my will.'

Some feelings may be more difficult for men to express, though some women may have difficulty expressing them too.

- Feelings of vulnerability. 'I wear a suit of armour, yet underneath I feel frightened a lot of the time and want nurturing.'

- Feelings of sensitivity. 'Going to the ballet last night was so beautiful that I wanted to cry.'

- Feelings of love towards children. 'I love my kids, though I don't know how to show it.'

Often both men and women have difficulty expressing positive feelings in their relationships.

- Acknowledging strengths. 'I'm always picking on her and yet I think she's a great person.'

- Expressing love. 'I never seemed to get around to saying what was in my heart and telling him I loved him. Now it's too late.'

- Accepting compliments. 'I really appreciate your saying that.'

EXERCISE
—12—

Feelings I find easy and difficult to express

INSTRUCTIONS

1. Take a piece of paper. At the top write FEELINGS I FIND EASY AND DIFFICULT TO EXPRESS. At the top left column write EASY, at the top of the right column write DIFFICULT.

2. In each column list the feelings you find easy and difficult to express. Table 3.1 may give you some ideas about the different feelings.

3. Do you detect any pattern in the feelings you have listed as either easy or difficult to express? If so, please specify.

4. Do you think the feelings you find either difficult or easy to express have been influenced by your sex-role or cultural conditioning? If so, please specify.

Sending feelings messages

In sending feelings messages you integrate verbal, body and voice messages and sometimes touch and action messages as well. Most of the considerations about the *appropriateness* of revealing personal information also apply to expressing your feelings. These considerations include: your goals, sensitivity to the receiver, amount, breadth, depth, timing, target person and social context. You may think taking so many considerations into account is likely to make you wooden and dull. However, you probably take most of these into account anyway. Also, not expressing your feelings well may make it more difficult for you to express them later: for example, others may be less willing to listen.

Exercise 13 has been designed to increase your awareness that in sending feelings messages you are a chooser not only in *what* you say, but in *how* you say it. For example, Louise's mother died recently and she wants to communicate to her boyfriend Rob how sad she feels. Her composite feeling of sadness message might include the following elements.

- *Verbal messages.* Words Louise might use include: 'I feel sad, low, miserable, unhappy, depressed'. Phrases she might use include: 'I feel really low', 'I feel under a cloud', 'I've got the blues'. Louise might also state the reasons for her sadness in an 'I feel . . . because . . .' statement.

- *Voice messages.* Louise's voice messages might include: sighing, speaking slowly, a monotonous delivery, and speaking quietly.

- *Body messages.* Louise's body messages might include: corners of mouth turned down, tears, sniffling, slouched body posture, and also moving closer to Rob for a hug.

Practice is important in learning to express your feelings. The more you hold back unnecessarily, the harder it may be for you to break this habit. Nobody's perfect. In expressing feelings, often just having a good try is more than adequate. Feelings are processes. You can only state how you have felt in the past or how you feel at the moment. You may feel differently in future, even as a result of just being able to state your feelings.

EXERCISE
—13—

Sending feelings messages

INSTRUCTIONS

1. For each of the following feelings write down:
   - (a) verbal messages
   - (b) voice messages
   - (c) body messages

   which you could use to express the feeling appropriately in *your* relationships.

love	anger
fear	anxiety
happiness	boredom
shame	depression

2. Look at the feelings you listed in Exercise 12 as difficult for you to express. For each of these feelings write down:

(a) verbal messages
(b) voice messages
(c) body messages

which you could use to express the feeling appropriately in *your* relationships.

ACTION MESSAGES

Suit the action to the word, the word to the action.
William Shakespeare

Action speaks louder than words.
Anon

Woody Allen was once asked whether he had ever taken a serious political stand on anything. He replied: 'Yes, for twenty-four hours I refused to eat grapes'. Had he been serious, his actions would have spoken louder than his words. In today's slang, the messages you send through your actions are 'the bottom line'. Discrepancies between your words and actions can seriously erode the trust which is the foundation of any serious loving relationship.

If you love someone you try to act in loving ways towards them. You are concerned for their happiness and development. Your loving is a gift of yourself displayed through your words and actions. Loving actions can be small yet have much meaning for the recipient. These might include: a letter, a card, a poem, a surprise gift, going out to a favourite restaurant, to more mundane actions like not leaving your stockings or socks around and doing your share of the household chores. Some couples initiate and worsen their conflicts because thay have stopped doing positive things for each other. Also, partners may be poor at signalling what they like and picking up such messages from each other.

The importance of genuineness in your words and actions is pervasive. Below are a few illustrations of people's actions not matching their words.

Simon, 46, is always telling Simon junior, 12, that he wants him to be his own man. However, the only public school to which he is prepared to send his son is the one where he went himself.

Justin, 24, has told his boss Debbie that he is no longer prepared to work late at short notice. Debbie comes up to him one hour before he is due to go home with a 3-hour job which *must* be done tonight. Justin stays behind and does it.

Andy, 46, is a college lecturer who has written a book on the importance of family life. He is married with 2 young children. Gradually, it emerges that he has been having an affair with his secretary, Roberta.

Lesley, 19, says she believes in equality of the sexes. However, when she goes out on a date, her boyfriends always end up paying.

Each of the above vignettes was built around a major theme where actions can contradict words.

- *Non-possessiveness/possessiveness*. You may talk respect for the individuality of your loved ones and yet act in controlling ways towards them.

- *Assertion/lack of assertion*. Assertion entails, where appropriate, backing up your words with your actions.

- *Trust/mistrust*. Trust entails keeping your formal and informal contracts or else openly attempting to renegotiate them.

- *Equality of the sexes*. Equality means that *both* sexes have to give up some of their traditional privileges.

Promises, promises, promises. A good definition of a 'phoney' is someone whose action messages fall far short of their verbal, voice and body messages. The importance of sending good action messages in initiating, developing and maintaining stable loving relationships cannot be overemphasized.

This book is about the technology of loving relationships. In this chapter I have tried to be a human engineer who shows you the component parts of how you send information. You cannot not send messages. My hope is that by spelling out the body, touch, voice, verbal and action components of sending information you will be in a stronger position to gain more control over your loving skills as the book proceeds.

CONCLUDING SELF-TALK

I am always sending information about myself to others. These messages can be broken down into five main categories: body, touch, voice, verbal and action messages. The messages I send are influenced by many considerations, including my goals, my skills strengths and weaknesses, social rules and my upbringing, including my sex-role and cultural conditioning. I can choose to develop my loving skills by disclosing myself better. This means improving my skills within each of the five categories. Additionally, it means improving my skills of matching my words with my actions, and my body, touch and voice messages with my words.

Being a rewarding listener

The reason why we have two ears and only one mouth is that we may listen the more and talk the less.

Zeno of Citium

A riot is at bottom the language of the unheard.

Martin Luther King

*T*he next two chapters focus on the skills of being a rewarding listener. Listening is one of the most power-ful psychological rewards that you can give. However, how many people are there in your life with whom you feel you can be very open and share the secrets of your heart? The answer for some of you will be none. Probably for most of you there are not as many highly rewarding listeners as you would like. Varying degrees of unrewarding behaviour that masquer-ade as listening are widespread. Here's an analogy:

- mild psychological punishment: *occasionally* not being listened to;
- moderate psychological punishment: *sometimes* not being listened to;
- severe psychological punishment: *mostly* not being listened to; and
- a psychological death penalty: *never* being listened to.

How rewarding a listener are you? To what extent do you inflict varying degrees of psychological pain and punishment on others? The emphasis in this book is on exploring how *you* can be a loving person to others rather than on how others treat you. There is a common illusion that, while others frequently listen poorly, one's own listening is good and is just 'doin' what comes naturally'. For those not born deaf, the capacity to hear sounds is natural. However, the skills of understanding and decoding the meanings of most sounds require learning. Furthermore, rewarding listening involves observation and, hence, learning the skills of decoding body as well as verbal messages.

Why is listening such a fundamental skill?

Being a rewarding listener is a fundamental skill of being a loving person. Below are some of the reasons.

- *Affirming another.* Rewarding listening affirms, unrewarding listening disconfirms. When children grow up, the quality of listening of the adults around them is almost as vital for their psychological development as food is for their physical development. Children who have been sensitively listened to are not only likely to be accepted by others, but to accept themselves as well. Their sense of worth is intact. Furthermore, they have had the safety to express and explore their feelings. Thus they have been helped to acquire the capacity for *inner* listening, listening to and trusting their own feelings and reactions, which is an essential part of *outer* listening, listening to others. Additionally, having at least one parent who listens well provides them with a secure base to engage in exploratory behaviour and make personal experiments. Children who have not been adequately listened to are likely to be more out of touch with their feelings, insecure, anxious, angry and aggressive. Even if unintended, unrewarding listening perpetrated on a regular basis constitutes a significant form of psychological violence. Disconfirmation of the core of one's being on a daily basis by a thousand unkind listening cuts is the stuff out of which severe mental illness is made. In adult life, listening can also affirm or disconfirm. Perhaps the most frequent complaint in distressed relationships is that either or both partners no longer listens.

- *Knowing another.* Rewarding listening allows another to feel safe and to strip away the social masks that they wear for protection. You no longer need make so many assumptions about what they think and feel since they tell you anyway. Loving another person involves knowing them in their separateness and prizing it. Your listening skills help you to know them on their terms. In doing so, you transcend your egocentricity. Also, no one can know the weight of another's burden unless told.

● *Knowing yourself.* Listening effectively to others provides you with valuable information about yourself. Though you may not always like what you hear, remaining open to others gives you the opportunity to grow from their feedback. Defensiveness or tuning out to information that is discrepant with your picture of yourself is a major corroder of loving relationships. It is highly unrewarding to the sender. Instead of your being in an *open* communication system in which you and your partner feel free to share what you think and feel, there can develop a *closed* communication system. Here you and your partner tiptoe around each other's fragile egos at the expense of honesty. Each partner knows what triggers the other's unrewarding listening behaviours and may find it easier to avoid painful confrontations. A further result of this is that partners get progressively alienated from themselves through not having the courage to be a rewarding listener when faced with difficult feedback.

● *Building trust and stability in a relationship.* Perhaps the major find from research into self-disclosure is that intimacy levels of disclosures tend to be matched (Cozby, 1973). Your gradually telling your secrets and my gradually telling you mine is a process that depends on us being willing to listen to each other as well as to disclose. Trust is built as much from acceptance of our disclosures as from our willingness to disclose.

Rewarding listening also builds trust and stability in relationships by helping partners prevent and manage problems. If partners are able to say what they think and feel, misunderstandings are less likely to occur based on misperceptions of each other's positions. Additionally, if partners listen to each other when conflicts occur, they stand a much better chance of resolving their difficulties to their mutual satisfaction.

● *Bridging age, sex and cultural differences.* Every person has a potential set of blinkers depending upon their life's circumstances. How can you know what it is like to be old, dying, female, male, Scottish, Welsh, Irish, a Pakistani migrant, a Vietnamese refugee, an Aboriginal Australian or a Maori if you are not from one of these groups? However, if you relate to someone with a different set of life's circumstances, they can greatly assist you in understanding them if you reward them by listening well. Similarly, if they are rewarding listeners for you, together you build bridges and not walls.

REWARDING LISTENING: A NINE-SKILLS APPROACH

The remainder of this chapter and most of the next describes nine key skills of being a rewarding listener. Some of the skills overlap. They are not presented in any rigid order of importance.

Skills of rewarding listening

Skill 1:   knowing the difference between me and you
Skill 2:   possessing an attitude of respect and acceptance
Skill 3:   sending good body messages
Skill 4:   sending good voice messages
Skill 5:   using openers, small rewards and open questions
Skill 6:   rewording
Skill 7:   reflecting feelings
Skill 8:   reflecting feelings and reasons
Skill 9:   avoiding unrewarding 'don'ts'

SKILL 1: KNOWING THE DIFFERENCE BETWEEN ME AND YOU

Don't judge any man until you have walked two moons in his moccasins.

American Indian Proverb

If the people to whom you relate are to feel that you receive them loud and clear, you need the ability to 'get inside their skins' and 'see the world through their eyes'. At the heart of rewarding listening is a basic distinction between 'you' and 'me', between 'your view of you' and 'my view of you' and between 'your view of me' and 'my view of me'. Now 'your view of you' and 'my view of me' are both inside or internal viewpoints, whereas 'your view of me' and 'my view of you' are both outside or external viewpoints. The skill of listening to and understanding another person is based on your choosing to acknowledge the separateness between 'me' and 'you' by getting into their internal rather than remaining in your external viewpoint.

If I respond to what you say in a way that shows an accurate understanding of your viewpoint, I am responding *as if inside* your *internal viewpoint*. If, however, I choose not to show an understanding of your viewpoint, or lack the skills to do so, I respond from my external viewpoint. In short, if I respond to you as if inside your internal viewpoint, I respond to you from where you are. If I step outside your internal viewpoint, I respond in an external way that reflects more where I am or think you should be than where you are.

Below are some examples of *external viewpoint* responses by a listener.

> 'I'm interested in what's going right for you, not what's going wrong.'
> 'You should always respect your parents.'
> 'My advice to you is to drop him.'
> 'You have troubles. Let me tell you mine.'

Responding as if in the internal viewpoint entails you in understanding talkers on their terms. This involves careful listening and allowing talkers the psychological space to tell their own story. Furthermore, it entails decoding their messages, especially if not clearly sent. This includes understanding voice and body as well as verbal messages. Below are examples of *internal viewpoint* responses by a listener.

> 'You feel that the last months have been terrible for you.'
> 'You have mixed feelings about getting married.'
> 'You found the thought of unemployment scary.'
> 'You're thrilled that she finally said "I love you".'

Exercise 14 asks you to identify whether the listener has responded as if from the talker's internal viewpoint. Some of the responses may seem a little artificial since they have been devised to make the point of the exercise clear. Answers for the exercise are provided at the end of the chapter.

EXERCISE
—14—

Understanding another's internal viewpoint

INSTRUCTIONS

This exercise consists of a number of statement–response excerpts from different relationships. Three responses have been provided for each statement. Write IN or EX by each response according to whether you consider it is *as if inside* the speaker's *internal* viewpoint or from an *external* viewpoint.

Example

Husband to wife
Husband: I'm worried about the kids. They always seem to be out late these days and I'm beginning to feel that I scarcely know them.

Wife
EX   (a) If you took a bit more interest you would know them better.
IN   (b) You're concerned that you're becoming distant from the kids because you see so little of them.
EX   (c) You're a good dad and deserve better than this.

Exercise

1. Girlfriend to boyfriend
   Girlfriend: I think your Mum's great. I hope I can be as energetic as her when I'm her age.
   Boyfriend

      (a) Mum likes you too.

      (b) Wait until you get to know her better.

☐ (c) You think Mum's super and admire her vitality.

2. Student to teacher

Student: I'm finding the workload very heavy. I'm depressed at missing out so much on my social life.

Teacher

☐ (a) You feel down since you're all work and no play.

☐ (b) All students have to work hard to pass these exams.

☐ (c) Life isn't much fun for the staff either.

3. Child to parent

Child (crying) I've just been beaten up by Eric. He's a big bully. I hate him.

Parent

☐ (a) You poor boy.

☐ (b) Big boys don't cry.

☐ (c) You hate that nasty Eric.

4. Friend to friend

Friend A: Let's go to the beach this weekend and see if we can meet some neat guys.

Friend B:

☐ (a) You would like me to go to the beach with you this weekend to try to meet some males.

☐ (b) I've got other plans for this weekend.

☐ (c) That's no place to meet them.

SKILL 2: POSSESSING AN ATTITUDE OF RESPECT AND ACCEPTANCE

It is one thing to know intellectually the difference between listening from the internal and external viewpoints and quite another to implement it in practice. Even professional counsellors and psychotherapists, who are trained to respect their clients' right to make their own choices, can become external when they mean to be internal. It is much more difficult in personal relationships where you are not protected by the rules and limited contact of psychotherapy. In Chapter 1, I mentioned that self-love was integral to your capacity to love another. Self-love entails respecting and accepting yourself as a worthwhile, yet fallible, human being. Having a basic attitude of acceptance of yourself as a *person* means that you can still endeavour to change those of your specific *behaviours* that do not work for you. You do not have to accept them too.

Table 4.1 Relationship between level of self-acceptance and ability to accept others

(a) *Confident person*

Lack of self-acceptance	Lack of acceptance of others
Self-acceptance	Acceptance of others

(b) *Unconfident person*

Lack of self-acceptance	Lack of acceptance of others
Self-acceptance	Acceptance of others

The extent to which you are able to respect and accept yourself is reflected in the level of acceptance and respect, and hence quality of listening, you are able to offer another. Table 4.1

depicts the relationship between your level of self-acceptance and how much you can accept others on their terms. The table is a simplification because in close personal relationships you will be put to the test, when you and your partner are angry or in conflict, regarding your own level of security and acceptance. Unless you discipline yourself, good listening can be the first casualty of a conflict. Consequently, self-acceptance should be extended to mean accepting yourself enough to control your temper and stay tuned in to your partner when the going gets rough.

Barriers to an accepting attitude

An accepting attitude involves respecting another as a separate and unique human being with a right to their own thoughts and feelings independent of your own. This does not mean that you agree with everything they say. However, you are secure enough in yourself to respect it as their version of reality. You do not need to use barriers and filters to protect you from hearing the full range of their messages. These barriers manifest themselves both internally and externally. They manifest themselves internally in that you operate on, distort and filter out certain elements of the messages you receive. At worst you may deny or block out the whole of an incoming message. The barriers manifest themselves externally in subtle and not so subtle voice and body cues to others that they should edit what they say. Also, in the more obvious verbal 'don'ts' to avoid in being a rewarding listener. These are listed in Chapter 5.

What are some of the main barriers and filters that act as sources of interference to your receiving another loud and clear? All of them are related to your sense of worth and to how much debilitating anxiety you possess. The stronger you are emotionally, the less need is there for you to use barriers and filters, so the more open you are to others. Barriers to an accepting attitude include the following.

- *Strong feelings.* Experiencing strong positive or negative feelings can interfere with your listening. Earlier I mentioned how hard it can be to stay open to another when either of you is angry and in conflict. Strong positive feelings can also contribute to your not adequately hearing another.

  Alice, 18, thought that Mark, 19, was the most

terrific boy she had ever met. Mark liked Alice, but still wanted to go out with other girls. He first tried hinting to her that he did not want to spend all his free time with her and she did not get the message. Mark now thinks he is going to have to be much more direct with her.

- *Trigger words and phrases.* Trigger or 'red flag' words and phrases are those, when used by others, that you find emotionally charged. Most trigger words and phrases get their emotional impact because what they say and the tone of voice in which they are said are perceived as put-downs. Each individual has their own triggers. Many of these are 'You' messages: For example 'You're weak', 'You screwed it up', 'You failure' and 'Can't you do anything right?' Adjectives like 'thoughtless', 'clumsy' and 'effeminate' can also act as trigger words. Being talked down to can trigger negative emotional reactions: for example, 'You should really follow my advice' or 'You do as you're told'.

  Dan and his Dad are not close on the surface, but have a lot of feeling for each other underneath. Dan finds himself tuning out to his Dad every time he uses phrases like 'When I was your age' and 'Be a man'.

  Positive words and phrases can also trigger feelings that interfere with your listening. For example, flattery like 'Gee, you're wonderful Mr/Mrs Murgatroyd . . . I really admire you' may contribute to your not hearing other feedback that is less flattering.

- *Unfinished business.* Unfinished business can interfere with your being open to another. For instance, if you have just had a row with a shop assistant you may be less ready to listen to your children who want to discuss their day at school. Also, if you still have strong unresolved feelings about something that has occurred earlier in a relationship, you may listen less well to current information until the earlier issue has been processed.

- *Anxiety-evoking topics.* For reasons connected with how you were brought up, certain topic areas may be anxiety-evoking. You may either not like discussing them at all or get defensive when positions are presented that differ from yours.

A sensitive topic for Liz is her religion. She feels that her Roman Catholic faith gives her a good framework for living. She gets very upset when her faith is challenged, and she responds defensively.

Ken, 19, was brought up in a home where sex was not openly discussed. He gets very nervous at some of the locker room talk he hears where people tell dirty jokes and boast about their sexual conquests.

- *Prejudice(s)*. Again for reasons connected with your upbringing, you may tune out to people who are different from you by reason of, amongst other things, their age, sex, sexual preference, culture, race, social class, physical disability, intelligence level.

Below are a couple of examples.

Homosexuality is a sensitive topic for Herb. He constantly draws attention to homosexual tendencies in others. However, it is impossible to hold a rational discussion with him about gay rights. He simply does not want to listen.

Trudy, 26, dislikes old people. She does not seem to realize that they were young once too. Also, that they have thoughts and feelings that merit respect just as much as her own. She treats old people coldly and maintains her distance from them.

- *Anxiety-evoking people*. There may be specific people or categories of people with whom you feel anxious and, hence, do not listen to them well. These may include: your parents, your relatives, friends of the same or other sex, strangers and authority figures.

Sally, a 35-year-old nurse, has a poor relationship with her boss Cassie. Sally finds Cassie 'makes her nervous'. A consequence of this is that she follows Cassie's instructions poorly. Sally then gets even more nervous when Cassie criticizes her for not paying attention.

- *Anxiety-evoking situations*. Anxiety and threat are present to a greater or lesser degree in all situations. Below are some common situations where people may feel vulnerable and hence their own agendas may preclude their fully listening to others.

Going on your first date with a different person.
Going to a party where you do not know anyone.
Meeting for the first time your girlfriend/boyfriend's parents.
Having to answer questions after a public talk you have given.
Going for a job interview.
Being teased on a sensitive topic.
Making love for the first time.

Many of the above illustrations involve coping with new situations. However, even when you have either been for a number of job interviews or fielded questions after a number of talks, you may still experience some debilitating anxiety that interferes with your listening.

- *Bringing the past into the present.* Sometimes you may inappropriately transfer reactions and feelings from your past into your present. These may be either positive or negative feelings. Here are two examples:

    Nancy and Brad are a couple in their early thirties. Nancy knows that she reminds Brad of his mother. Sometimes she thinks he has difficulty acknowledging how different she is from his mother.

    Arthur, a single man aged 42, moved into the house next to Helen, a widow in her early sixties. Helen had had a disastrous relationship with her previous neighbour, another bachelor called Rod. Her first remark to Arthur was: 'People around here are going to take a long time getting used to you'.

- *Information different from your self-picture.* You may find it hard to keep assuming an accepting attitude when the information you receive differs from your picture of yourself. People differ in their thresholds for being open to such information. Positive as well as negative information can be denied and distorted.

    Rachel tells Bruce she finds him good looking. Bruce looks shy and replies 'Oh, not really'.

    Janet is a career-oriented school teacher who prides herself on her professional approach. One day she gets feedback from her class that they find her approach dull and prefer that of another teacher.

Janet gets angry and thinks that they do not appreciate all the work she puts into her lessons.

- *Physical barriers*. Physical considerations may contribute to your being less accepting of others than you might be. For instance, fatigue, illness, the discomfort of being too hot or too cold, and external noise may all affect how well you listen. The stresses of your life may contribute to your being depressed, irritable and tense. None of these feelings is conducive to your being open and accepting of another person.

Above I have discussed 10 barriers and filters to your adopting an attitude of respect and acceptance for the speaker when you listen. This list is far from exhaustive. Exercise 15 asks you to explore barriers and filters that may prevent you from being an accepting listener.

EXERCISE
—15—

Assessing my barriers to an accepting attitude when I listen

INSTRUCTIONS

Assess yourself in terms of how much each of the following internal barriers interferes with your possessing an accepting attitude when you listen.

Internal barrier	My assessment
Strong feelings	
Trigger words and phrases	

Unfinished business	
Anxiety-evoking topics	
Prejudice(s)	
Anxiety-evoking people	
Anxiety-evoking situation	
Bringing the past into the present	
Information different from my self-picture	
Physical barrier	
Other(s)	

Summarize the extent to which you see yourself possessing an accepting attitude when you listen to:

(a) your spouse/partner/girlfriend/boyfriend, and
(b) your friends.

SKILL 3: SENDING GOOD BODY MESSAGES

To be a rewarding listener, you need to convey your attention and interest. Sometimes this is referred to in the counselling literature as attending behaviour (Ivey, 1971). Many of the points in training counsellors in this skill are relevant to everyday interaction. However, especially once you get to know each other, you can be much more flexible in your relationships. Too much formality is counterproductive. Some of the main body messages by which you can show your attention and interest are as follows.

- *Physical availability*. People who are always off to the next event in their busy lives choose not to find time to listen adequately to those to whom they relate. Loving relationships require an investment of quality time. If this is not forthcoming, sooner rather than later either or both parties are likely to feel that they are not being adequately listened to. If you are rarely or never available to listen, you have withdrawn much of your interest and attention from the other person.

- *Open and relaxed body posture*. Physical openness means facing the speaker not only with your face but with your body. You need to be sufficiently turned towards the other person so that you can receive all their significant facial and body messages. A relaxed body posture, provided you do not sprawl, conveys the message that you are emotionally accessible. If you do sit in a tense and uptight fashion, the listener may either consciously consider or intuitively feel that you are too bound up with your personal agendas and unfinished business to be fully accessible to them.

- *Slight forward lean*. Whether you lean forwards, backwards or sideways is another aspect of body posture. If you lean too far forward you look odd and others may consider that you invade their personal space. If you lean far back, others may find this distancing. A slight forward trunk lean can both encourage the talker and avoid threat, especially at the start of relationships.

- *Positive use of gestures*. The head nod is perhaps the most common gesture in listening. Each head nod can be viewed as a reward to the talker signifying your attention. Head nods need not mean that you agree with everything they say. On the negative side, head nods can also be a powerful way of controlling a speaker and not showing an accepting attitude. Unconditional acceptance then gets turned into conditional acceptance. Arm and hand gestures can also be used to show your responsiveness to the speaker. However, listeners who gesture either too little or too much with their heads and arms can be discouraging. Other negative gestures include: tightly crossed arms and legs that act as barriers, hands clenched together, finger drumming, fiddling with your hair, your hand over your mouth, ear tugging, and scratching yourself, to mention but some.

- *Good use of gaze and eye contact.* Good eye contact means looking in the other's direction so that you allow the possibility of your eyes meeting reasonably often. There is an equilibrium level for eye contact in any relationship, depending upon: cultural and social rules, the degree of anxiety in each partner, the nature and state of development of the relationship, and the degree of attraction involved. Staring at another threatens. Looking down or away too often may indicate that you are tense or uninterested. Good gaze behaviour indicates your interest and also enables you to see important facial messages. Additionally, gaze can give you cues about when to stop listening and start responding. However, the main cues used in sychronizing conversations are verbal and voice messages rather than body messages (Argyle, 1983).

- *Appropriate facial expressions.* A friendly relaxed facial expression, including a smile, initially demonstrates interest. However, as the other talks, your facial expressions need to show that you are tuned into what they say. For instance, if another is serious, weeping or angry, you need adjust your facial expression to indicate that you observe and hear what they communicate.

- *Sensitivity to physical distance and height.* In Chapter 3, I mentioned the various zones of intimacy for different kinds of conversations. Rewarding listening entails respecting these zones. If you move too quickly into another's personal space, they may both feel uncomfortable and move away. If you are physically too far away, not only do they have to talk louder but they may

perceive you as emotionally distant. The most comfortable height for conversations is if your heads are at the
same level. If you persist in standing when someone seated
talks to you, this is likely to feel awkward for them. Additionally, if listeners sit in higher or lower chairs than
speakers, this is also off-putting.

• *Appropriate use of touch.* When people date there may be
high levels of touch as they listen to and get to know one
another. Their body contact as they listen and talk may
include: holding hands, a semi-embrace, and sitting close
so that their legs touch. In many relationships, touch can
be an effective way of showing concern for someone who
is hurting and in pain. Demonstrations of concern include
touching another's hands, arms, shoulders and upper
back. The intensity and duration of touch should be sufficient to establish contact and yet avoid creating discomfort. Part of being a rewarding listener includes
picking up messages about the limits and desirability of
your use of touch.

Both *within* your body messages and also *between* your body
messages and your voice and verbal messages, congruence
increases the chances of your being perceived as a rewarding
listener. For instance, you may be smiling and at the same time
either fidgeting or tapping your feet. Your smile may indicate
interest, your foot tapping impatience, and your overall
message may be one of insincerity.

When you listen, the message can be: 'It ain't the words you
hear, but how you hear them'. For instance, the damaging
effects of poor listener body messages were highlighted in a
study by Haase and Tepper (1972). They asked counsellors to
rate a number of ten-second videotaped interactions between a
'counsellor' and a 'client'. They found that even good verbal
understanding messages could be reduced to poor ones when
the counsellor uttered the message without eye contact, in a
backward trunk lean, rotated away from the client and from a
far distance. In short, sending good body messages is a crucial
part of the loving skill of being a rewarding listener. Exercise
16 asks you to explore your behaviour in this regard.

EXERCISE
—16—

How rewarding are my body messages when I listen?

INSTRUCTIONS

Assess how rewarding you consider your body messages are when you listen, by completing the following worksheet.

Body message	My assessment
Physical availability	
Open and relaxed body posture	
Slight forward lean	
Positive use of gestures	
Good use of gaze and eye contact	
Appropriate facial expressions	
Sensitivity to physical distance and height	
Appropriate use of touch	

Congruence within my body messages	

1. Summarize how rewarding or unrewarding you consider your body messages are when you listen.

2. Identify specific skills weaknesses in your body messages as you listen, and set goals for change.

EXPERIMENT
——3——

What happens when I vary my body messages as a listener?

INSTRUCTIONS

Part A: assessment

Completed in Exercise 16.

Part B: make an 'If . . . then . . .' statement

Design an experiment in which you systematically try to improve one or more of your body message skills weaknesses when you listen. Make an 'If . . . then . . .' statement along the lines of '*If* I change (a), (b) and/or (c) when I listen in my relationship with John/Jane Doe, *then* these consequences (to be specified) are likely to follow'.

Part C: try out and evaluate your changed behaviour

Try out your changed behaviour. Assess its positive and negative consequences for yourself and others. Have your predictions been confirmed or disconfirmed? Has the experiment taught you something about how you can strengthen your skills of sending better body messages when you listen? If so, what?

Informal experiment

Another option is to play a game with a friend in which you hold a conversation on a topic of mutual interest.

First 2 minutes: you converse normally.

Second 2 minutes: you try to send good body messages when listening as your friend talks.

Third 2 minutes: you try to send poor body messages when listening as your friend talks.

Evaluation period: discuss what it felt like receiving and sending poor body messages. Your evaluation session may be more educational and fun if you play back a video of your 6-minute conversation. Then reverse roles and repeat the second and third parts of the experiment.

SKILL 4: SENDING GOOD VOICE MESSAGES

The emotional atmosphere you provide when you listen can be greatly enhanced by your voice messages. Talkers need to feel that you are responsive to their feelings. One of the main ways you can do this is by sending voice messages that neither add nor subtract emotional meaning and emphasis.

Below I look at the voice messages mentioned in Chapter 3 in terms of being a listener who responds appropriately.

- *Volume*. You need to respond at a level that is comfortable and easy to hear.

- *Pace*. It creates a more relaxed atmosphere if you do not talk too fast when you respond. Also, in general, interrupting is to be avoided.

- *Emphasis*. It is important that your voice is expressive in accurately picking up the major feelings and feeling nuances of speakers.

- *Tone*. High-pitched and shrill voices can be off-putting. A harsh tone can threaten.

- *Enunciation*. If you do not respond clearly then that can interrupt the speaker's train of thought.

- *Accent.* Heavy accents can be very difficult to listen to, especially if accompanied by poor use of grammar and language. Again, this may interfere with the speaker's train of thought.

- *Firmness.* Speaking in a weak and diffident voice may indicate that you have problems and deter the speaker. Too much firmness overwhelms.

- *Use of pauses and silences.* Your use of pauses and silences can enhance your capacity to be a rewarding listener. If you are making it easy for speakers to tell their stories, it is often a good idea to pause after each of their utterances to see if they wish to continue. Also, good use of silences can both allow speakers more psychological space to think things through before speaking and also to get in touch with their deeper feelings.

EXERCISE
—17—

How rewarding are my voice messages when I listen?

INSTRUCTIONS

Assess how rewarding you consider your voice messages are when you listen, by completing the following worksheet.

Voice message	*My assessment*
Volume	
Pace	
Emphasis	

Tone	
Enunciation	
Accent	
Firmness	
Use of pauses and silences	

1. Summarize how rewarding or unrewarding you consider your voice messages are when you listen.

2. Identify specific skills weaknesses in your voice messages as you listen, and set goals for change.

SKILL 5: USING OPENERS, SMALL REWARDS AND OPEN QUESTIONS

Openers, small rewards and open-ended questions each require use of a few words as well as of good voice and body messages. They each make it easier for the speaker to talk.

Openers

Openers or permissions to talk are brief statements indicating that you are prepared to listen. They can occur at any time in a relationship. The message contained in all of them is: 'I'm interested and prepared to listen. I give you the opportunity of sharing with me what you think and feel'. A good time to use an opener can be when you sense someone has a personal agenda that bothers them and needs a little encouragement to share it. Such an opener may be a response to another's body messages. Examples of openers are:

> 'How was your day?'
> 'You seem a bit down today.'
> 'You look really happy.'
> 'Is there something on your mind?'
> 'Would you like to talk about it?'
> 'I'd like to hear your viewpoint.'

When using openers, you require sensitivity to the other's reactions. They may neither be ready to talk nor consider you the right person with whom to talk. They certainly may not want information dragged out of them. However, sometimes you rightly sense that they want to talk, but have difficulty doing so. Here follow-up remarks like: 'It's pretty hard to get started', and 'Take your time' may further help the speaker open up. Poor body messages can totally destroy the impact of an opener. For example, if a dad looks up and says 'What's on your mind son?' and then looks down and continues working on his car, his son is likely to feel discouraged rather than encouraged about opening up.

Small rewards

Small rewards are brief verbal expressions of interest designed to encourage the speaker. The message they convey is: 'I am with you. Please go on'. Small rewards can be used for good or ill. On the one hand, they can reward people for talking to you from their internal viewpoint. On the other hand, they may range from crude to subtle attempts to take others out of their internal viewpoint by shaping what they say. For instance, you may say 'Tell me more' whenever someone says what you want to hear, yet remain silent when they do not. Below are some examples of verbal small rewards, though perhaps the most frequently used, 'Um-hmn', is more vocal than verbal.

Um-hmn	Sure
Please continue	Indeed
Tell me more	And
Go on	So
I see	Really
Oh	Right

Interesting	Ah
Then	Yes
I hear you	You're not kidding

Open questions

You may use questions in ways that either help speakers to elaborate their internal viewpoints or lead them out of their viewpoints, possibly into yours. Open questions allow speakers to share their internal viewpoint without curtailing their options. Closed questions restrict another's options for responding. They often give only two options, 'yes' or 'no'.

> *Open question*: How do you feel about Alison?
> *Closed question*: Do you like Alison?

Bolton (1979) observes: 'Closed questions are like true/false or multiple choice test questions, while open questions are like essay questions' (pp. 44–45). Closed questions may have various negative outcomes. You may be perceived as leading and controlling the conversation. You may block another from getting in touch with and listening to themselves and responding *from their internal* viewpoint rather than *to your external* viewpoint. You may set the stage for an interrogation. Since closed questions can be disincentives to talking, they can create silences in which the stage is set for further closed questions. Even open questions require to be used sparingly. I do not mean to imply that you never use closed questions. It depends on the goals of your listening. They are useful if you wish to collect information. However, they can be dangerous if you wish to allow another to let you inside their internal viewpoint.

CONCLUDING SELF-TALK

Rewarding listening is a fundamental skill of loving. If I listen well I affirm others, know them and myself better, build trust and stability in my relationships, and help bridge age, sex and cultural differences. I can improve my skills of being a rewarding listener. I can become more conscious of when I listen from my external viewpoint rather than from the speaker's internal viewpoint. I can work on my barriers and filters to possessing an attitude of respect and acceptance when I listen. I can discipline myself to send body and voice messages that encourage rather than discourage speakers. Additionally, by using openers, I can make it easier for people to start opening up to me. Furthermore, by using small rewards and open questions, I can help them to keep sharing their internal viewpoint.

ANSWERS TO EXERCISE

Exercise 16
1. (a) EX;   (b) EX;   (c) IN.
2. (a) IN;   (b) EX;   (c) EX.
3. (a) EX;   (b) EX;   (c) IN.
4. (a) IN;   (b) EX;   (c) EX.

— 5 —

Responding helpfully

No one would talk much in society if he only knew how often he misunderstands others.

J.W. von Goethe

I only desire sincere relations with the worthiest of my acquaintances, that they may give me the opportunity once in a year to speak the truth.

Henry Thoreau

*R*ewarding listening requires you to be able to respond helpfully. You need to provide the gift of your listening so that another genuinely feels that you have understood them. Reaching out to another includes sensitively receiving and understanding their messages as well as sending yours. Furthermore, you have to communicate your understanding back to them so that they know you have received them loud and clear.

> Lucy, 17, had a boyfriend Ron, also 17. About a year ago Lucy's parents split up. This had numerous practical and emotional consequences for her. Whenever she tried to speak to Ron about her pain she felt that he did not understand her. Furthermore, she wondered if Ron even wanted to hear about it since his family life had been very happy.

> Marge and Tom are a couple in their forties. Tom manages a small company of which Marge is the co-owner. Over the past months Tom has developed a relationship with Maria, the production manager of the company. This has had a devastating effect on his relationship with Marge. Also, when she points out that such goings-on are not good for company morale, she feels he tunes out and cannot face the negative consequences of his actions.

In each of the above instances, separateness and alienation are encouraged by poor listening skills. Ron remained unaware that he was not hearing Lucy loud and clear. Tom's own needs and defences got in the way of his fully hearing Marge's feedback. The above vignettes come from my private practice. Stories such as the above are commonplace inside and outside family relationships. Getting on top of the inner enemy of your own anxiety and responding to another with accurate understanding and kindness can require considerable discipline. It is a form of love in which you may have to be tough with yourself.

The first part of this chapter continues the discussion of the skills of rewarding listening in which you try to make it easy for another to share their internal viewpoint. The latter part of the chapter looks at confrontation, a responding skill that involves stepping out of the speaker's internal viewpoint.

Reflective responding

In this book the term *reflective responding* is used as a shorthand term for responding with understanding as if in the speaker's internal viewpoint. Reflective responding entails tuning in to and 'mirroring' with your verbal, voice and body messages the crux of the meaning contained in the verbal, voice and body messages of another. Prior to discussing the skill in more detail, here are a couple of brief examples.

Patient to friend
Patient: 'When I first heard I'd got terminal cancer, my world fell apart. I'm still pretty shaken and frightened at the thought of death.'
Friend: 'You feel scared about dying and are still reeling from the news of your cancer.'

Wife to husband
Wife: 'With the children nearing the end of their education I want to build more of a life for myself. I don't want to hang around the house all the time. I want to get out and be active.'
Husband: 'You're determined to carve something outside the home for yourself and not stay brooding over an empty nest.'

When assessing how good a reflective response is, it is sometimes helpful to think of a three-link chain: *first*

statement – reflective response – second statement. Good
reflective responses allow the opportunity for another's second
statement to be a continuation of the train of thought contained in their first statement. Bad reflective responses do not.

Uses of reflective responding

When people are first introduced to the skill of reflective
responding they frequently express reservations.

> 'It's so unnatural.'
> 'People will just think I'm repeating everything they say.'
> 'It gets in the way of my being spontaneous.'
> 'It makes me too self-conscious.'

When learning any new skill, from driving a car to driving a
golf ball, there is a period where you are likely to have to concentrate extra hard on making the correct sequence of choices
that make up the skill. Reflective responding is no exception. If
you work and practise at a skill, you ultimately are likely to
own it as a 'natural' part of you. It is natural to the extent that
it feels natural. One of the main reasons why reflective
responding seems so unnatural at first is that unhelpful ways of
responding, such as judging, are firmly installed in many
people's loving skills. Thus you may need not only to learn a
new skills strength, but also to unlearn a current skills
weakness.

Reflective responding should not be used all the time, but
flexibly incorporated into your repertoire of responses. There
are many occasions when reflective responding may help you.

- When you need to show that you have understood.

- When you need to check out that you have understood.

- When others need to experience their feelings as valid.

- When others struggle to understand themselves.

- When others require help in expressing thoughts and
  feelings.

- When others are trying to manage personal problems or
  make decisions.

- When you need to be clear about another's position in a disagreement.

- When you wish to ensure that the responsibility for a decision or course of action in their lives rests with the other person.

- When you wish to maintain and enhance your relationship by setting aside a regular time for listening to each other.

However, there are other occasions when you may gain from either not using reflective responding or using it sparingly.

- When you consider someone talks too much and it is time communication became more two-way.

- When it is important that you share your internal viewpoint.

- When you wish to match the level of intimacy of another's disclosures.

- When someone expresses praise or appreciation to you.

- When you are aware that you are listening as a means of avoiding defining and asserting yourself.

- When you feel too tired or hassled to listen properly.

- When you are unable to be accepting.

- When you consider another's solution might damage either yourself and/or them.

SKILL 6: REWORDING

There is a joke about a counsellor, who firmly believed in reflective responding, being seduced by a client.

Client: I quite like you.
Counsellor: You quite like me.
Client: I think you're kinda cute.

Counsellor: You think I'm kinda cute.
Client: I find you attractive.
Counsellor: You find me attractive.
Client: I find you really attractive.
Counsellor: You find me really attractive.
Client: I find you so attractive that I would like to go to bed with you.
Counsellor: You find me so attractive that you would like to go to bed with me.
Client: Yes, why don't we go ahead and do it?
Counsellor: I can't go to bed with you, I'm your counsellor.
Client: Well, you're fired as my counsellor. Let's go to bed!

In the above sequence, the counsellor has boringly and mechanically repeated what the client has just said. For most people, that would be sufficient to cool their ardour. As a frustrated husband once said to his wife: 'If I had wanted someone to repeat everything I said after me, I would have married a parrot.' If you are to avoid wooden reflective responses, you need to work on two subskills: rewording and reflecting feelings.

The reason that it is important to reword or paraphrase is that you drive speakers crazy if you repeat them all the time. This does not mean that you never use their words, but you do so sparingly. However, when you reword, you try to stay close to the kind of language they have used. Below are a few basic examples.

Wife to husband
Wife: 'Go to hell.'
Husband: 'You're really mad at me.'
Friend to friend
First friend: 'I'm depressed.'
Second friend: 'You've got the blues.'
Divorcee to friend
Divorcee: 'It just hurts that all our mutual friends now see only Jim' (her ex-husband).
Friend: 'It's painful that friends you knew as a couple have stayed friends only with Jim.'

A good rewording of verbal content can provide a mirror

reflection that is clearer and more succinct than the original utterance. It may be appreciated by speakers with such comments as 'That's it' or 'You've got me'. In other instances, rewordings may be insufficient. They only focus on words. The voice and body messages need to be reflected as well.

Exercise 18 is designed to make you more aware of the degree to which you have choice in responding to verbal content. For each statement, many rewordings may be appropriate. Answers are provided at the end of the chapter.

EXERCISE
—18—

Reflecting words by rewording

INSTRUCTIONS

Part A: single rewording

Reword the content of each of the following statements into clear and simple language. Use 'you' or 'your' where the speaker uses 'I' or 'Me'. Remember there is no single correct answer.

1. 'It bothers me when you don't respond.'
2. 'I appreciate the help you've given me.'
3. 'I shall miss my girlfriend when she's away.'
4. 'I couldn't help laughing when he screwed up.'
5. 'You're having me on.'
6. 'Everybody here seems to pick on me.'
7. 'I get so frustrated when I can't concentrate.'
8. 'He's a handsome guy and doesn't know it.'
9. 'Stop trying to manipulate me.'
10. 'I find it difficult to show positive feelings.'

Part B: multiple rewording

Think of at least three different ways to reword the content of the following statements.

1. 'I've always been shy in social situations.'
2. 'I'm very fearful of people getting psychologically close to me.'
3. 'I feel shut out by her and don't know why.'

SKILL 7: REFLECTING FEELINGS

Most often it happens that one attributes to others only the feelings of which one is capable onself.

André Gide

The more faithfully you listen to the voice within you, the better you will hear what is sounding outside.

Dag Hammarskjöld

A sure way of helping people to experience your understanding is to be sharp at picking up their feelings. Reflecting feelings may be viewed as *feeling with* another's flow of emotions and being able to communicate this back to them. It entails offering an expressive emotional companionship. You respond to another's music and not just to their words. Also, when you reflect feelings, you give another the opportunity to listen more deeply to their own feelings.

Reflecting feelings involves both receiver skills and sender skills.

Receiver skills
Understanding another's face and body messages.
Understanding their voice messages.
Understanding their words.
Tuning into the flow of your own emotional reactions.
Taking into account the context of another's messages.
Sensing the surface and underlying meanings of another's messages.

Sender skills
Responding in ways that pick up the other's feelings words and phrases.
Rewording feelings appropriately, using expressive rather than wooden language.
Using voice and body messages that neither add to nor subtract from the emotions being conveyed.
Checking out the accuracy of your understanding.

There is a risk that constant reflective responding focusing on feelings just encourages people to wallow in them. For instance, Neil may persist in feeling sorry for himself when discussing his relationship with Nicole, which is not going well. Judgement is needed in how much and when to reflect feelings. For instance, you might use a reflective response to allow Neil to express his feelings and, then, possibly ask a question like 'Well, is there anything you think you could do to help your situation?'

Picking up feelings words and phrases

Let's start with the obvious. A good but not infallible way to discuss what another feels is to listen to their feelings words and phrases. Sometimes people ask: 'Well, what did you feel?' just after they have already been told. Sometimes feelings words are not the central message. For instance, Sandra may say 'It's just great' that her mother is getting married again, at the same time as her voice chokes and her face looks sad because the corners of her mouth are turned down. While the forthcoming marriage may be great for her mother, Sandra's voice and body messages indicate her doubts about how great it will be for her.

Below is an example of someone using feelings words and phrases that communicate what he means.

> *Mick to Frances:*
> 'I really enjoyed our date last night. It was just great. Even after so little time I feel there may be something special between us. When can we meet again?'
> Mick's feelings words and phrases: 'really enjoyed', 'just great', 'something special between us', and 'can we meet again?'

Exercise 19 attempts to help you become more disciplined at listening for verbal messages about feelings. It then builds on your rewording practice in Exercise 18 by asking you to reword the feelings words and phrases that you identify. Answers are suggested at the end of the chapter.

EXERCISE
—19—

Identifying and rewording feelings words and phrases

INSTRUCTIONS

For each of the following statements: (a) identify the words and phrases the speaker has used to describe how he or she feels; and (b) provide rewordings of these words and phrases that accurately reflect how the speaker feels.

1. Tony to Wayne
   'I find being without a job depressing. I'm young and want to get ahead. Right now my prospects look bleak.'
   Tony's feelings words and phrases:
   Rewordings of feelings words and phrases:

2. Eileen to Tricia
   'I'm determined to be my own woman. It's exciting to think I could have a successful career.'
   Eileen's feelings words and phrases:
   Rewordings of feelings words and phrases:

3. Sophia to Mario
   'I wish my folks got on better. I hate seeing them getting old and being so unhappy.'
   Sophia's feelings words and phrases:
   Rewordings of feelings words and phrases:

4. Tim to Colleen
   'Who the heck does he think he is telling me what to do? If I didn't need the job I would tell him to go to hell.'
   Tim's feelings words and phrases:
   Rewordings of feelings words and phrases:

Picking up voice and body messages

Your job as a listener is to receive information in a way that shows emotional responsiveness to speakers. To do this you need to integrate the mirroring of voice and body messages into your overall responses. Much of this can be done by varying your voice inflections and facial expressions. For instance, if a hypothetical suicide-prone friend says 'I feel terrible', you could adjust your voice and facial expression to mirror somewhat a sense of desperation. This need not prevent your voice and face also expressing warmth and sympathy.

Reflecting feelings entails expressive listening and responding. The reflection of feelings needs to be accurate in two ways. First, the feelings need to be correctly identified. Second, the level of intensity of the feelings needs to be correctly expressed. At one extreme there is the wooden responder who continuously subtracts from the level of intensity of the speaker. At the other extreme is the melodramatic responder who overemphasizes the speaker's intensity of feelings. In British, Australian and New Zealand cultures there may be a tendency when responding either to ignore or to subtract from the level of intensity of the speaker rather than to overemphasize feelings.

Another consideration in reflecting feelings is whether, and the degree to which, the speaker is prepared to acknowledge their feelings. For instance, as a listener you may infer that a parent is absolutely furious with a child. However, the parent may not be able to handle such an observation since it clashes with their self-image of being an ideal and loving parent. Thus you need to use your judgement in choosing how much feeling to reflect.

Children tend to express their emotions very openly. As you grew up you received and internalized numerous messages about which emotions it was appropriate for people of your social characteristics, family background and sex to express where and when. Consequently, many emotional messages 'come out sideways' rather than being expressed loud and clear. As such they are heavily encoded and need to be decoded. Even if they are decoded accurately, there is the further issue of whether the sender is sufficiently self-aware to acknowledge them if reflected back.

Exercise 20 is about observing feelings from voice and body messages. The first time you do the exercise, focus on the more obvious manifestations of anger, friendship, sadness and anxiety. Later you may wish to list some of the ways a negative emotion like anger may be expressed when it 'comes out sideways' rather than gets expressed directly. For instance, the speaker may both smile and clench his or her fist. In other words, you receive a mixed message that requires decoding.

Some answers to Exercise 20 are suggested at the end of the chapter.

EXERCISE
—20—

Picking up feelings from voice and body messages

INSTRUCTIONS

By filling in the blank spaces, indicate what voice and body messages might serve as cues for you to pick up each of the following feelings.

Non-verbal cue	Anger	Friendship	Sadness	Anxiety
Tone of voice				
Voice volume				
Eye contact and gaze				
Facial expression				
Posture				
Gestures				

Assess your effectiveness at picking up from their voice and body messages the feelings of your loved ones and friends.

Reflecting feelings from verbal, voice and body messages

You receive so many verbal, voice and body messages from others, how do you know which ones really count? There is no simple answer. Some people communicate their feelings loud and clear with a good matching of verbal, voice and body messages. Others' styles of communicating feelings interfere with their effectiveness: for example, either communicating less intensity of feeling than is the case or communicating some feelings loud and clear, but having difficulty expressing other feelings. Then there are a host of factors disrupting sending clear feelings messages, depending upon: the situational context; the person to whom the message is being sent; the sex of the sender; cultural rules; the attending skills of the listener; and whether or not the sender had a good night's sleep and is in a reasonable temper today.

What you try to do is: (a) decode the *overall* message accurately, and (b) formulate an emotionally expressive reflective response that communicates back the crux of the speaker's feelings. People generally feel you understand them better if you reflect their feeling at the front of your response, even though they may not have communicated it first. Here is an example.

Gina has just failed an important maths test.
Gina's verbal message: 'I flunked maths and have to retake it. I'm so disappointed with myself'.
Gina's voice message: quiet voice, emphasis on 'so disappointed', voice lowers and trails away for 'with myself', sighs.
Gina's body message: down at mouth, pale, tearful, slouched posture, moves slowly.
Possible reflection of feeling: 'You're bitterly upset with yourself'.

The reflection of feeling is said somewhat tentatively to check out whether Gina considers it accurate. There is a risk of your putting feelings into another's mouth which are either only partially accurate or even downright inaccurate. As you reflect Gina's feelings your voice messages convey kindness and concern and your body messages convey interest and attention. Because Gina feels bitter disappointment with herself, you emphasize the words 'bitterly upset' in your reflective response.

If you are not confident that you have picked up the speaker's feelings accurately, you can make your response even more tentative. For example you could say to Gina: 'I think I hear you saying you now feel bitterly upset with yourself – have I got you right?' This may not be as good as pinpointing the feeling accurately with less hesitation, but it is better than rushing in and getting it wrong.

SKILL 8: REFLECTING FEELINGS AND REASONS

One kind of reflective responding that is often helpful entails reflecting back both feelings and reasons. You are not making an interpretation or offering an explanation from your external viewpoint. Rather, where reasons have been provided for a feeling by another, you reflect these back in a 'You feel . . . because' statement that mirrors their internal viewpoint. Here is an example.

> Charles: 'I have my law exams coming up and it's vital for my career to get a good grade. My whole future depends on it. I'm so worried.'
>
> Mark: '*You feel* really anxious *because* you have these make-or-break exams imminent.'
>
> Charles: 'Yes, I can't sleep properly any more and I'm not eating well. I have a constant feeling of tension and wonder what I should do.'

Here Mark correctly identified Charles's worry and anxiety rather than blocked its discussion. Mark's 'You feel . . . because' response showed more understanding than if he had stopped after saying: 'You feel really anxious'. The 'because' part of Mark's statement succinctly stated the crux of Charles's view of the cause of his worry. Charles was able to use this reflective response not only to elaborate his feelings but also as a stepping-stone to wondering about how he should handle them. Reflective responding focusing on Charles's *feelings and their causes* is helping him move toward *taking action* to manage them better.

Exercise 21 requires you to reflect feelings and reasons in a standard 'You feel . . . because . . .' format. People who start listening-training often have trouble both identifying feelings and stating them accurately. The exercise tries to make sure you do this first before moving on to reflect the reasons for the feeling. Some possible responses to Exercise 21 are provided at the end of the chapter.

EXERCISE
—21—

Reflecting feelings and reasons

INSTRUCTIONS

For each of the following statements formulate a 'You feel . . . because . . .' response that rewords the speaker's main feeling and clearly states the crux of their explanation for it.

1. Maureen to Vince:
   'I hate being teased. I just hate it. I'm no different from the other girls and yet they seem to enjoy ganging up on me. It makes me feel so angry and lonely.'

2. Merle to Don:
   'I've got this neighbour who wants her little boy to play with mine. I would like to please her and yet her boy is very naughty. I feel confused and wonder how best to handle her.'

3. Amy to Tania:
   'Though it's not what we planned, I'm pregnant. I'm surprised how strongly I feel about having the baby. Fortunately, John wants it too.'

4. Helmut to Ian:
   'I get annoyed when people don't understand my relationship with Tom. Sure we are emotionally very close, but what's wrong with that? Some people can't understand intimate friendships between guys.'

SKILL 9: AVOIDING
UNREWARDING 'DON'TS'

We're all of us sentenced to solitary confinement inside our own skins for life.

Tennessee Williams

You cannot and should not listen to others all the time.

However, if you love people, you try to help them out of their solitude. You endeavour to avoid making the kind of responses that close them up rather than help them to unfold and blossom. Many of the characteristic ways in which you respond to others in everyday conversation are *not* particularly helpful in encouraging them to share their internal viewpoint. A distinction is sometimes made between a counselling conversation, where the counsellor listens carefully to the client, and a social conversation, cynically described as 'Two people taking turns to exercise their egos'. Counsellors are trained to make the listening choices that help clients to feel safe and accepted. This includes avoiding the kinds of threatening verbal responses prevalent in everyday conversations.

If people are going to give you the gift of revealing themselves, they need psychological safety and space. Such safety and space is both quantitative and qualitative. If you are either not physically accessible or, when you are, you monopolize the conversation or keep interrupting, you are scarcely giving another the *quantity* of safety and space they need. However, you can also preclude them from having the *quality* of safety and space they need by choosing to respond in ways that show lack of respect for the importance of their internal viewpoint. This not only makes it more difficult for others to talk to you, but it also interferes with their listening to themselves. A tragedy in many close relationships is that often, unintentionally through their skills weaknesses, friends, partners and lovers put each other down when they listen. You may wish to express your caring by helping your friends or partner. However, instead you may communicate that they are not absolutely free to talk about and to be themselves.

Below are some of the 'don'ts' to avoid if you wish to be a rewarding listener. This is not to say that you should never use some of the following ways of responding in your relationships. Rather that you need be aware of their possible negative consequences before choosing to use them.

- *Directing and leading.* Taking control of what another can talk about.
  'I'm interested in what's going right for you, not what's going wrong.'
  'I would like you to talk about your relationship with your mother.'
  'Let's focus on how you get on at work.'

● *Judging and evaluating.* Making judgemental statements, especially those indicating the speaker falls short of your standards.
'I don't think you should be seeing her.'
'You've made a real mess of your life.'
'You are not very good at expressing yourself.'

● *Blaming.* Assigning responsibility in a finger-pointing way.
'It's all your fault.'
'You started it.'
'I'm all upset now because of you.'

● *Getting aggressive.* Making statements that are designed to cause pain and belittle another.
'Can't you ever do anything right?'
'You fool!'
'Idiot!'

● *Moralizing and preaching.* Patronizingly telling another how they should lead their lives.
'You should always respect your parents.'
'Honesty is the best policy.'
'Sex is not everything in life.'

● *Advising and teaching.* Adopting an 'I know what is best for you to do' style of responding. Not giving another space to reach their own conclusions.
'My advice to you is to drop him.'
'No wonder you're lonely. You need to go out and meet people.'
'You need to spend more time outdoors.'

● *Not accepting another's feelings.* Telling people that their feelings should be different from what they are.
'You shouldn't be feeling so sorry for yourself.'
'Only sissies get nervous.'
'I don't see why you're so happy.'

● *Inappropriately talking about yourself.* Talking about yourself in ways that interfere with another's disclosures.
'You have troubles. Let me tell you mine.'
'I think I'm a good listener. A lot of people tell me that.'

'I am going to tell you my experience so that you can learn from it.'

- *Interrogating.* Using questions in such a way that another feels threatened by unwanted probing.
'Do you masturbate? If so, what are your fantasies?'
'Tell me about your previous relationships.'
'What are your weaknesses?'

- *Reassuring and humouring.* Trying to make others feel better more for your sake than theirs. Not acknowledging their true feelings.
'We all feel like that sometimes.'
'You can get by. I know you can.'
'Look, I've made you laugh. It can't be that bad.'

- *Labelling and diagnosing.* Playing the amateur shrink and placing a label or diagnostic category on another.
'You have a hysterical personality.'
'You're paranoid.'
'You're a real neurotic.'

- *Over-interpreting.* Offering explanations that come from your external viewpoint and bear little similarity to what another might have thought of by themselves.
'I think that you are afraid of me and that is why you don't go out with me more.'
'Your indecision about getting a job is related to your fear of failing to live up to your father's standards.'
'The fact that you were not loved as a child makes it hard for you to show your affection for me.'

- *Distracting and being irrelevant.* Confusing the issue by going off in another direction or creating a smokescreen.
'Let's go some place else.'
'Let's change the subject.'
'Do we have to talk about this? Why don't we have some fun?'

- *Faking attention.* Insincerely pretending to be more interested and involved in what is being said than you are.
'That's so interesting.'
'I would never have believed it.'
'Oh, really.'

• *Placing time pressures.* Letting the speaker know that your availability for listening is very limited.
'I've got to go soon.'
'You had better be brief.'
'I'm very busy these days.'

A major 'don't' that is not listed above is that of breaking confidences. If you are a leaky sieve you are about as welcome as a leaky condom! All the above 'don'ts' focused on verbal responses. However, as shown earlier, discouraging voice and body messages can be just as devastating. Exercise 22 aims to help you explore which of your present ways of responding interfere with your being a rewarding and safe person with whom to open up.

EXERCISE
—22—

How safe am I to talk to?

INSTRUCTIONS

Using the scale below, rate each of the following 'don'ts' of rewarding listening according to how much you respond that way in relationships that are important for you.

Frequently	2
Sometimes	1
Never	0

Don'ts   *Your rating*

1. Directing and leading

2. Judging and evaluating

3. Blaming

4. Getting aggressive

5. Moralizing and preaching

6. Advising and teaching

7. Not accepting the other's feelings

8. Inappropriately talking about myself

9. Interrogating

10. Reassuring and humouring

11. Labelling and diagnosing

12. Over-interpreting

13. Distracting and being irrelevant

14. Faking attention

15. Placing time pressures

Look at the times that you have rated 2 or 1 and assess the consequences in your relationships of each of these ways of responding.

USING REWARDING LISTENING SKILLS IN YOUR DAILY LIFE

Let us now see if changing some of your existing listening choices in your daily life has positive consequences for you.

Undoubtedly you already possess some listening skills strengths. Perhaps, like most people, you can build on these strengths if, in a more systematic fashion, you use the rewarding listening skills just described. The focus of Experiments 4 and 5 is on improving your skills of helping another to share their internal viewpoint. Remember to accompany your changed verbal behaviours with good voice and body messages.

EXPERIMENT
——4——

What happens when I use openers and small rewards?

INSTRUCTIONS

Part A: assessment

Review the section on openers and small rewards at the end of Chapter 4. Then for the next 24 hours behave as you normally do and monitor your use of openers and small rewards in your daily life. It may assist you if you keep a log of your behaviours with the following headings.

Time	Other person(s) involved	My use of openers and small rewards

Part B: make an 'If . . . then . . .' statement

Design an experiment in which you systematically use openers and small rewards. Make an 'If . . . then . . .' statement along the lines of: '*If* I change (a) and/or (b) in my relationship(s) with (one or more specific people), *then* these consequences (to be specified) are likely to follow'.

Part C: try out and evaluate your changed behaviour

Try out your changed behaviour. Assess its positive and negative consequences for yourself and others. Have your predictions been confirmed or disconfirmed? Has the experiment taught you something about how you can be a more rewarding listener by improving your use of openers and small rewards? If so, what?

EXPERIMENT
——5——

What happens when I use reflective responding skills?

Part A: assessment

Through completing the exercises so far in this chapter, you should already have some idea of how well you use reflective responding. For the next 24 hours listen as you normally do and monitor your use of reflective responding in your daily life. It may assist you if you keep a log of your behaviours with the following headings.

Time	Other person(s) involved	My use of reflective responding

Part B: make an 'If . . . then . . .' statement

Design an experiment in which you systematically use reflective responding (though don't overdo it!). Make an 'If . . . then . . .' statement along the lines of: '*If* I use reflective responding more in my relationship(s) with (one or more specific people), *then* these consequences (to be specified) are likely to follow'.

Part C: try out and evaluate your changed behaviour

Try out your changed behaviour. How well did you use reflective responding? Assess its positive and negative consequences for yourself and others. Have your predictions been confirmed or disconfirmed? Has the experiment taught you something about how you can be a more rewarding listener by improving your use of reflective responding? If so, what?

BEYOND THE INTERNAL VIEWPOINT: CONFRONTATION

So far I have focused on being a rewarding listener so that you make it easy for another to share their internal viewpoint. However, there are also times when you may help another by not responding from their internal viewpoint. Though it may seem strange, confrontation can be an important and helpful loving skill.

What is confrontation?

Your fantasy of confrontation may be that you are sitting in the 'hot seat' whilst others psychologically attack you and try to strip you of your defences. Admittedly this is one form of confrontation, but not the sort advocated here. The skill I wish to convey is that of challenging another's existing perceptions so that they can work with more and better information. Each of you lives in the world of your own perceptions. Sometimes a challenge or confrontation from outside can broaden and deepen your horizons. Egan (1977) views confrontation as an *invitation* to another to examine his or her style of relating and its consequences for self and others. Needless to say, *how* you confront is very important.

Confronting inconsistencies and possible distortions of reality are two kinds of confrontation that you can include in your repertoire of loving skills.

1. *Confronting inconsistencies.* When someone talks to you, you can experience inconsistencies in the messages they send you. Such inconsistencies may include the following.

   - Inconsistency between verbal, voice and body messages.
     'On the one hand you say that you are fine, but on the other I catch a note of pain in your voice and see you looking tearful.'

   - Inconsistency between words and actions.
     'You say you love your children from your former marriage, but you rarely try to see them and are behind on your maintenance payments.'

- Inconsistency between past and present utterances.
  'You now say you hate her, but a week ago you were saying how much you loved her.'

- Inconsistency between your view of you and my view of you.
  'You say that you see yourself as unattractive, but I genuinely do not see you that way.'

- Inconsistency between your view of you and others' view of you.
  'You see yourself as pulling your weight in doing the chores, but you seem to be getting a lot of messages that other members of the family see you differently.'

2. *Confronting possible distortions of reality.* When people talk to you they may make statements like:

   'They're all out to get me.'
   'I have no friends.'
   'I'm a terrible mother.'
   'I'm no good with women/men.'
   'He/she doesn't love me any more.'
   'I'm no good at anything.'
   'I can't do anything about it.'
   'They made me do it.'

All of the above are possible examples of faulty thinking that may be harming rather than helping the speaker. One of your responding choices is to make a reflective response within the speaker's internal viewpoint. Another is to confront the speaker's version of reality. People often trip themselves up by jumping to conclusions on insufficient evidence ('I have no friends') and by thinking in black-and-white terms ('Either I'm perfect or I'm no good at all'). Also, they may fail adequately to own responsibility for their thoughts, feelings and actions ('They made me do it'). You need to use your judgement as to whether you go on listening within their internal viewpoint or you confront their possible distortions of reality.

How to confront

My emphasis here is on using confronting to help another expand and explore their perceptions. The starting point is their internal viewpoint rather than yours. There may be other occasions in your relationships, for instance confronting a conflict, when the starting point may be your viewpoint. This is covered in a later chapter.

How you confront involves verbal, voice and body messages. Here are some possible verbal messages.

- *Confronting inconsistencies.* A common response here is that of '*On the one hand you say . . ., but on the other hand . . .*'. For example, '*On the one hand you say* that you are fine, *but on the other hand* I catch a note of pain in your voice'. This is often shortened to 'You say . . ., but . . .'. For example, '*You say* that you are fine, *but* I catch a note of pain in your voice'.

- *Confronting possible distortions of reality.* Here a good form of words is: 'You say . . ., but what's the evidence?' For example, 'You say that you have no friends, but what's the evidence?' Such a response reflects the speaker's internal viewpoint and then invites them to produce evidence to support it. They may then make a remark like: 'Well, Kathryn never phones me up any more.' Then you may confront them again with a question like: 'Is there any other way of looking at this?' With each of the two questions 'What's the evidence?' and 'Is there any other way of looking at that?' you invite the speaker to produce their own evidence to confirm or disconfirm their version of reality rather than do it for them. On other occasions you may suggest some evidence from your viewpoint for their consideration.

Below are some guidelines for how to confront.

1. *Start with reflective responding.* Always start your response by showing that you have heard and understood the speaker's message. Then build on this with your confronting response. This way you are more likely to keep the speaker's ears open to what comes from your viewpoint.
2. *Where possible, help speakers to confront themselves.* By reflecting inconsistency, you allow speakers to choose their own conclusions about it. Similarly, by asking speakers to search for evidence to back their statements, you help them to confront themselves. Assisting others in self-confrontation often leads to less resistances than directly confronting them from your external viewpoint.

3. *Do not talk down.* Keep your confrontations at a democratic level. They are invitations for exploration rather than papal *ex cathedra* statements. Avoid 'You' messages. A major risk in confronting others is that they perceive what you say as a put-down rather than as helpful.

4. *Use the minimum amount of 'muscle'.* Only confront as strongly as required to achieve your goal. Heavy confrontations can create resistances. Though sometimes necessary, they are generally to be avoided.

5. *Avoid threatening voice and body messages.* Try to avoid threatening voice and body messages, like sighing and finger pointing.

6. *Leave the ultimate responsibility with the speaker.* Allow speakers to decide whether your confrontations actually help them to move forward in their exploration. Many of your confrontations may involve slight challenges which, if well timed and tactfully worded, are unlikely to elicit a high degree of defensiveness.

7. *Do not overdo it.* Nobody likes persistently being challenged. You create an unsafe emotional climate for the speaker. You can help others move forward with skilled use of confronting responses. You can block them and harm your relationship if you confront too often and too clumsily.

EXPERIMENT
—6—

What happens when I use confronting skills?

INSTRUCTIONS

The approach to this experiment is more informal than that of the previous experiments since you do not control when another offers you the chance to use your skills.

Part A: confronting inconsistencies

For a 48-hour period use the skills of confronting inconsistencies described in the chapter whenever you consider it appropriate in your daily life. Extend the time period for the experiment if necessary. Keep a log with the following headings.

Date and time	Details of my confronting inconsistencies	Consequences of my confronting inconsistencies

Summarize what you have learned from the consequences of changing your confronting inconsistencies behaviour.

Part B: confronting possible distortions of reality

Whenever an appropriate occasion occurs in the next 3 days, use the skills of confronting possible distortions of reality by another or others in your relationship(s). Extend the time period for the experiment if necessary. Keep a log with the following headings.

Date and time	Details of my confronting possible distortions of reality	Consequences of my confronting possible distortions of reality

Summarize what you have learned from the consequences of changing your confronting possible distortions of reality behaviour.

CONCLUDING SELF-TALK

Reflective listening is a rewarding listening skill that I can use in my relationships. It involves mirroring the crux of the speaker's verbal, voice and body messages so that they feel accurately understood. Component skills of reflective responding include: rewording, decoding and reflecting back feelings, and reflecting back speakers' reasons for their feelings. There are numerous pitfalls that I must try to avoid if I wish to be safe to talk to.

There are occasions when I may help another more by responding to their messages from my viewpoint than from theirs. Confronting is a skill that I can use to challenge their existing perceptions and, I hope, to expand them for their benefit. Two major kinds of confrontation are: confronting inconsistencies and confronting possible distortions of reality. How I confront is important since clumsy confrontations are threatening and lead to defensiveness.

ANSWERS TO EXERCISES

Exercise 18
The following are suggestions, though other answers might also be appropriate.

Part A

1. 'You feel upset when I don't reply.'
2. 'You're grateful for my assistance.'
3. 'You're going to be lonely when (name of girlfriend) isn't around.'
4. 'You couldn't control your enjoyment of his mistake.'
5. 'You feel I'm making a fool out of you.'
6. 'You feel we all gang up on you.'
7. 'You become very irritated when you can't keep your mind on something.'
8. 'You feel he's a good looking boy and isn't aware of it.'
9. 'Quit attempting to take me places where I don't want to go.'
10. 'You have trouble expressing affection.'

Part B

1. 'You've always been bashful in company.'
   'You've always been timid when socializing.'
   'You've always been anxious with people.'
2. 'I'm afraid of intimacy.'
   'I find close relationships scary.'
   'I get worried by emotional nearness.'
3. 'I feel excluded by her and can't find the reason.'
   'I feel pushed away by her and can't understand it.'
   'I feel rejected by her and have no explanation for it.'

Exercise 19
Other rewordings than those suggested below may also be appropriate.

1. Tony's feelings words and phrases: 'depressing', 'want to get ahead', 'bleak'.
   Rewordings of feelings words and phrases: 'a downer', 'wish to be successful', 'unpromising'.
2. Eileen's findings words and phrases: 'determined', 'exciting', 'successful'.
   Rewordings of feelings words and phrases: 'resolved', 'thrilling', 'good'.
3. Sophia's feelings words and phrases: 'wish', 'got on better', 'hate', 'being so unhappy'.
   Rewordings of feelings words and phrases: 'would like', 'be on friendlier terms', 'loathe', 'being so miserable'.
4. Tim's feelings words and phrases: 'Who the heck', 'need the job', 'go to hell'.
   Rewordings of feelings words and phrases: 'Who on earth', 'want the money', 'get lost'.

Exercise 20
Below are some illustrative voice and body messages. There are many others.

Non-verbal cue	Anger	Friendship	Sadness	Anxiety
Tone of voice	Harsh	Warm	Soft	Timid Hesitant
Voice volume	Loud	Easy to hear	Quiet	Quiet
Eye contact	Direct	Good, but unobtrusive	Averted	Averted Very intermittent

Facial expression	Clenched teeth	Smile	Tearful Mouth turned down	Strained
Posture	Rigid	Relaxed	Slouched	Tense
Gestures	Fist clenched Finger pointing	Arm round shoulder	Holds head in hands	Finger tapping

Exercise 21

1. 'You feel mad and isolated because you loathe being treated and picked on as though you're different.'
2. 'You feel torn because you have mixed feelings about pleasing your neighbour and yet not wanting your son to play with her naughty boy.'
3. 'You feel amazed at the strength of your feelings because your pregnancy wasn't planned and yet you really want the baby.'
4. 'You feel upset because people misunderstand your feelings for Tom.'

— 6 —

Overcoming shyness and making initial contact

Venus favours the bold.
Ovid

Gather ye rosebuds while ye may
Old Time is still a-flying,
And this same flower that smiles today
To-morrow will be dying.
Robert Herrick

*A*n essential loving skill is the ability to step out of your solitude and make initial contact with others. It is an area that can cause much agonizing. Let us look at two young women who go to the same party where neither knows anybody else well.

> Kay arrives at the party having made a big effort to overcome her nerves about going at all. Though attractive, she thinks that people do not find her so. On arrival at the party she is given a drink and introduced to a group of people. She listens to them politely, but never makes a contribution of her own. When later a young man called Craig tries to engage her in conversation, she becomes very quiet and averts her gaze. She appears tense and lacking in warmth and vitality.

> Sara goes to a party excited and determined to do her best to have a good time. She is not afraid to go up to people whom she thinks look interesting and introduce herself. When conversing she appears interested in what others say and participates in a lively and unforced way. Since she wants to meet new people she moves around. Even if she does not find someone with whom to develop a

relationship, she will have enjoyed herself and helped others to do likewise.

Both Kay and Sara are attractive. Assuming it is a reasonably good party, both should be able to make an enjoyable time for themselves. However, Sara has much better making-contact skills than Kay. Consequently, the chances of Sara finding people who wish to see her again are greater than those of Kay. Kay is far from alone in finding difficult situations involving groups of new people. Below I focus on some of the skills that Kay, and possibly you, too, might use to reach out and make contact with others. I have divided the chapter into three main sections: defining shyness, combating shy thinking and making-initial-contact skills.

DEFINING SHYNESS

I am afraid to tell you who I am, because, if I tell you who I am, you may not like who I am, and it's all that I have.

John Powell

Dictionary definitions of shyness emphasize words like bashful, timid, wary, uneasy in company and avoiding contact. Shyness is a problem for children, adolescents and adults alike. Based on a large-scale shyness survey mainly conducted on American college students, Zimbardo (1977) found that more than 80 per cent reported that they were shy at some points in their lives. Of these, over 40 per cent considered themselves presently shy. Zimbardo's data focus on people who admit their shyness. My position is that anxiety is present in *all* social interaction to a greater or lesser degree, even though much of it goes unacknowledged. When meeting new people you wear a social mask to influence and control their reactions to you. You stage manage their impressions of you. Your underlying anxieties can play a big part in blocking you from making good person-to-person contact. Instead, you risk treating yourself and others as objects to be manipulated rather than as people to be loved.

What is shyness? Though not exhaustive, below are some considerations for defining shyness and for assessing how shy you are:

- *Feelings.* Feelings associated with shyness include:

anxiety	insecurity
bashfulness	loneliness
confusion	mistrust
embarrassment	shame
fear	tension
humiliation	vulnerability

- *Physical reactions.* Physical reactions associated with shyness include:

blushing	nausea
feeling faint	perspiring
knotted stomach	pounding heart
mind going black	shaking
mouth going dry	shallow breathing

- *Thoughts.* Thoughts associated with shyness include the following.

Self-talk about myself
It's OK to be shy
It's not OK to be shy
I am a solitary person
I am uninteresting
I am weak
I lack self-confidence
I am not as good as others
I might get hurt or rejected
I lack social skills
I need approval
I can't take embarrassment

Self-talk about what others think
Others accept my shyness
Others notice my physical symptoms
Others may reject me
Others may think I'm incompetent
Others may consider me uninteresting
Others pay close attention to my behaviour
Others are shy too and understand
Others get uncomfortable with me

Thinking skills weaknesses
Additionally, shyness gets sustained by other thinking
skills weaknesses such as: unrealistic personal rules,

misperceiving, misattributing cause, and predicting wrongly. I discuss each of these skills weaknesses shortly.

- *Verbal, voice and body messages*. Illustrative verbal, voice and body messages associated with shyness include the following.

Verbal messages
Keeping silent or talking as little as possible
Low self-disclosure
Being too ready to agree

Voice messages
Speaking quietly
Stammering
Loudness masking insecurity

Body messages
Avoiding or escaping from situations
Averting gaze
Smiling too much
Tight body posture

Conversational skills weaknesses
Additionally, shyness gets sustained by poor conventional skills, including: use of openers, listening, coordination of switching from talking to listening and back, keeping the conversation flowing, and ending conversations.

Defensive roles
Many people handle their anxieties in social situations by wearing masks or acting out defensive roles (Powell, 1969). These roles include: aggression, clowning, conforming, cynicism, inappropriate flirting, monopolizing, putting themselves down, and playing the strong, silent type.

- *People*. You may be more shy with some kinds of people than others. Zimbardo's (1977) shy students were shy with the following categories of people in descending order: strangers, the opposite sex, authorities by virtue of their knowledge, authorities by virtue of their role, relatives, elderly people, friends, children and parents.

- *Situations*. Situations associated with shyness include the following.
Meeting people for the first time

Asking someone for a date
Giving a talk in front of a group of people
Participating in a discussion group
Asking for help (for example, when ill)
Going to a party
Situations requiring assertiveness (for example, returning
something to a shop)
Interviews
Having a conversation with a person of the other sex
Going to a dance/disco
Showing your body in a non-sexual context
Situations involving sexual intimacy

In the above section I have attempted to provide a much
fuller definition of shyness than that indicated by dictionary
definitions like bashful or timid. Additional dimensions are
how severe you perceive your shyness to be, either across the
board and/or for specific situations, and whether or not you
consider shyness to be a problem for you. Exercise 23 asks you
to assess your current experience of shyness.

EXERCISE
—23—

My experience of shyness

INSTRUCTIONS

Fill in the worksheet below by assessing your current experience of shyness in each of the dimensions listed. Give
specific illustrations where possible. Consult the text if in
doubt about the meaning of a dimension.

Dimension	My assessment
Feelings	
Physical reactions	

Thoughts	
Verbal messages	
Voice messages	
Body messages	
Conversational skills weaknesses	
Defensive roles	
People with whom I'm shy	
Situations in which I'm shy	

1. To what extent do you see that any shyness you possess is influenced by considerations relating to your biological sex and to your culture? If so, please explain.

2. Summarize how shy you currently perceive yourself to be. What are the consequences for yourself and for others?

COMBATING SHY THINKING

If you are shy now, many early learnings contributed to it. These include the examples set by your parents. Zimbardo (1977) observes: 'In general, then, about 70 percent of the time parents and children share the same shyness label; they tend to be shy together' (pp. 62–63). Also, the consequences provided by others for your reaching out behaviour undoubtedly contributed. However, now your problem is how to stop sustaining your shyness if it interferes with your attaining your relationship goals. One of the main ways in which you sustain your shyness is by thinking shy. Your use of thinking skills can either support or oppress you (Nelson-Jones, 1989). I now present five thinking skills in which you can alter the balance more in the direction of self-support than self-oppression to overcome your shyness.

Attributing cause accurately

Attributions are the explanations, interpretations, or reasons you tell yourself for what happens. How you explain your shyness influences whether you either work to overcome it or stay stuck. There are a number of misattributions or faulty explanations for shyness which may weaken your motivation for change. These explanations are often partial truths, but the error is to treat them as whole truths. Below are some possible misattributions concerning shyness.

- 'It's my genes.' This is the position that you are shy by nature rather than by nurture. Though people may have different biological pronenesses to anxiety and fearing rejection, a considerable part of shyness represents learned behaviour that is sustained by your current thinking and action skills weaknesses.

- 'It's my unfortunate past.' Your unfortunate past or 'What others did to you' may have contributed to your acquiring some skills weaknesses associated with shyness. However, you sustain your shyness by 'What you do to yourself'. If you have had a very unfortunate past you may require counselling help to provide the nurturing and healing you never received from your natural parents. However, many people, with or without professional help, have learned to overcome skills weaknesses caused by their unfortunate pasts.

- 'Others must make the first move.' Some of you may play a passive rather than an active role when meeting new people. It is as though you wait for events to happen to you rather than take an active part in shaping events. You are letting others assume the responsibility for helping you out of your shell. This may not happen. Sometimes the passivity is reinforced by social rules. For instance, females are expected to be less forward and take fewer risks in making social contact than males. This may have negative consequences for both shy females and males: for shy females, because they have been insufficiently helped to develop initiating skills; and for shy males, because they feel the full pressure of the expectation that males initiate. A major theme of this book is that each person must assume responsibility for making the choices that work best for them. Sitting or standing around waiting for 'things' to happen is frequently not the best choice.

- 'It's all my fault.' You may consider that everything that goes wrong in social situations is your fault. You may fail to take into account that, when two people relate, each has a responsibility for the success of the contact, not just you. Your hypersensitivity to feelings of embarrassment and willingness to blame yourself may erode rather than help you gain the confidence to work on your shyness.

- 'I've tried before.' You may have tried to overcome your shyness before and been unsuccessful. However, this need not be your guide to the future. For instance, this time you may try harder, understand your shyness better, possess better skills at managing it, and be better at enlisting the support of others. The fact that you have tried before does not mean that you cannot now learn new and better skills to help you succeed.

- 'I can't stand setbacks.' Setbacks are part of learning any new skill. Also, problems like shyness are a part of living. Your unrealistic expectations about the learning process and smoothness of life make you vulnerable to setbacks. You can develop the skills of learning to handle shyness rather than to oppress yourself when faced with setbacks.

The above are attributions or explanations not only of how you became shy but also of why you remain shy. Did any of them have the ring of truth for you? If so, work hard at challenging the faulty thinking that these misattributions represent. Below are some examples of more realistic attributions.

- 'Though like many people I'm naturally sensitive, my shyness has been largely learned.'

- 'Though others undoubtedly contributed to my becoming shy, I currently sustain my shyness through skills weaknesses that I can work to overcome.'

- 'It is not up to others to make the first move to help me out of my shyness since I am responsible for making the choices in life that work best for me.'

- 'I am only responsible for my own behaviour in social situations rather than accepting total responsibility for what happens.'

- 'Though I've tried before, circumstances are different now and with more understanding of how I've sustained my shyness I can develop new and better skills to overcome it.'

- 'Setbacks in my attempts to overcome my shyness are both challenges and may also be valuable learning experiences.'

Coping self-talk

Coping self-talk is another thinking skill for managing feelings of shyness (Meichenbaum, 1983, 1985). The idea is that during your waking hours you continuously engage in an internal dialogue or perform self-talk. The goals of coping self-talk are to calm your anxieties and to help you deal effectively with the task at hand. Thus coping self-talk contains two major elements: *calming* self-talk and *coaching* self-talk. Coping self-talk is about *coping* or 'doing as well as I can' rather than about *mastery* or 'being perfect' and 'having no anxiety'. Coping is a much more realistic goal than mastery. Altering your goal from mastery to coping is likely to increase your self-support and to decrease your self-oppression. You now possess an attainable standard toward which to strive.

Coping self-talk involves replacing negative self-talk statements with helpful ones. Reverting to the examples at the start of the chapter of Kay and Sara going to the party, their self-talk was as follows. Note how Kay oppresses herself and Sara supports herself.

Kay: 'I know that I am going to find this party difficult. Everybody is looking at me. I feel unattractive. I don't want to make a mistake. I'm feeling tense and, when this happens, I know it will only get worse.'

Sara: 'I enjoy parties and meeting new people. Though I get a little anxious with strangers I know I can overcome it. I have developed some good party skills and these usually work. All I have to do is my best.'

In coping self-talk, calming and coaching statements tend to be interspersed. Two important areas of *calming* self-talk are as follows.

- Telling yourself to stay calm. Simple self-statements include: 'Keep calm', 'Relax' and 'Just take it easy'. Additionally, you can instruct yourself to 'Take a deep breath' or 'Breathe slowly and regularly'.

- Telling yourself you can cope. Simple self-statements include: 'I can handle this situation' or 'My anxiety is a signal for me to use my coping skills'.

Coaching self-talk can help you to cope with shyness in the following ways.

- Specifying your goals. For example, 'I will go up and talk to a minimum of three new people at the party'.

- Breaking tasks down. Thinking through the steps needed to attain your goal.

- Concentrating on the task at hand. You instruct yourself like pilots who talk themselves through to difficult landings.

You may use coping self-talk before, during and after stressful social situations: for example, going to a party full of strangers or out with a new date. Possible coping self-talk statements for *before* a stressful social situation include:

'This anxiety is a sign for me to use my coping skills.'
'Calm down. Develop a plan to manage the situation.'
'I know if I use my coping skills I can manage.'

Possible coping self-talk statements for *during* a stressful social situation include:

> 'Take my time. Breathe slowly and regularly.'
> 'Relax. I can manage if I just take one step at a time.'
> 'I don't have to be liked by everyone. All I can do is as best as I can.'

Possible coping self-talk statements for *after* a stressful social situation include:

> 'Each time I cope it seems to get easier.'
> 'I'm proud of the way I'm learning to manage my fears.'
> 'I've shown myself that I can do it now.'

Another area in which you can use coping self-talk is when if, like me, you are prone to potentially destructive self-doubt when starting close relationships. For example, if you had a very successful date a couple of evenings ago, but have had no further contact with your date since then, you may handle your insecurity in negative ways like putting yourself down and possibly later coming on too strong. Instead, tell yourself to calm down, realistically appraise the feedback you received on your date (much of which may have been very positive), and either initiate contact or wait and see what happens. If you cannot trust yourself to remember the positive feedback, write it down.

EXERCISE
—24—

Using coping self-talk to manage shyness

INSTRUCTIONS

1. Identify any negative self-talk you may use that contributes to shyness and social incompetence.

2. Identify a specific social situation that you find stressful. Write out at least three coping self-talk statements for each of

(a) before,
(b) during, and
(c) after the situation.
It may help if you write each statement on a 3 × 5 card for practice and use-in-emergency purposes.

EXPERIMENT
——7——

What happens when I use coping self-talk skills to manage shyness?

Part A: assessment

Look back at your answer to Exercise 24.

Part B: make an 'If . . . then . . .' statement

1. The 'If . . .' part of your statement relates to rehearsing, practising and then using your self-talk statements before, during and after the social situation that you find stressful. Rehearsal and practice is important. Spend at least two separate periods rehearsing and practising your self-talk as you imagine yourself coping with anxiety before, during and after the stressful social situation.
2. The 'then' part of the statement indicates the specific consequences you predict will follow from the changes in your behaviour.

Part C: try out and evaluate your changed behaviour

Try out your changed behaviour. How well did you use coping self-talk? Assess its positive and negative consequences for yourself and others. Have your predictions been confirmed or disconfirmed? Has the experiment taught you something about how you can support yourself with coping self-talk? If so, what?

Choosing realistic personal rules

Your personal rules are the 'do's' and 'don'ts' by which you lead your life. Each of you has an inner rule-book that guides your living and loving. If your rules are self-supporting they can motivate and help you to attain realistic goals. However, if your rules are self-oppressing, they leave you open to a triple dose of self-downing. For example, Marty has a rule that he must be successful on all his first dates. However, his first date with Ann does not go well, so this activates his first dose of self-downing. His second dose of self-downing is because he then becomes anxious and depressed about his dating ability. His third dose of self-downing is because he now starts devaluing not just his dating ability but his whole worth as a person.

Albert Ellis (1980) has coined the term 'mustabation' to refer to rigid personal rules characterized by 'musts', 'oughts' and 'shoulds'. He has a simple ABC framework for showing how people's thinking affects their feelings and behaviour.

A – the activating event
B – your beliefs about the activating event
C – emotional and behavioural consequences

Ellis regards the emotional and behavioural consequences to be determined by your beliefs in relation to the activating event rather than by the activating event itself. I prefer the term personal rules to beliefs.

Let's look at a specific incident regarding Kay at the party.

A Craig, after conversing with Kay, circulated.
B Kay's personal rule is 'I must be approved of by everyone'.
C Kay felt depressed because Craig moved away and she then left the party early.

Kay's thinking at B represents irrational or unrealistic personal rules. The rule 'I must be approved of by everyone' involves a mustabatory overgeneralization in which Kay unnecessarily lays her sense of personal adequacy on the line. Craig may or may not have moved away because he was not particularly interested in Kay. Even if Craig was not interested in Kay, Kay does not have to win Craig's approval; there are other males on the planet.

Three important unrealistic personal rules that contribute to people sustaining their shyness are:

1. I *must* be liked and approved of by everyone I meet.
2. I *must* never reveal anything about myself that might be viewed negatively.
3. I *must* never make a mistake in social situations.

Unrealistic rules such as these need to be identified and their consequences for your happiness and fulfilment rationally assessed. You then need to reformulate your unrealistic rules into realistic rules that work for rather than against you.

Reformulating involves substituting self-supporting for self-oppressing characteristics in specific personal rules. Some of the main characteristics of self-supporting personal rules include the following.

- *Expressing preferences rather than demands.* You distinguish clearly between your non-absolutistic preferences and your absolutistic mustabatory demands.

- *A coping emphasis.* Managing or coping with situations rather than being perfectionist in regard to them.

- *Being based on your own valuing process.* Your rules are not just rigid internalizations of parental, sex-role and cultural directives.

- *Flexibility.* Where appropriate, being amenable to change.

- *Absence of self-rating.* Your rules lead to a functional rating of specific characteristics according to whether they are useful for attaining your goals rather than to a global rating of your personhood.

Below are more realistic reformulations of the shyness-engendering personal rules cited earlier.

1. Though I might prefer to be universally liked, it is unreasonable and unnecessary to demand that this be the case. I can meet my needs for friendship and affection if I only meet some people who like me and whom I like.
2. Nobody's perfect. If I am to have honest and open relationships I need to reveal my vulnerabilities as well as my strengths.
3. To err is human. Though I would prefer not to make mistakes I can use them as learning experiences.

Exercise 25 focuses on managing shyness through identifying your unrealistic personal rules and reformulating them into realistic rules. As mentioned earlier, rules are frequently unrealistic when they contain words like 'must', 'ought' and 'should'. See if you can identify some of the rules that may be contributing to your being tense in social situations. Then attempt to arrive at either confidence-engendering reformulations of these rules or, at the very least, reformulations that help you contain your anxiety.

EXERCISE
—25—

Identifying and reformulating personal rules to manage shyness

INSTRUCTIONS

1. Make a list of any major unrealistic personal rules that contribute to your being shy in social situations. Make a list in four categories:

   (a) rules learned from my parents
   (b) rules on account of my biological sex
   (c) rules specific to my culture
   (d) others.

   If a rule fits into more than one category, give priority to listing it in (b) or (c), if relevant.

2. Assess the consequences for yourself and others of your possessing these unrealistic personal rules.

3. Reformulate each unrealistic rule so that it offers a realistic standard for your future behaviour.

4. Cassette-record your reformulated rules and play them back at least once a day for the next week.

Choosing to perceive accurately

I deal with the area of perceiving and misperceiving briefly here in relation to shyness. A more detailed discussion follows later in the book. If you are shy, the way you perceive many situations is likely to sustain your discomfort. Each person

carries within them some pain and insecurity. Without necessarily knowing it, you can be so influenced by your self-doubts
that you jump to unwarranted perceptual conclusions. These
perceptual conclusions are often self-oppressing in four main
ways. First, implicit in them is a low opinion of your worth.
For instance, 'He/she doesn't like me' may be an accurate perception. However, it can also be an inaccurate perception
based on your underlying doubts about your worth. Second,
they distort the thoughts, feelings and actions of others. Third,
they engender avoidable negative feelings, such as depression
and anxiety. Fourth, they may lead you to behave against your
own best interests.

Often people are unaware that they may jump to the first
perceptual conclusion rather than say to themselves 'Stop . . .
think . . . what are my perceptual choices?' Psychiatrist Aaron
Beck (1976) observes that frequently people have *automatic*
thoughts and perceptions that influence their emotions. Either
they are not fully conscious of these thoughts and images or it
does not occur to them that they warrant special scrutiny. Beck
collaborates with his patients in the scientific or detective work
of identifying these self-oppressing perceptions or 'what you
tell yourself'. These perceptions are related to your
mustabatory personal rules. For example, if you have a rule 'I
must be liked by everyone all the time', this is likely to sensitize
you to look for cues of rejection.

When exploring upsetting perceptions the ABC framework
needs altering slightly to:

A   The activating event
B   Your perceptions
C   Emotional and behavioural consequences

The consequences for you of A are influenced by your
perceptions of A at B. They *do not* automatically follow from
A. You have a choice of how you perceive at B.

Here is an example within the ABC framework.

A   Craig talks to Kay at the party and then circulates.
B   Kay perceives: 'Craig does not like me'.
C   Key feels depressed and leaves the party early.

However, there were many other perceptions Kay might have
had at B. These include:

'Craig is sensible in wanting to circulate at a party.'
'Craig liked me enough to come and talk to me.'
'I need to improve my conversational skills if I am going to hold the interest of guys like Craig.'
'There are other guys at the party so why worry about Craig.'
'I quite liked Craig but I didn't find him that fascinating.'

If you are like Kay and have a tendency to jump to negative perceptual conclusions, how can you combat this? First, become aware of your tendency. Second, identify the signals that you may be oppressing yourself. These include negative feelings about yourself and others without good cause and self-defeating behaviour that distances you from others. Also, you can identify the kinds of people and situations associated with your self-downing. Third, monitor your thinking in specific situations and practise making the connections between upsetting feelings and upsetting perceptions. Fourth, question your perceptions by logical analysis and search for better explanations. This process involves you engaging in the following kinds of self-talk.

'Stop . . . think . . . what are my perceptual choices?'
'Are my perceptions based on fact or inference?'
'If they are based on inference are there other ways of perceiving the situation that are more closely related to the factual evidence?'
'If necessary, what further information do I need to collect?'
'What is the perception I choose because it represents the best fit in relation to the factual evidence?'

Let's assume that Kay has some skills in choosing the most realistic perception. She went back in her mind over her contact with Craig and assessed the evidence for her 'He does not like me' perception. On doing this she discovered that there were *no facts* to support this conclusion and that it was an inference on her part. She generated alternative perceptions such as the five perceptions listed above. She decided that all five taken together constituted an appropriate way to perceive what had happened at the party. None of them involved putting herself down.

EXERCISE
—26—

Choosing how I perceive in shyness situations

INSTRUCTIONS

Part A: generating different perceptions

For each of the following scenarios, generate at least three different perceptions.

(a) At a disco somebody of the other sex whom you do not know winks in your direction.

(b) You go out on a first date, it goes well, and 5 days later you have had no contact from your date.

(c) At a party a person whom you met 15 minutes ago pays you a compliment on how you dress.

(d) Somebody at a social gathering looks at you and then looks away.

Part B: perceiving differently in a specific shyness situation

1. Choose a situation in which you have felt shy or socially uncomfortable.

2. Make a worksheet in the following format.

Situation	Upsetting perception(s)	Different perceptions

3. Write down the situation and, in the upsetting perception(s) column, any perceptions associated with your shyness in that situation. Assess the realism of your upsetting perception(s) by logical analysis.

4. In the different perceptions column, write down as many different perceptions of the situation as you can generate. Then evaluate which has the best 'fit' for explaining the situation.

5. Assess the ways in which the emotional and behavioural consequences of your 'best fit' perception(s) would have been different from those of your original perception(s).

Predicting gain and loss

A study of depressed and non-depressed students by psychologists Paula Pietromonaco and Karen Rook (1987) found differences in their decision-making style. Depressed students were significantly less likely to assign weight to the potential benefits of acting in social situations and significantly more likely to assign weight to the potential risks. Furthermore, for decisions about initiating social contact and establishing intimacy, depressed students expressed a greater reluctance to take the target actions than did the non-depressed students. If you are shy, this does not necessarily mean that you are depressed. However, I have cited the above study because many shy people have a similar pattern of overestimating risk, underestimating reward and hence being less prepared to act.

You lead your life into the future rather than into the past. Predictions are thoughts and images about the probability of future events. However, past circumstances in your life may adversely colour your view of your future. You need to view the future realistically. For some of you, obtaining the gain may be the risk. As one psychiatrist kidded: 'There is only one thing worse than not getting what you want, and that is getting it!'

There are a number of thinking errors that shy people are prone to when predicting the future. These include:

- *Underestimating reward and overemphasizing risk.* Your balance sheet is based on erroneous accounting so you conclude you do not have the funds to act.

- *Overgeneralizing.* Drawing a broad conclusion from a specific observation. For instance, 'Mary turned down my request for a date, so therefore all girls will in future'.

- *Black-and-white thinking.* Thinking in either–or terms. For instance, 'If I go out with Kevin he is either going to love me or hate me'.

- *Catastrophizing.* Making out that the negative consequences of not achieving your goal will be much worse than is justified.

- *Personalizing.* Predicting that you will be more the centre of attention than is warranted.

- *Self-rating.* Predicting that the outcomes of what you do are not only positive or negative in themselves, but have global implications for your worth as a person.

- *Underestimating strengths and resources.* Misperceiving your social strengths and resources and your capacity to cope with adverse feedback.

In my private practice I find that I can help many shy people by building up their skills of generating and evaluating rewards.

Sean, aged 30, had little experience of dating women; his longest experience lasting 3 dates. In his church group, Sean was on a committee with Suzanne who had been friendly to him and whom he wondered if he should ask out. Sean questioned 'Why bother to take the risk of seeking the reward?' With his counsellor, Sean generated both the potential risks and rewards of taking this initiative. He was already expert at acknowledging risks and needed to learn that: 'It is in my interests to look at rewards as well as risks in my decisions'. His list of potential rewards for asking Suzanne out included the following:

'I might have a chance of a strong relationship.'
'I might gain more experience in developing relationships.'
'This might contribute to helping me become happier.'
'I might gain confidence and a more positive self-image.'
'I might develop my ability to express my feelings more.'
'I might give myself the opportunity of Suzanne taking some of the initiative too.'

Sean evaluated the rewards of asking Suzanne out as outweighing the risks. She later became his first steady girlfriend.

The most conclusive way of gauging the accuracy of your predictions is, like Sean, to put them to the test. Reality testing your previously negative predictions may become easier if you carefully break tasks down, take small steps before larger steps, rehearse what you are going to do and, where appropriate, seek the support of other people.

EXPERIMENT
——8——

What happens when, if feeling shy, I alter the way I predict reward and risk?

Part A: assessment

1. Think of a particular person with whom you would like either to initiate or to deepen a relationship and yet have felt inhibited from doing so.
2. Make up a worksheet with the following format.

Rewards from acting (+s)	*Risks from acting (−s)*

3. On the worksheet first list your *current* predictions of reward and risk. These are the ones which, on balance, may inhibit you from acting. Then draw a line under each list.
4. Now generate as many *extra* predictions of reward and risk as you can and list them in the appropriate columns after your underlines. Pay particular attention to generating rewards.
5. Assess your revised list of rewards and risks and, if appropriate, set yourself goals to alter your behaviour.

Part B: make an 'If . . . then . . .' statement

Make an 'If . . . then . . .' statement along the lines of '*If* I implement my changed behaviour (specify), *then* (a), (b), (c), etc. predictions are likely to come true'.

Part C: try out and evaluate your changed behaviour

Try out your changed behaviour. Assess its positive and negative consequences for yourself and the other person. Have your predictions been confirmed or disconfirmed? Has this experiment taught you something about how you can support yourself by predicting reward and risk more accurately? If so, what?

In the preceding pages I have taken what psychologists call a 'cognitive' or *thinking* skills approach to shyness. If you are shy you may already possess the *action* skills of making contact in your repertoire. You just need the confidence to use them. Other shy people, along with many who would not consider themselves shy, need to develop their action skills of making contact. These action skills are often closely interrelated with thinking skills.

MAKING INITIAL CONTACT SKILLS

A group of you in a room together for the first time can either be a collection of separate existences locked within your own skins or you can start to make contact with each other. There are different stages in making contact. Here the main focus is on helping you to make effective choices when first meeting people. This is the important time in which you make and receive first impressions. During this period you may plant the seeds for relationships to grow later. Alternatively, you may curtail opportunities either by choice or by mistake. When meeting people for the first time you need to communicate: (1) liking of and interest in the other; (2) absence of threat; and (3) an initial definition of yourself. You communicate that you are a rewarding rather than a negative person.

Openers

Getting started and breaking the ice is easier if you have developed a repertoire of appropriate opening remarks. You can choose from those conversational openers and ice-breakers those appropriate to the different situations in which you find yourself. Making initial contact is usually done by way of small talk as you 'feel' each other out psychologically to see if you want the contact to continue and on what level. *Safe talk* is another way of viewing *small talk*. The level of disclosure is usually low in terms of intimacy. Trust and mutual acceptability has yet to be established. However, in situations where you are unlikely to meet again, a 'strangers on the train' phenomenon can occur in which disclosures may be surprisingly intimate.

Below are some suggestions for conversational openers and ice-breakers. The list is by no means exhaustive. Some of you may have your favourite opening gambits that have worked well for you in the past. If so, why change? Others of you may wish to build up your repertoire.

- Introduce yourself:
  'Hello, I'm (or 'my name is') _____.'

- Offer something:
  'Can I get you a drink?'
  'Would you like some peanuts?'

- Exchange basic information:
  'What brings you here?'
  'Where do you live?'
  'What line of work are you in?' etc.

- Pass comments relevant to the occasion, possibly followed by a question:
  'I like this hot weather. Do you?'
  'It's a great party. Do you agree?'
  'I've just arrived. What's happening?'

- Give compliments, again possibly followed by a question:
  'I like your dress.'
  'You are a really great dancer.'
  'I like your dress. Where did you get it?'
  'You are a really great dancer. Where did you learn?'
  'I like your sense of humour.'

- Bring up topical subjects:
  'What do you think of the election?'
  'What do you think of the new Arts Centre?'
  'Have you been watching _____ television series?'

- Try self-disclosure:
  'I feel nervous because this is the first time I've been here.'
  'I'm so relieved and happy. I've just heard that I have passed my exams.'
  'I went and saw the film _____ yesterday and really enjoyed it.'

- Encourage others' conversation:
  'That's interesting'   'Uhm uhm'   'Tell me more'
  'Really'   'Did you?'   'Oh'

Body and voice messages

Two important body messages in starting typical interactions are eye contact, 'catching someone's eye', and having your body openly oriented toward the other person (Duck, 1986). Your head and face play an important role in rewarding others. Smiling can indicate linking and absence of threat. However, it can be overdone and then appear like a phoney mask. Others pick up whether your body messages match what you say. Lack of genuineness, or incongruence, is likely to distance you from others. A reasonable amount of gaze should be maintained. People gaze nearly twice as much when listening as when talking (Argyle, 1983). Too little eye contact may indicate bashfulness or lack of interest. A high degree of eye contact may be seen as domineering or possibly indicating sexual attraction. Of course, you may be choosing to convey the latter. Appropriate nodding of your head when you listen is another way of being rewarding and reducing threat when you first meet.

Voice messages are very important. Good speech is easy to hear and relaxed. Shy people often need to work on speaking louder. For instance, Adrian is a shy student who talks very softly so as not to draw attention to himself. Sometimes, without being fully aware, you may show your nervousness by speaking very quickly or by slurring your words. Even those without obvious impediments may need to work on the quality of their speech.

Keeping conversations flowing

A basic conversational sequence involves three steps: speaking–switching–listening. You coordinate who has the floor by sending voice, body and verbal cues. For instance, you may avert your gaze, stop your 'uhms' and not make a listening response if you think it is your turn to speak.

Three ways in which you can help keep a conversation flowing are: using your rewarding listening skills, using questions to draw the other out, and having things to talk about yourself. There are a number of obvious ways in which you can keep yourself informed: reading newspapers and magazines; looking at the TV news; and keeping up to date on the latest developments in your specific areas of interest, for instance by watching your local football team or the latest movies. You may also use jokes to loosen up the conversation. However, you may need to practise them in advance so as not to blow the punch line.

More often than not meeting new people involves searching for common ground. This is partly to find safe talk with which to fill or structure time. In general, people find silences awkward when they do not know each other well. However, this searching for common ground is also part of the exploration of whether you later wish to become friends, lovers or marital partners. It can entail finding out specific factual information, for instance a shared hobby or a mutual friend. It can also include discovering emotional information that is possibly more implicit than explicit: for instance, mutual liking, compatibility and closeness. In initial contacts a process of coordination takes place in at least two ways: you test out whether or not you wish to continue the contact and you also coordinate the direction and intimacy of your disclosures.

You cannot *not* communicate. Your voice, words and body always send out messages. However, you can choose what and how you reveal and define yourself to others. Furthermore, the way you reveal and define yourself will influence not only the level of intimacy of others' disclosures, but also how they react to yours. The way you present yourself and your activities to others guides and controls the impressions others form of you. An analogy may be made with the theatre where the players are engaged in manipulating the audience's impressions. However, suspending others' disbelief can interfere with the starting and developing of relationships. They may perceive you as insincere. Consequently, you are faced with a set of choices concerning how open and honest to be about yourself at each stage in the conversation.

Ending conversations

Shy people and even those not so shy sometimes have trouble in ending conversations. There are numerous reasons why you may choose to end a conversation, ranging from boredom to having to go when you would really rather stay conversing with someone you find attractive. Breaking eye contact, starting to edge away, making your body orientation less open, holding out your hand are all body messages that you wish to go.

How you end the conversation can have positive or negative consequences for your subsequent relationship. If you wish to meet again, you can show appreciation, for example, 'I very much enjoyed talking with you' said with a smile and with voice messages that indicate you are sincere about it. You could also reinforce this with a comment like 'I hope we meet again'. If your feelings are even more positive you could say something like 'I wonder if we could get together again some time'. If your feelings are negative, your disengaging body messages can become more pronounced, even to the extent of holding out the palm of your hand as a stop signal. You can make closure comments like 'Well, that's about the sum of it' and 'I must be off now' said in a firm voice. Also, you avoid smiling too much.

Making a date

Since the position in this book is that of equality between the sexes, both females and males are encouraged to initiate when they want to meet somebody again. Receiving messages from another that they might be interested in dating involves using your decoding skills. Even then you may get it wrong. Males especially may be too ready to read sexual messages into the friendliness of the other sex. Verbal messages that convey interest in dating include: compliments, making it clear that you have noticed the other in the past, reflecting the other's feelings, being helpful, and asking the other questions about themselves. Body messages include: eye contact, absence of arm and leg barriers, not looking elsewhere when conversing, and light touching with or without humour. Vocal messages include animated speech involving variations in emphasis.

Dating is often done on the telephone. Some of the thinking skills discussed earlier are highly relevant to asking someone out. Coping self-talk can help you calm your anxieties as well as stay focused on the task at hand. Possessing realistic personal rules can prevent you from oppressing yourself with exaggerated fears about rejection. Predicting gain as well as risk can assist you in taking the risks that may bring you the gain.

Additional telephone skills include:

- *Clearly identifying yourself.* For example 'Hello, this is Jane/John Doe. We met at the Smiths' barbecue last week'.

- *Sending an 'I' message request.* For example, 'I was wondering whether you would like to come out for a movie / cup of coffee / drink (state one only) with me this weekend?'

- *Offering specific alternatives.* If the answer is 'yes', be prepared to offer specific alternatives, for example of different movies or of different places for coffee. Make sure to make your suggestions in such a way that the other person feels safe discussing them.

- *Stating your agreement clearly.* At the end it can be useful to summarize your agreement: 'Just to confirm I'll call round at your apartment at 8 p.m. this Friday to go to _____ movie. I look forward to seeing you then.' Misunderstandings over first meetings are not the best ways to start relationships.

- *Taking refusals politely.* The other person has a perfect right to turn you down. Hopefully, they do it with tact. Their courage in refusing you merits respect and you should politely end the conversation.

EXERCISE
—27—

Assessing my making-initial-contact skills

INSTRUCTIONS

Using the worksheet below assess your making-initial-contact skills.

Skills area	My assessment
Openers	
Body messages	
Voice messages	
Keeping the conversation flowing	
Ending conversations	
Making a date	

1. Summarize how you see your skills strengths and weaknesses in making initial contact.

2. How do you see your making-initial-contact skills being influenced by sex-role and cultural considerations?

3. Set yourself specific goals for improving your making-initial-contact skills weaknesses.

CONCLUDING SELF-TALK

If I am shy I am one of the large numbers of people who admit to this. However, everyone experiences some anxiety in social situations. One way I can combat my shyness is by developing self-supporting and discarding self-oppressing thinking skills. Such thinking skills include: accurately attributing the cause for my shyness; using coping self-talk; choosing realistic personal rules, especially regarding approval and rejection; not jumping to unwarranted perceptual conclusions; and predicting reward as well as risk. Whether I'm shy or not I may gain from developing my making-initial-contact skills. These include conversational skills like openers, coordinating who has the floor, keeping the conversation flowing and ending conversations. Additionally, I may need to work on my telephone dating skills.

7

Choosing relationships

We are never so defenceless against suffering as when we love, never so helplessly unhappy as when we have lost our loved object or its love.

Sigmund Freud

Charm: that quality in others of making us more satisfied with ourselves.

H.F. Amiel

*T*his chapter explores how you go about choosing an intimate relationship. It must be viewed in conjunction with the next chapter on deepening relationships. Choosing a long-term partner is a process that starts with casual dating in which partners are not identified as a couple, progresses to serious dating in which partners are identified as a couple, and ends with marriage or *de facto* marriage (Hutson, Surra, Fitzgerald & Cate, 1981). Hutson *et al.* (1981) distinguish between four types of courtship:

Type 1: Accelerated–arrested courtship, with a rapid initial move towards marriage slowing down just before final commitment.
Type 2: Accelerated courtship, a smooth and rapid transition towards marriage.
Type 3: Intermediate courtship, slower than the first two types, but more rapid than the fourth.
Type 4: Prolonged courtship, where relationships '. . . took a relatively retarded and rocky path toward marriage' (p. 76).

The above courtship periods ended in marriage. However, a filtering in or out process takes place in choosing whom to date, during casual dating and during serious dating. As the divorce statistics show, the filtering process also takes place during marriage. Furthermore, it takes place when partners cohabit outside marriage.

The stark fact is that most intimate relationships start in hope and end in pain. This raises the issue of whether many partners could be making better choices about with whom to relate. If they were better initial choosers they might increase their chances of achieving stability, happiness and fulfilment in their relationships.

An important skill in maintaining a loving relationship is that of selecting a partner. This chapter starts by exploring some potential sources of error in how people select their partners. I then discuss some criteria for selection. These criteria go beyond vague statements like 'we love each other' and 'we get on really well with each other'. In Chapter 8, on deepening relationships, I not only discuss how relationships develop but also how the filtering in or out process continues.

MAKING UNREALISTIC CHOICES

Love is blind; friendship closes its eyes.

Anon

How can you avoid unnecessarily landing yourself in an unhappy relationship? There are no guarantees. All relationships go through cycles of alienation and affection and have their lows as well as highs. You have to steer a course between *pollyannaism*, 'everything will turn out for the best', and undue *pessimism*, 'everything will turn out for the worst'. Even if it does turn out for the worst, you may have experienced some good times along the way.

In the previous chapter, when discussing overcoming shyness and making initial contact, I emphasized being clear about gains as well as about risks. In this chapter on choosing long-term relationships I emphasize being realistic about risks as well as about gains. Forewarned is forearmed. Below are some reasons why, when choosing a partner, the quality of your decision-making may be adversely affected.

- *Poor decision-making skills.* Even at the best of times, you may be poor at making decisions in a systematic and rational way. Samuel Butler once said that: 'Life is the art of drawing sufficient conclusions from insufficient premises.' You may possess a decision-making style that interferes with your having the mature fusion of 'head space' and 'heart space' necessary for wisely choosing a partner. You may get too anxious and hypervigilant. In this process you may fail either to take into account or to weigh adequately relevant information. Alternatively, you may either make decisions impulsively or be passive and just conform to what others expect of you. Good decisions depend not only on collecting sufficient information but also on your ability to perceive and assess it accurately.

- *Insufficient sense of your identity.* It is a paradox that most people have to make critical decisions about choice of partner and career when young and inexperienced. Your level of security and knowledge of your own wants and wishes may be insufficient at this stage. When choosing a relationship, my personification of me chooses my personification of you. However, I may not really know myself. Instead what I call 'I' or 'Me' may be a clutter of attitudes, values and rules taken over from other people, such as my parents, as if they were my own. I may perceive you in terms of their values and not mine. You may do the same to me. The risk of this is that, as either or both of us grow into more autonomous persons, we get badly out of step with each other. Our relationship, instead of being built on the rock of stable yet flexible identities, has been built on the sand of unstable and possibly rigid identities.

- *Falling victim to impression management.* When people date they package themselves to get the other to perceive them favourably. Imagine getting ready for a new date. In varying degrees the girl is 'out to get' the guy and the guy is 'out to get' the girl. Depending on how far out of touch they are with their own valuing processes and identity, the people you date 'sell' themselves as though they are commodities. They emphasize their assets or selling points and strictly control the flow of information about their perceived liabilities. It can be hard to get to know another person well when, both consciously and unconsciously, they are putting on an act for your consumption. Appearances can be deceptive. For example, conflicts may be smoothed over so as not to interfere with the goal of winning the other's affection. However, later on, in the routine of daily living, these conflicts surface.

Some people are very adept at manipulating appearances to conceal their negative points. However, others have hidden assets that become more apparent as you get to know them better.

• *Idealization of the other.* A combination of the myth of romantic love, your own insecurities and your date's skills of impression management may lead you to idealize them. You see in them what you want to see. You may fail to acknowledge adequately messages that contradict your ideal picture. Furthermore, you may fail to realize that they may not be as interested in you as you are in them.

• *Unrealistic relationship expectations.* There are a number of other unrealistic expectations besides the myth of the ideal partner that may build hidden weaknesses into your relationships. Below are some of them.

'People who are in love live happily ever after.'
'Love overcomes all.'
'Love lasts for ever.'
'I can change him/her.'
'My marriage/partnership is not going to run into trouble; it can't happen to me.'
'People will always be the same.'
'My partner and I should meet all of each other's needs.'
'Real love involves the complete fusion of two separate individuals.'

Partners who enter relationships may be unaware of some of their hidden assumptions and expectations. They may fail to realize that, because they expect too much, they set themselves up for a fall. Furthermore, they remain unaware that a conflict between each partner's inter-dependence and autonomy is at the heart of all close relationships. To pretend that it does not exist is a huge retrograde step in being able to manage it constructively.

• *Looking for a role.* Some people may be heavily influenced to get married because they have been brought up to see marriage as their main role in life. They seek to marry a role rather than a person. They get married to secure the structure and trappings of married life without paying sufficient attention to the realities of having a loving relationship with their spouse. Because of the traditional emphasis on females being the homemaker, women especially may feel the pressure to get into the married role. This includes motherhood and being able to raise a family. Disparaging remarks like 'old maid' and 'on the shelf' are made about single females after a certain age. Males also may get married to present a more socially acceptable image to the world: for instance to advance their careers.

- *Immature loneliness.* People search for companionship to avoid loneliness. The pain of loneliness is a major way by which nature ensures that people relate. However, there are different reasons for being lonely. Some of these may make you vulnerable to making poor relationship choices. For example, some people possess neither the security nor the skills to be able to spend much time on their own. Because they are more incomplete than they need be they risk unwisely saying 'yes' to a relationship. Young people who leave their homes and family networks may especially feel under pressure to establish a substitute home before they are emotionally ready. Getting into a relationship on the rebound when you feel undervalued and your self-esteem is low can be another example of loneliness contributing to poor choosing. Also, getting into a permanent relationship when you are geographically isolated and with little opportunity for adequate choice of a partner has distinct risks attached to it.

- *Transference.* The psychoanalytic movement in particular has emphasized that people relate to others on the basis of their past experiences with similar people. For example, children who have had difficulty with their parents may react negatively to subsequent authority figures. In close personal relationships, without being aware of it, you may both perceive and react to the other in terms of a previous relationship: for a male this may be his mother or a former girlfriend. Transference reactions can be positive or negative. Either way they are not a sound base on which to make relationship choices. You need to react to others as they are, not because they remind you of someone else.

- *Infatuation.* If you are infatuated with another you are inspired with extravagant and unreasoning passion.

Physical attraction is probably the main stimulus for people starting relationships. However, albeit very important, it is only one criterion in choosing a permanent relationship. Infatuation is a state of heightened emotionality which burns itself out. Infatuation and lovesickness are part of being alive. However, where possible, protect yourself from making major commitments until you have come down to earth and made a more realistic appraisal. Where there is a strong sexual attraction it is all too easy to misperceive each other and to rationalize away potential difficulties in your relationship.

- *Giving in to family pressures.* In discussing having an insufficient sense of your own identity I mentioned how you may have internalized parental values. Without having your parents *physically* around you may still *psychologically* choose a partner to suit them. This may both restrict your field of choice as well as build instability into your relationship. The same can happen when families openly put pressure not to marry out of their culture, class, religion or whatever else, even though their children may strongly prefer someone different. Conformity and rebellion are two maladaptive ways of handling this kind of pressure. By conforming you inhibit or bury your true feelings and settle for less than you might have been. By rebelling you overreact and may get into an unstable relationship that you later regret. Though difficult, having the courage of your convictions and using assertion skills are the best ways to manage family pressures to act against your interests. With the trend toward later marrying and both males and females having their own incomes, family pressures on mate selection probably carry less weight than in the past.

The above list of possible distortions in choosing long-term partners is not exhaustive. You may think of others as well. You double the chances of distorted choosing if you take into account that both you and your partner may misperceive each other. I have focused on choosing long-term partners rather than friends. This is for a number of reasons. Friendships are easier to get out of. They do not involve children. Also, you are less likely to be so sexually and emotionally involved when choosing your friends. Exercise 28 encourages you to explore whether you have some skills weaknesses when it comes to choosing a long-term partner.

EXERCISE
—28—

Exploring my possible skills weaknesses in choosing a long-term partner

INSTRUCTIONS

Write down your assessment of how each of the following skills weaknesses might interfere with your capacity to choose a suitable long-term partner.

Skills weakness	My assessment
Poor decision-making skills	
Insufficient sense of my identity	
Falling victim to impression management	
Idealization of the other	
Unrealistic relationship expectations	
Looking for a role	
Immature loneliness	

Transference	
Infatuation	
Giving in to family pressures	
Others not listed	

1. Summarize your possible skills weaknesses in being able to choose realistically a long-term partner.

2. To what extent are your possible skills weaknesses influenced by your biological sex and by your culture?

MAKING MORE REALISTIC CHOICES

Persons are fine things, but they cost so much; for thee I must pay me.

Ralph Waldo Emerson

There can be little liking where there is no likeness.

Aesop

This section explores some considerations for realistically choosing a long-term partner. Especially if marriage is intended, what you make is a choice for all seasons. What matters to you in the short term may be different from what matters in the long run. Sternberg considers that among the things that increase in importance as relationships grow are willingness to change in response to each other and willingness to tolerate each other's imperfections (Trotter, 1986). Additionally, the sharing of values, especially religious values, becomes more important. Others have observed a shift from passionate love to compassionate love (Cunningham and Antill, 1981).

Choosing a long-term relationship is a process that takes place over an extended period of time. Though the initial saying 'yes' to another human being may be on first sight or meeting, it takes time to gather appropriate evidence to justify your initial choice. Also, you have to feel ready for a relationship. Intuition as well as physical attraction plays a large role in getting relationships started. The intuitive little child inside you may feel an emotional attraction to the intuitive little child inside another. You may feel unexpectedly safe and comfortable in another's presence. It is as though you have been friends for some time.

Couples tend to be similar in many ways. Argyle and Henderson (1985) observe: 'They are more similar than by chance in age, social class, religion, height, intelligence, values and beliefs and in some measures of personality' (p. 105). This is not surprising in that people tend to meet each other in fairly circumscribed social settings. Though complementarity may add spice and interest, most relationships need to be grounded in a high degree of similarity. However, it helps if the rocks in your head fit the holes in your partner's.

Below are a series of considerations in choosing a long-term relationship. You cannot assess another person's suitability in isolation from yourself. There is no such thing as the perfect partner or the perfect relationship. Trade-offs, compromises and negotiations are inevitable. Each person and each couple will weigh the importance of the following considerations differently. Also their importance for either or both partners is likely to change over time. This either enhances closeness or can get partners badly out of step.

● *Physical attractiveness/sexual compatibility.* Ever since the film *10*, many people have been measuring physical attractiveness on a simple scale ranging from 1, 'not at all attractive', to 10, 'extremely attractive'. Especially for males physical attractiveness may be a very important consideration in starting a relationship. Individuals tend to match themselves on physical attractiveness. People who consider themselves less likely to be accepted may trade down to a less attractive partner. Physical attractiveness is not just a matter of natural attributes. How the individual uses body language, for instance use of gaze and eye contact, also contributes to it.

With the increase in premarital sex, sexual compatibility is becoming more important in the choice of a long-term partner. Passion as expressed by kissing, hugging, touching and making love needs to be satisfactorily given and received. Furthermore, partners need to be able to talk freely about their sexual relationship, including sharing their fantasies.

• *Emotional responsiveness.* Each partner needs to be emotionally responsive to the other. Warmth and caring need to be openly given and received. Additionally, partners need to be sufficiently in touch with themselves that they can be spontaneous and express a range of feelings. Genuineness in the expression of feelings is very important. Verbal, voice, body, touch and action messages should speak in the same direction. If you experience someone as either cool and unresponsive to you or 'blowing hot and cold', warm one moment and pushing you away the next, this at the least merits further exploration.

• *Capacity for intimacy.* In his book *The art of loving*, Fromm (1956) emphasized the importance of knowledge in loving relationships. Your willingness to be known can help me relate to you as you are, rather than in terms of my inaccurate personification of you. Your openness and ability to reveal yourself as a fallible human being helps me to know you. It also makes it easier for me to drop my social masks and defensive façades. Capacity for intimacy and emotional responsiveness come together in that if you can feel free to disclose not only personal information but also your feelings then you share the flow of your being with me. This encourages me to do the same. Our relationship becomes a vibrant process rather than something which is static and dull. We have an open rather than a closed communication system.

• *Respect.* Respect means concern that, within our interdependence, you see me as I am and allow me to grow as a separate human being. Possessiveness and control are the antithesis of respect. You are secure enough in yourself that you allow me the psychological space to be myself. You are capable of helping me and taking pleasure in my unfolding. You do not need me to constrict myself so that you can sustain a false picture of yourself. I am a person in my own right and not an object for your use. A good test of whether another respects you or not is that of how well they listen to you. Poor listeners tend to be too bound up with their own agendas to respect you fully.

- *Considerateness and caring.* Considerateness means thoughtfulness and having regard for another's feelings. It consists of both presence of the desirable qualities of care and kindness and also absence of the undesirable quality of insensitivity to others. Considerateness involves being aware of another's needs and, where reasonable, trying to meet them. This can involve being positive in finding out their needs as well as reacting. Being considerate shows that you care. Caring plays a very important role in people's judgements of love (Steck, Levitan, McLane and Kelley, 1982). Additionally, caring was one of the three main components in Rubin's (1970) Love Scale. Illustrative items were: 'I would do almost anything for _____'; 'One of my primary concerns is _____'s welfare'; and 'I feel responsible for _____'s well-being'.

  Considerateness also involves avoiding inconsiderateness. If someone does not try to minimize the negative consequences of their actions on you they are inconsiderate. They lack the sensitivity to avoid hurting you unnecessarily. What counts is 'me' rather than either 'you' or 'you and me'. They may behave like spoiled little girls or boys.

- *Sense of humour.* Does the child in the other person appeal to the child in you? Do they have a similar sense of fun and humour? Do you enjoy kidding and playing together? Enjoying each other's sense of humour can both enhance the good times and ease the bad times in your relationship. In a British opinion survey (MORI, 1983), having a good sense of humour was rated above looks in qualities thought desirable in a partner.

- *Openness to experience.* If you are open to your experience you are able to perceive incoming information without distorting or denying it. This is highly relevant to a person's capacity to maintain a long-term relationship in a number of ways. First, the more each of you can perceive yourself and the other accurately, the sounder the information base you have for transacting your relation-ship. Second, if a person is rigid, defensive and not willing to look at their own behaviour this is a critical danger signal in regard to entering a long-term relationship with them. Rather more frequently than you would like, you may find yourself being held solely responsible for conflicts and misunderstandings. Third, openness to experience allows another person to change and grow, to be responsive to your changes and growth, and to renegotiate how you wish to relate in light of these changes.

- *Trustworthiness/commitment.* All relationships involve contracts of varying degrees of implicitness and explicit-ness. These contracts or agreements relate to such matters as not engaging in sexual activity with others, not criticizing the other in public, standing up for the other person in public, keeping confidences, keeping promises and generally acting in a reliable and dependable way. Another aspect of trust is that of trusting another not to reject or hurt you needlessly. The notion of commitment is closely allied to that of trust. A committed partner does not breach trust. Instead a committed partner keeps trust by staying with the relationship through the hard times which inevitably occur.

- *Loving skills strengths.* Though most people do not think · of their relationships in skills terms, there is no reason why you should not. Throughout this book various skills for ini-tiating, maintaining and developing relationships are described. You can assess the loving skills of a person with whom you are considering a long-term relationship. You may experience this as rather calculating. However, the success of your relationship heavily depends on how well each of you sends and receives messages and manages your anger and differences. Rather than rush into a relation-ship, it may pay you to spend some time allowing conflicts to emerge and then trying to deal with them. The engage-ment period is a time of increased commitment when couples can assess each other's loving skills more closely. Cohabitation offers a further opportunity for this.

- *Shared pleasant activities.* One of the main approaches to helping depressed individuals is to encourage them to increase the number of pleasant activities in which they are involved (Lewinsohn, Munoz, Youngren & Zeiss, 1986). Similarly, if relationships are to remain happy, you need to engage in a reasonable number of shared pleasant activities. You can still enjoy individual activities as well. You need space apart from each other as well as together. Frequent conversations, both intimate and less intimate, are an important way of keeping in touch with each other both emotionally and practically. Couples vary in the activities they enjoy. Some illustrative pleasant activities include: going for a walk, eating together informally, playing indoor games, playing outdoor games, gardening, having friends around, going to the cinema or theatre, and going to a disco. If you enjoy doing things together this is a good omen for your relationship. However, the activities each of you enjoys are likely to change over the course of your relationship. You may then need to work to keep sharing some pleasant activities.

• *Compatibility of values.* Values are the underlying principles and priorities on which people base their lives. They are people's philosophy of life. At any time you and your partner have a profile of values, some of which are more important than others. Differences in values are inevitable. However, you need to feel comfortable with each other's major values to sustain a long-term relationship without great strain.

Below are some values that you may or may not share with a person you are considering as a long-term partner.

Friendship. Being joined to others outside your relationship by mutual intimacy and interests.
Family life. Having and being part of a family. Valuing parenthood.
Religious. Acknowledging the need for connectedness to some ultimate and superhuman power.
Materialistic. Values centred on the accumulation and control of money.
Aesthetic. Appreciating beauty and good taste, with special reference to the arts such as music, literature and painting.
Intellectual. Valuing analytic and rational pursuits.
Social. Helping others. Showing social concern.
Sensual. Valuing the pleasures of the flesh.

Hedonistic. Valuing fun and having a good time.
Career. Valuing having a career.
Practical. Valuing practical pursuits and, where practical matters are concerned, self-reliance.
Outdoors. Appreciating and valuing being out of doors. Liking being in communion with nature.
Athletic. Valuing participation in sport.
Autonomous. Valuing independence and thinking for yourself. Valuing enterprise.
Conventional. Appreciating tradition. Valuing obedience and conformity to the status quo.
Self-actualizing. Being committed to personal growth and development.

Values are the basis on which you and your partner develop goals for your relationship. You may discover on closer examination that each of you wants and expects different things. This need not be an insuperable obstacle if you can resolve the value conflicts to your mutual satisfaction. However, major unresolved value conflicts are unlikely to go away. Under these circumstances, you should then consider whether it is worth the risk of committing yourself to a long-term relationship.

● *Compatibility of personal rules.* In Chapter 2, I mentioned that each individual possesses an inner rule book of personal rules for living that they bring to their relationships. These rules are of varying degrees of flexibility and represent their values. They manifest themselves in every area of a couple's functioning: for example, how the family income is earned, how the family income is spent, use of leisure time, time spent with friends, sex, how to communicate with each other, how to manage anger and conflict, household chores, visiting relatives and raising children. Sometimes, given flexibility on both sides, differences in personal rules can be negotiated to arrive at a mutually satisfactory solution. On other occasions the differences may be more intractable: for instance differences concerning size of family and education of children. Where possible, find out in advance if either partner feels unable or unwilling to work through a major difference. This may influence your decision about making a longstanding commitment to the relationship.

- *Sex-role compatibility.* This is a transitional period in which traditional sex-roles are being challenged. People enter heterosexual relationships with different personal rules about sex-roles. In a transitional period the differences may be greater than in a period where sex-roles are heavily dictated by tradition. Sex-role issues permeate every area of heterosexual relationships from making love, doing the washing up, to earning and spending the couple's income. Difference in how partners perceive sex-roles can often be worked through by discussion and negotiation. However, where major differences remain, these are best acknowledged and taken into account in any decision about a long-term commitment.

- *Others.* There are other considerations you may wish to take into account. These include practical considerations such as: sleep, food and music preferences; the difference in your ages; and what sort of parent you think your partner might make. Where possible, think through in advance what you are looking for in a partner. Then you may have to be prepared to compromise.

EXERCISE
—29—

Choosing a long-term partner

INSTRUCTIONS

Write down your assessment of how important each of the following considerations is for you in choosing a long-term partner. For each consideration indicate what in particular you should look out for.

Consideration	Importance and what to look out for
Physical attractiveness/ sexual compatibility	

Emotional responsiveness	
Capacity for intimacy	
Respect	
Considerateness and caring	
Sense of humour	
Openness to experience	
Trustworthiness and commitment	
Loving skills strengths	
Sharing pleasant activities	
Compatibility of values	
Compatibility of personal rules	
Sex-role compatibility	
Others	

Write out a summary of your main priorities in choosing a long-term partner.

CONCLUDING SELF-TALK

I can increase my chances of happiness and fulfilment if I develop my skills in choosing a long-term partner. Many factors may contribute to my making a poor choice. These include: poor decision-making skills, insufficient sense of my identity, falling victim to impression management and unrealistic relationship expectations.

Partners may value different qualities at different stages in their relationships. Consequently, I need to make a choice for all seasons. This means not only taking into account physical attractiveness, sexual compatibility and how well we get on now, but also taking longer-term considerations into account. Considerations relevant to the long term include how open the other is to new experience and how compatible our values are. I need to look closely before I leap into a long-term relationship, especially one involving children.

8

Deepening relationships

Only connect!
E.M. Forster

Behold me! I am worthy
Of thy loving, for I love thee!
Elizabeth Barrett Browning

*C*hoosing and deepening relationships are interrelated. At each stage of your relationships, you and those to whom you relate may choose either to develop or not to develop them further. In this chapter, I explore some of the ways in which bonds between partners may be deepened and strengthened.

Rewardingness, reciprocity and rules

Rewardingness, reciprocity and rules are the 3 Rs of developing and deepening relationships. Let us examine each in turn.

- *Rewardingness.* The main goal in life of most people is to be happy (Nelson-Jones and Strong, 1977). People seek out experiences that are rewarding for them. Furthermore, a fundamental psychological principle is that people are more likely to repeat behaviours that have rewarding consequences for them than those which do not.

  The notion of rewardingness permeates relationships in a number of ways (Argyle and Henderson, 1985). First, each partner looks for rewards. In loving relationships these include the rewards of giving as well as of taking. Many of these rewards involve voice, body, touch and action messages rather than just words. Second, relationships are likely to deepen if partners can increase the range and depth of their rewardingness for each other. Areas of mutual rewardingness include intimacy, caring and sex. However, if either partner considers and resents the exchange of rewards being in imbalance, this puts the relationship at risk. Third, relationships are more likely to be maintained if partners are able to sustain a high level of rewardingness for each other. At the very least, the rewards or satisfactions from staying in the relationship need to exceed the perceived rewards from being out of it. Fourth, relationships are likely to end when the rewards of being free of them consistently exceed the rewards of staying in them.

- *Reciprocity.* Most long-standing relationships are grounded in some form of reciprocity in the giving and receiving of rewards (Azrin, Naster & Jones, 1973). Cunningham and Antill (1981) observe: 'It is indisputable that most human relationships are based on considerations of equity and exchange' (p. 31). Put simply, you meet my needs and I meet yours. Happy relationships involve a preponderance of positive reciprocity or mutual rewardingness. This is especially the case where each partner genuinely cares for the growth and development of the other. Sometimes there can be imbalance as one partner *willingly* donates his or her strength to draw out the potential for loving of the other partner. In his book *Becoming Partners*, Carl Rogers (1973) recounts the moving story of how Joe's steady trust in the potential for growth of Irene was able to free her from the unhappiness of her upbringing and two previous marriages. In distressed relationships, there is either a preponderance of negative reciprocity in which partners trade negative behaviours or there is an imbalance in the exchange of positive behaviours which is resented. Table 8.1 is a schematic representation of reciprocity of rewardingness.

Table 8.1 Schematic representation of reciprocity of rewardingness in happy and distressed relationships

a. *Happy relationships*

Positive reciprocity

| You are rewarding for me | $\xleftrightarrow{+S}$ | I am rewarding for you |

b. *Distressed relationships*

Negative reciprocity

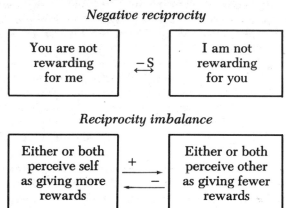

The analysis of reciprocity in Table 8.1 is a simplification. This is for many reasons. For example, you could be trying to show your love for me and I either might not perceive it or push you away. Alternatively, you might not know how to show your love for me because I am inhibited in telling you how to do it. Furthermore, when I appreciate what you do I may be poor at expressing this appreciation. Additionally, we may either be mutually rewarding in some areas and not in others or offer different levels of reward in different areas. There are many other possible disclaimers. However, the basic point remains: some degree of reciprocity of rewardingness is critical to deepening and maintaining long-term relationships between equals.

• *Rules.* Each of you brings your personal rules to your relationships. However, your relationships also have their own formal and informal rules or contracts. The purposes of these relationship rules are to provide guidelines and to clarify expectations for your own and your partner's behaviour. They prevent your having to think each issue through from scratch every time it occurs. Argyle and Henderson (1985) observe that relationship rules are of two main kinds: those about providing rewards and those about avoiding inflicting costs. Rules about intimacy, for example 'sharing news of success', about caring, for example 'showing emotional support', and about exchange of specific rewards, for example 'give birthday cards and presents', come in the first category. Rules about faithfulness, for example 'restricting sexual activity to the other partner', and privacy, for example 'respect each other's privacy' and 'keep confidences' come in the second category.

Relationships take place in social contexts. Consequently, many of the rules will reflect cultural, social and family mores. However, relationships also take place between two unique individuals who have the capacity to choose which relationship rules work for them. Thus partners have the potential to move beyond playing out *roles* in relation to each other to create rules which allow them to express their individuality as *persons*. These rules are likely to emphasize concepts such as reciprocity and rewardingness. However, they can be fresh, spontaneous and negotiated between equals rather than, for good or ill, unthinkingly taken on from others.

THE INTIMACY BOND

Things are seldom what they seem,
Skim milk masquerades as cream.
Externals don't portray insides,
Jekylls may be masking Hydes.

Sidney Jourard

By means of what he considered his atrocious verse, Jourard (1964) made the point that of all living forms, humans are capable of *being* one thing and *seeming* from their actions and talk to be something else. He emphasized that effective loving involves both partners knowing and relating to each other as they are. People who do not truly know each other cannot love each other.

Deepening loving relationships involves having the courage to discard impression management, social masks and defensive façades. It involves the movement towards dropping all those concealing rather than revealing behaviours that protect you from knowing yourself and being known to another. Self-disclosure involves both revealing personal information and also expressing your feelings. In Chapter 3, I discussed these dimensions of self-disclosure from the viewpoint of sending verbal messages. Here I explore the effects of self-disclosure on how relationships develop.

Revealing progressively more intimate information

Raul and Connie have been dating for a month. At first Connie thought Raul was the strong, silent type. As he disclosed more of himself, she was surprised to find out how sensitive and emotional he was, how much he valued his close friendships, and how willing he was to listen to her talking about her goals in life. Raul, on the other hand, was learning that Connie was a very determined young lady who wanted to combine having her own business and raising a family. He admired her openness and willingness to share her doubts about her femininity. This made it easier for him to share his doubts about not being the typical male and his feelings of hurt at the teasing he had received because of this. Also, both Connie and Raul were able to share their doubts about their physical attractiveness.

In choosing whether or not to deepen a relationship one of the main ways in which you psychologically feel each other out is by making progressively more intimate disclosures. Altman and Taylor (1965) indicate that as relationships develop there is both increasing breadth of disclosure and also increasing depth. The process of deepening a relationship involves you in matching the intimacy level of each other's disclosures prior to disclosing at a still more intimate level. You move beyond safe talk to talk that has increasingly more risk attached to it. The main risk is that of rejection. Another major fear is lack of confidentiality. In short, two important ways that you deepen a relationship are either by *first making* a more intimate disclosure or by *matching* a more intimate disclosure when another takes the first risk. If you both wish to develop your relationship you are likely to coordinate the deepening of the intimacy level of your disclosures. More often than not there is no smooth progression to more intimate disclosures, rather a jagged line in that direction.

Progressively sharing more intimate information involves you in revealing your vulnerabilities as well as your strengths. Some of you may feel the need to present yourselves in a positive light all the time. The effect of this 'boasting' can have on others is at least threefold. First, they fail to get to know you properly since you wear a mask. Second, they may find themselves in a psychologically negative exchange with you since they are the only person in the relationship who is vulnerable and makes mistakes. Third, because they feel threatened, they edit what they say to you.

There are a number of explanations for why the progressive matching of the intimacy level of disclosures deepens relationships. One explanation is that your disclosure is a reward to another indicating liking. This needs to be matched if the relationship is to remain in balance. Another explanation emphasizes how disclosures are received. If your disclosure is met with acceptance by another, this not only establishes them as less threatening and more alike, but also gives them permission to make a similar disclosure. Consequently, by accepting disclosures as well as by disclosing, trust gets developed.

Expressing your feelings about the relationship

Acknowledging, owning and openly expressing your feelings is a major way in which the intimacy bond gets developed. Partners increasingly feel free not only to talk about themselves but to express themselves. As such they move beyond playing two-dimensional roles to relating to each other as three-dimensional persons. Furthermore, your relationship becomes an active process rather than relating to each other in rigid and stereotyped ways.

While you should always acknowledge all of your significant feelings, you have a choice as to when and how best to express them. You need to work toward an open communication system in which each partner feels free to express her or his feelings rather than assume that this exists from the start. Expression of feelings can damage as well as enhance relationships.

An important aspect of expressing feelings is the giving and receiving of feedback. Egan (1977) calls this skill immediacy or 'you–me' talk. He distinguishes between *relationship* immediacy, 'Let's talk about how we've been relating to each other recently', and *here-and-now* immediacy, 'Let's talk about what's going on between you and me right now as we're talking to each other' (p. 235). 'You–me' talk involves the giving and receiving of feedback either about our relationship or about what may be being left unsaid between us right now. Here I focus mainly on expressing feelings about a relationship in ways that may do more good than harm.

Below are a few guidelines for expressing feelings about a relationship.

● *Become aware of your feelings.* Try to get in touch with what you truly feel. Avoid parroting other people's feelings as if they were your own. If you are confused about your feelings be prepared to share this. Your feelings about your relationship may become clearer as you discuss them with the other person involved.

● *Send 'I' messages.* Feelings by definition are subjective. By your use of words, own your feelings and avoid making others responsible for them.

● *Be genuine.* Use voice, body, touch and action messages that match what you say. As with all communication, giving feedback is not just a matter of *what* you say but *how* you say it.

● *Express positive as well as negative feelings.* Psychologist Irene Kassorla (1984) stresses the power of stating 'honest positives'. Honest positives are genuinely held positive thoughts and feelings about another person. They are a valuable form of feedback in their own right. Also, they can be interspersed with negative feelings to prevent the other person feeling under attack from a barrage of negative comments. Here is a brief example.
Negative feelings only: 'I'm seeing too much of you'.
Positive and negative feelings: 'I want to keep seeing you but I need more space for myself'.

● *Share persistent negative feelings.* Rogers (1973) stresses the importance of sharing persistent negative feelings. He observes that if this sharing '. . . is firmly based in the attitude, "I want to share myself and my feelings with you, even when they are not all positive", then a constructive process can almost be guaranteed' (p. 209). These feelings might include boredom with your sexual relationship, annoyance with the way the household chores are distributed, and disappointment that a partner is failing to take adequate care over his or her appearance.

● *Invite discussion.* Do not 'hit and run'. Respect the other person's right to respond to your feedback. 'You–me' talk involves two-way sharing and discussion of feelings about your relationship. Relationships where communication goes only one way are headed for, if not already on, 'the rocks'.

● *Be prepared to look at your own behaviour.* Your feelings take place in the context of a relationship in which both you and your partner influence each other. You may have contributed to your negative feelings either by mis-perceiving your partner or by behaving negatively. It is to be hoped that, when confronted, you are open enough to acknowledge any role you may have played in generating your negative feelings.

EXPERIMENT
——9——

What happens when I am more open about sharing my feelings in a relationship?

1. *Expressing positive feelings*

Part A: assessment

1 Think of a relationship which you think you could improve if you shared more of your positive feelings toward the other.
2 For an appropriate period, say 3 days, monitor how you send positive and negative messages to the other person.
3 List all the positive feelings that are left unsaid in your relationship.

Part B: make an 'If . . . then . . . ' statement

Make an 'If . . . then . . .' statement along the lines of '*If* I express these positive feelings (specify), then these con-sequences (specify) are likely to follow'.

Part C: try out and evaluate your changed behaviour

Try out your changed behaviour. Assess its positive and

negative consequences for yourself and the other person. Have your predictions been confirmed or disconfirmed? Has this experiment taught you something about the power of expressing positive feelings rather than leaving them unsaid? If so, what?

2. *Expressing negative feelings*

   If appropriate, carry out the above experiment but this time focus on expressing a negative rather than a positive feeling. Follow the guidelines for expressing feelings about another person.

THE CARING BOND

All truly loving relationships are characterized by a high degree of caring. This caring involves affection, interest in and concern for each other's welfare and growth. The quality of caring is important. It can represent what Maslow (1962) terms '. . . B-love (love for the Being of another person, unneeding love, unselfish love) and D-love (deficiency-love, love need, selfish love)' (p. 39). When caring represents deficiency love it may be *manipulative*, 'I show caring to you because I want something in return', *oppressive*, 'I care for you whether or not you want my care', *dependency-engendering*, 'I care for you because I do not want you to be free', and *aggressive*, 'I care for you so you should darned well show more caring for me'. Caring based on deficiency love is pseudo-caring. In the early stages of dating you have insufficient information to know whether the caring expressed by another is superficial or the real thing. As you get to know each other better you collect more evidence on which to make an accurate assessment.

Where caring represents being-love, your reward is in the giving as well as the receiving of caring. Fromm (1956) observes: 'Love is the active concern for the life and growth of that which we love' (p. 22). You prize the being of the person you love and are motivated by a consideration of their interests. There is a happy fusion between what is best for them and what you want for yourself. Your caring is an end in itself and not the means to an end. You respect the individuality and separateness of your partner and do not seek to manipulate, possess or control.

As relationships develop you find out whether you and your partner reciprocate a satisfactory level of caring. You discover not only how much your partner cares for you but also how much you care for your partner. You need to cut through your own pseudo-caring as well as that of your partner. It is easy to think that you care for another person more than you do when you are in a romantic haze characterized by infatuation and idealization. In the day-to-day realities of curlers and dirty shirts you may feel otherwise. Also, you will be challenged to care for your partner when you are in conflict and do not like their behaviour.

Since caring plays such a central role in the deepening and maintenance of loving relationships, below I describe it more fully. First I start with statements about caring. Then I discuss verbal, voice, body, touch and action messages showing caring.

- *Statements about caring.* The following are statements that people might make to describe how they care for a partner.

  'I try to be there for him/her when she/he is upset.'
  'I want her/him to feel emotionally supported by me.'
  'I try to tune into what she/he is going through and show that I understand.'
  'If she/he ever really needs me, I will come running.'
  'I feel responsible for her/his welfare.'
  'I feel protective about her/him.'
  'Her/his happiness is important to me.'
  'I try to avoid doing things that hurt her/him.'
  'I try to show her/him that I care.'
  'I like doing things to brighten her/his life.'
  'I like standing up for her/him in her/his absence.'
  'I always remember birthdays and anniversaries.'
  'However hurt and angry I feel, I always try hard to understand her/his position.'
  'I value her/him growing as a separate person within the context of our relationship.'
  'I want to help her/him attain her/his goals.'

  The above statements of caring contain the following themes: emotional support, showing understanding, concern for another's welfare, desire to give happiness and to avoid hurt, and respect and support for the other's individuality.

- *Verbal messages.* Verbal messages of caring include obvious statements such as 'I love you', 'I care for you' and 'I want to help you'. Additionally, you may pay each other compliments. Each partner in a relationship may have difficulty openly expressing their caring for the other. If this is the case, the other person may wrongly conclude a lack of caring. Unless rectified, this perception damages the relationship. Furthermore, words of caring need to be matched by actions. The development of a relationship can flounder if either party is perceived as insincere. Another way you can show caring is through the quality of your listening responses. Do they indicate that you care enough to understand the internal viewpoint of your partner? Additionally, confrontations, in which you challenge another to grow and not settle for less than their full humanity, can be very caring.

- *Voice messages.* Voice messages are extremely important in expressing caring. If your vocal music is wrong, you negate the effect of your fine words. Characteristics of caring voice messages include warmth, sympathy, expressiveness and interest. Your voice conveys kindness rather than harshness and disinterest.

- *Body messages.* Your body messages can support or negate your verbal messages of caring. When sending caring verbal messages your gaze, eye contact, body orientation and facial expression all need to demonstrate your interest and concern for the other. Similarly, when others share their problems you need to show good attending and listening body skills.

- *Touch messages.* Support and caring can be expressed by a hug, a half-embrace, an arm over the shoulder, a touch on the arm, a hand on top of or holding a hand, amongst other ways. As with all touch messages, you are in another's close intimate zone and consequently must be very sensitive to picking up cues about their willingness to be touched. Nevertheless, touch can be a wonderful way to express your caring.

- *Action messages.* Action messages indicating caring include: looking after each other when ill; being prepared to do your share of the household chores; giving birthday cards and presents; initiating pleasant events such as meals out; showing affection through flowers; poems and other spontaneous gifts; and being available to help out in times of need. Additional action messages include the presence of small helpful, and the absence of small unhelpful, daily behaviours: for instance, making a cup of tea or coffee in the morning and not leaving the bathroom basin dirty. These small repetitive indications of caring or lack of caring can have a large cumulative effect on how rewarding relationships are perceived to be. This, in turn, affects their future development for good or ill.

Sex-roles and caring

In Western cultures males are brought up to be *more* dominant, individualistic and independent than females. They are also brought up to be *less* nurturing, sympathetic and sensitive to others' feelings. Furthermore, some of the ways in which males show caring in their traditional sex-roles have to do with providing *things*, for instance the family income, rather than verbally supporting and showing affection to *people*. Thus, males more than females may have difficulties both in openly showing and also in receiving caring. Some males are very good at showing and receiving caring. Others may be better at either showing than receiving caring or the reverse. Some are good at neither.

Women may have their problems, too, in showing and receiving caring. However, it is more part of the traditional female sex-role to be rewarding in these ways. Disharmony can develop in relationships where partners experience a lack of reciprocity in the giving and receiving of caring. Despite their conditioning to be carers, females may be more dissatisfied with the amount of expressions of care they receive than males. This may be due to a lack of appreciation of their partner's true feelings for them or an accurate perception of their lack of caring. Many males need to be both more expressive in showing caring and also more relaxed about receiving it.

EXERCISE
—30—

Assessing my showing-caring behaviours

INSTRUCTIONS

Take one or more relationships that are important for you and, for each, fill in the following worksheet.

My assessment of my strengths and weaknesses in showing caring in my relationship with _____

Skills areas	My strengths	My weaknesses
Verbal messages		
Voice messages		
Body messages		
Touch messages		
Action messages		

1. Do you think your ability to *show* caring has been influenced by either sex-role or cultural considerations? If so, give examples.

2. Do you think your ability to *receive* caring has been influenced by either sex-role or cultural considerations? If so, give examples.

3. Do you think you need develop your showing-caring skills? If so, set yourself specific goals and develop and implement a plan to attain them.

THE TRUST BOND

Most people want security in this world, not liberty.

H.L. Mencken

If you can develop a relationship in which there is a deep level of trust you reciprocate the reward of security. Trust means a firm belief in the honesty and reliability of another. It implies a confident belief in their trustworthiness. As you develop relationships, especially close ones, a major underlying question you ask yourself is 'Can I trust this person?' At the point at which the answer becomes negative, the relationship will certainly deteriorate, if not be terminated.

Trust as acceptance

One way of looking at trust in personal relations centres on your fears of rejection. The question then becomes: 'Can I trust this person to accept me?' Against this criterion, progressive disclosure of more intimate information, revealing vulnerability and strength, and giving and receiving honest feedback all become ways of testing the trustworthiness of the other in relation to you.

Let us look at the progressive disclosure of personal information as part of the process of trust building. You show some trust in another by making a disclosure that is a little risky. If the other accepts and is supportive about your disclosure, trust is likely to be enhanced. Trust may be further enhanced if the other person risks disclosing at a similar level of intimacy. However, if the other person rejects your initial disclosure, you are unlikely to risk deeper disclosures and may even end the relationship. Where both of you feel relatively safe, you may be prepared to continue your trust testing and building by disclosing at a slightly deeper level and so on. Relationships end up at different levels of trust. Also, some people can be trustworthy in relation to certain areas of disclosure, but not in relation to others.

Though not so obvious, the same process takes place in relation to expression of feelings. Do not underestimate the role which anxiety can play in distorting communication even in the closest of relationships. People need to feel safe to get truly in touch with themselves and to be genuinely emotionally expressive. This aspect of trust-building can be subtle, complex and lengthy. Initial feelings of safety in the glow of romance may fade when differences surface. It is nearly impossible for people to wear permanent 'nice guy' or 'nice girl' masks.

Trust as commitment

> Betsy had been married 15 years and had 4 children aged 1 to 14. One evening at dinner her husband Bruce, a managing director of an import company, announced that he had fallen in love with Jane, whom he had interviewed for a secretarial position. A few weeks later when they were making love Bruce asked Betsy if he could call her Jane. Betsy has now divorced Bruce, who has set up house with Jane a few blocks from his former family home. Bruce just cannot understand why Betsy is so against taking up his offer to remain good friends despite their divorce.

Another way of looking at trust is to ask the question 'Can I trust this person to honour her/his commitments?' Betsy could not trust Bruce, though she tried to prevent herself from this realization for as long as she could. Trust involves being confident that the other person will abide by the formal and informal rules of your relationship even when out of your presence. Untrustworthy behaviour which is obvious to you includes breaking promises and commitments that you can check on. Untrustworthy behaviour that may deceive you includes lying, breaking confidences and cheating on you with a third party.

Another fact of trust as commitment is that of being willing to work on your relationship in the hard as well as in the good times. There is much to be said for a crisis or catastrophe approach for understanding the development of trust. There are misunderstandings, conflicts, arguments and crises in all close relationships. Partners can learn to trust themselves, each other and the relationship depending on how these difficulties are handled. They can find out that their relationship is not fragile, that each is prepared to accept the nastier part of the other without quitting, and that each is committed to making the relationship work. Difficulties in sound relationships provide challenges that the partners tend to constructively work through together, despite the pain they entail. In weak relationships, either or both partners do not have this level of commitment. Unresolved conflicts may lead to alienation which in turn can lead to their involvement with third parties and thus to the further breakdown of trust.

Being trustworthy

In developing and maintaining a relationship you too need to demonstrate your trustworthiness. You need to show characteristics like honesty, reliability, acceptance and commitment. If you are mean, suspicious, uncaring, hostile, selfish and competitive, people are unlikely to view you as trustworthy. Furthermore, given the tendency of partners to reciprocate each other's behaviour, you may make it more difficult for others to be trustworthy to you. For instance, if you persist in being aggressive, you sow the seeds of your own rejection.

EXERCISE
—31—

Developing trust and being trustworthy

INSTRUCTIONS

1. List some of the main ways that you assess whether you can trust another person enough to have a close relationship with her/him.

2. How easy do you find it to trust people? List some of the main positive and negative influences in your background on your ability to trust people appropriately.

3. How trustworthy are you? Take a piece of paper and draw a line down the middle. At the top of the left column write SKILLS STRENGTHS and at the top of the right column list SKILLS WEAKNESSES. Then list what you perceive your strengths and weaknesses in being a trustworthy person.

4. If appropriate, set yourself specific goals for being more trustworthy in your relationships and then monitor and evaluate your progress.

THE PLEASURE BOND

Nature knows no indecencies, man invents them.

Mark Twain

Physical attraction is a major stimulus for loving relationships. Nevertheless, you still have to coordinate how and when you integrate increased levels of sexual intimacy into your relationship. What Masters and Johnson (1975) call the pleasure bond is one of the main areas of reciprocity and rewardingness in the development and maintenance of loving relationships. Traditionally, intimate sexual behaviour was meant to be the preserve of marriage. Nowadays, sexual intercourse often takes place outside marriage though sometimes the couples later get married. A study by James (1983) showed that the frequency of sexual intercourse was highest in the two months after marriage, about four or five times a week, falling to just over twice a week from two to twenty years of married life, followed by a further decline.

Traditionally, the male was meant to be the expert in sexual behaviour (Masters and Johnson, 1975). This view is increasingly being challenged and now both sexes are encouraged to be equally responsible for expressing and sharing their sexuality (Alberti and Emmons, 1986). Effective sexual relationships take place *with* partners and not to them. Each partner needs to be actively involved in the process of giving and receiving pleasure. As such you need to extend your skills of disclosing and listening to your sexual relationships. Sender or disclosing skills include: taking initiatives, being playful, expressing wants, sharing fantasies, giving feedback, showing vulnerability, expressing pleasure and enjoyment, and showing gentleness and tenderness. Receiver skills include being responsive to verbal, voice, body and touch messages that help you give and receive pleasure and have a mutually satisfying experience.

This is not a book with a major focus on sexual relating. However, I stress the importance of trying to develop open communication in the sexual as in all other areas of your relationship. Despite the sexual revolution many are still inhibited in talking openly about sex. Both males and females have fears and anxieties over matters like body image and sexual performance. Additionally, many males need to become much more sensitive to the feelings of vulnerability that women have on account of their relative physical weakness.

There is no definite answer as to whether sexual satisfaction leads to emotional closeness or the reverse. Argyle and Henderson (1985) indicate that while sex leads to love for men the reverse may be true for women. Both sexes need to realize that effective sexual relating is not only 'doing what comes naturally', but requires the development and use of many skills of giving and receiving pleasure and of open communication. Those wishing more detail on sexual relating are referred elsewhere (for example, Comfort, 1972, 1973; Kaplan, 1974; Masters and Johnson, 1975; Brown and Faulder, 1977).

THE COMPANIONSHIP BOND

Celia and John have been living together for two months. Every evening when they come home from work they spend at least an hour having a drink and talking over the main events, thoughts and feelings of their days. On fine days they sit out in their garden to do this.

Jasmine and Mark went out for six months. The relationship ended because, whenever they did things together with some of Mark's friends, Jasmine was always critical of them.

Doug and Janet met because they were members of the same choral society. They enjoy singing together both informally at their homes and the rehearsals and concerts of their choir.

Diane is an ambitious young lawyer very wrapped up in her career. Her boyfriend Roger is getting fed up because she appears to put her career well above spending time with him.

An important loving skill is that of being a good companion with whom to share activities. Your relationship is more likely to stay fresh and be fun if you are sensitive and creative about doing things together. There is a limit to which you can hold intimate conversations without their being repetitive and boring. Much of your relationship is centred on activities of varying degrees of routine and enjoyment. Some of these activities are household chores which you both may decide to do. Others may be more enjoyable parts of your daily routine like having meals together, being in bed, watching TV and listening to music. Still others may be special events: for instance, eating out or going to a concert. Table 8.2 is an illustrative list of activities that you can do together. The home-based column assumes that you live either separately or together. You are also likely to want to do things on your own since neither of you can be expected to meet all of each other's needs. Also, your joint relationship may gain from the stimulus that each gets from your independent activities.

Table 8.2 An illustrative list of companionship activities.

Home-based	*Outside the home*
Eating informally	Going for a walk
Having a drink	Going swimming
Having a coffee	Going to the beach
Watching TV	Going on vacation
Listening to music	Playing outdoor games
Listening to the radio	Going to the cinema/theatre
Playing indoor games	Going to a concert/opera/ ballet
Being in bed	Going to a disco
Doing household chores	Going to a party
Preparing food	Going for a drive
Reading together	Going to the races
Interior decorating	Going to a sporting event
Gardening	Going to a talk
Sitting in the sun	Going to church
Massaging each other	Going shopping
Planning your finances	Visiting relatives
Having friends round	Visiting friends

How can doing things together help strengthen and deepen your relationship? First, you find out about each other's likes and dislikes and whether you are still compatible. Also, you discover whether each is committed to spending time with the other. Second, your companionship helps both you and your partner avoid loneliness. Third, many of the dull activities are less wearisome and many of the pleasant activities more fun through having someone to share them with. Fourth, shared activities provide a vehicle for your ongoing relationship conversation. They have an emotional as well as a functional purpose. Fifth, if you do enjoyable things together there is less room for potentially destructive third parties to enter your relationship. Sixth, sharing activities can be a source of strength during the rough times in your relationship. They may help you keep in contact, despite feelings of hurt, pain and anger.

THE DECISION-MAKING BOND

*You cannot be friends upon any other terms
than upon the terms of equality.*

Woodrow Wilson

Even when people start dating they have to negotiate numerous decisions with each other: what do to, where, when and so on. As relationships develop, the number of these decisions increases: for instance, decisions about what type of food to eat when cooking for each other, how much to see friends, and how to use touch in the relationship. As time goes by you develop relationship rules for many of these decisions so you do not have to keep thinking about them.

Issues of power and influence are present in all relationships. As you get to know each other better, you also get an indication of the extent to which power struggles and power plays, trying to get people to make decisions against their will, are likely to cause major disruptions. On the positive side, you also get an indication of whether together you can, without too much strife, make most of the host of decisions that close relating entails. The bond between you is likely to strengthen if you and your partner think that you can negotiate relationship decisions and rules to your mutual satisfaction. You feel you can mesh with and adjust to each other without too much difficulty. Your relationship comes under strain if either or both of you feels dissatisfied with how you handle power and decision making.

In traditional relationships the male tended to be more dominant in decision making than the female, though the female may have had certain areas in which she made most of the decisions, for example in the kitchen. In the present times of sex-role challenge and change, the traditional approach to decision making may build instability into your relationship. What happens if one of you, probably the woman, wants to move to a more equal distribution of power? Nowadays relationships may *be* more stable, as contrasted with *seem* more stable, if partners have equal power. This does not mean that you share all decisions. You may either share virtually all decisions or divide the decisions into his and her spheres of influence. However, you willingly agree to the division and are prepared to renegotiate it if it does not work. In theory equal power between partners is an ideal balance. In practice, the partner who commands the most financial resources, especially when the other does not have an income, is likely to have more power.

EXERCISE
—32—

Assessing how good I am at deepening relationships

INSTRUCTIONS

Assess your skills strengths and weaknesses in each of the following deepening-relationships areas. Answer *either* in general *or* in regard to a specific relationship.

Area	Skills strengths	Skills weaknesses
Intimacy		
Caring		
Trust		

Pleasure		
Companionship		
Decision making		

1. Summarize what you see as your main skills strengths and weaknesses in deepening relationships.

2. To what extent do you consider that your skills strengths and weaknesses have been influenced by *either* your cultural *or* your sex-role upbringing? If possible, cite specific examples.

3. Where appropriate, set yourself some realistic goals for deepening a relationship, plan how to attain them, implement your plan, and evaluate the consequences. You may wish to discuss this exercise with your partner.

POSTSCRIPT

There are many other ways in which partners develop bonds. For instance, as you get to know each other better it may become clearer that you share similar values. Also, as your relationship deepens you may commit yourselves to parenthood or buying a joint property. Deepening a relationship has risks as well as rewards. You may discover differences rather than similarities. This can be either positive or negative. The outcome depends on the nature of the differences and also on how well each of you copes with them.

CONCLUDING SELF-TALK

When deepening relationships I need pay attention to rewardingness, reciprocity and rules. I am more likely to stay in a relationship where we are both rewarding to each other and also have negotiated mutually satisfying relationship rules. There are a number of areas in which I can try to deepen my relationships. Six important areas are: intimacy, caring, trust, pleasure, companionship and decision making. I need to assess my skills strengths and weaknesses in each of these areas and change my behaviour accordingly. My attempts to deepen a relationship may create discomfort for either or both of us. How we cope determines whether the outcome is positive or negative for our relationship.

Assertion in relationships

Nothing is so strong as gentleness and nothing is so gentle as real strength

Ralph W. Stockman

*T*he late Abraham Maslow (1962) wrote: 'A person is both actuality and potentiality' (p. 10). The same may be said for relationships. Two people in a relationship are their own separate actualities and potentialities. They are also the actuality and potentiality of their relationship together.

If I am to be a loving person in my relationship with you I need to develop assertion skills in three interrelated areas.

- *Assertion for me.* I assert and define myself in regard to my personal goals. Here the emphasis is on preserving my rights, meeting my needs, and on expressing my positive and negative thoughts and feelings. This is an individualistic form of assertion that takes place in many situations other than my relationship with you, for instance in *my* job. An assumption for this kind of assertion might be: 'I possess sufficient self-love to assert myself to fulfil my potential'.

- *Assertion for you.* In a loving relationship I have a commitment for your happiness, growth and fulfilment. Consequently, I endeavour to help you to assert and define yourself in regard to your personal goals. I do not wish to possess or control you. Rather I try to help you become more of what you are capable of becoming. An assumption for this kind of assertion might be: 'I possess sufficient love for you to help you to assert yourself to fulfil your potential'.

- *Assertion for us.* I am concerned not only for each of us as separate individuals but also for the quality, health and vitality of our relationship together. When I assert myself within our relationship I am sensitive to helping us attain our relationship goals. Our happiness and development is important not just in the context of our separate lives but in relation to each other. We are an interdependent team committed to nurturing and building our relationship. An assumption for this kind of assertion might be: 'I possess sufficient love for each of us that I want both of us to assert ourselves to fulfil the potential of our relationship'. Below are two examples of assertion for us.

> Hugh and Pamela, both in their late forties, are approaching their 25th wedding anniversary. Both are committed to open communication in their relationship. Pamela considers that the timing of her assertion is very important. For example, if she knows that Hugh is under great pressure to meet work deadlines, she will wait for an opportune moment to request that he meets her needs for more time, companionship and for a head massage. She listens carefully to his reactions to her assertion and they work through its implications together. Hugh values Pamela both for her openness in stating her wishes and also for her considerateness. She is firm, yet tactful.

> Ernest and Maria have been going steady for five months. Early in their relationship Maria sensed that Ernest had difficulty in saying 'no' to her and in standing up to her when their views differed. Maria was very fond of him. Consequently, she showed her love by encouraging Ernest to be more open and direct and by demonstrating that she could handle his assertion and also his anger. Their relationship has deepened because both now feel they are able to be more honest in it.

The following is a brief definition of assertion for us.

Assertion in loving relationships entails developing an open communication system in which, for the benefit of our relationship, we strive honestly and considerately to express our positive and negative thoughts and feelings and to act constructively towards each other.

Non-assertion, aggression and assertion

Alberti and Emmons (1986) make a useful distinction between non-assertion, aggression and assertion. When dealing with perceived negative behaviour on the part of your partner, non-assertion entails being inhibited, submissive and possibly not mentioning it at all. Aggression entails unnecessarily putting your partner down, often by means of 'You' statements. Assertion means standing up for yourself and honestly expressing your feelings without either being inhibited or engaging in character assassination.

Below are some examples.

- You have cooked a special dinner for your partner who arrives an hour late without contacting you.

  Non-assertive: 'It's all right. Good to see you.'

  Aggressive: 'Damn you. Now the dinner is spoiled.'

  Assertive: 'I'm concerned at your being so late without contacting me. Was there a reason for this?'

- You live with somebody who rarely cleans the flat.

  Non-assertive: You say nothing, but resent it deeply.

  Aggressive: 'You lazy idiot. Do you think I like acting as your servant all the time?'

  Assertive: 'I'm annoyed because you almost always leave the cleaning to me. I want us to work out an arrangement so that we share the chores more evenly.'

You may also express your positive thoughts and feelings in non-assertive, aggressive and assertive ways.

- You have been wanting your partner to cut the lawn for

some time and he/she finally keeps his/her word and does it.

Non-assertive:	Be pleased, but say nothing.
Aggressive:	'That's great. It's about time you kept your word.'
Assertive:	'The lawn looks lovely. Thank you.'

The above examples focus on the verbal component of non-assertive, aggressive and assertive statements. However, the voice and body messages are also very important. Furthermore, to behave assertively you need to think assertively. It is to these thinking skills that I now turn.

THINKING ASSERTIVELY

There are a number of key thinking skills that enable you to behave more assertively. These are the same thinking skills necessary for combating shyness, though with some modification.

Attributing cause accurately

You may fail to be as assertive as you might be because you take a passive rather than an active stance to your relationship. Rather than assuming active responsibility for meeting your own and your partner's needs you may hinder your effectiveness through misattributions. These include:

'I'm naturally unassertive.'
'I'm the victim of my past.'
'My partner is there to meet my needs.'
'My partner should know what I think and feel.'
'I've tried before to improve our relationship.'
'It's his/her fault that I'm like this.'
'Nobody loves me, so why bother.'
'My partner should not need to be told that I love him/her.'
'My problems are so bad that I can't do anything about them.'
'My partner should be able to assert himself/herself without much support from me.'

'My partner and I should be able to communicate effectively without having to work at it in the rough times.'

The danger of all the above potentially faulty explanations for how you behave is that they are dead ends. You need to become aware both of your misattributions and also of their consequences for you and your relationship. You then need to distinguish between fact and inference and formulate attributions that are more conducive to the health of your relationship. Such attributions assume two main points: first, your and your partner's responsibility for your own thoughts, feelings and actions; and second, your joint responsibility for actualizing the constructive rather than the destructive potential of your relationship.

Using coping self-talk

You may engage in *negative* self-talk that blocks your assertiveness. Negative self-talk that impedes assertion includes

- *Emphasizing mastery rather than coping.* 'Unless my assertion succeeds totally it is a failure.'

- *Catastrophizing.* 'If I assert myself and then do not get what I want it will be a catastrophe.'

- *Negative self-labelling.* 'If I assert myself, then I am being selfish.' Butler (1981) states: 'Most women venturing into androgynous areas face a barrage of negative self-labels they must overcome before asserting themselves' (p. 60). These negative self-labels include: nagging, castrating, unfeminine, bossy, pushy, bitchy, menopausal and frigid. Also men who assert their nurturing and tender characteristics may have to overcome negative self-labels. These labels may include: weak, emotional, pansy, soft, wet and effeminate.

Coping self-talk is the antidote to negative self-talk. In coping self-talk calming and coaching elements tend to be interspersed. Below is an example of coping self-talk before, during and after Pamela asserts herself in requesting that Hugh spend more time with her.

Before: 'Calm down. What are my goals. Just think through what are the skills I need to use to attain them.'
During: 'I feel anxious. However, I know Hugh cares for me and for the welfare of our relationship. I need to keep cool and say what I have to say.'
After: 'I feel good that I said what was on my mind in a way that he could hear. I don't need to feel so anxious next time.'

The goals of coping self-talk are to help you contain your anxieties and to stay focused on what you want to achieve. If you have a difficult assertion situation in your relationship, it may help to rehearse and practise your coping self-talk before your face-to-face assertion. This you can do by visualizing the scene and talking yourself through it. Where possible, visualize potential difficulties and setbacks and talk yourself through them as well.

Choosing realistic personal and relationship rules

As you grew up you may have been subject to many pressures not to be assertive. Furthermore, you may have lived with people who demonstrated inhibited or aggressive ways of attempting to meet their needs within their relationships. There are many sources from which, rightly or wrongly, you may have internalized faulty assertion rules. Below I mention some of these sources with reference to learning to become non-assertive in your relationships. Also I provide some illustrative unrealistic rules that may later interfere with your achieving open relationships.

- Your family.
  'You must avoid conflict and commenting on unusual behaviour.'
  'You must not openly talk about sex.'

- Your religion.
  'You should care for others rather than look after your needs.'
  'You should always be gentle and self-effacing.'

- Your gender.
  'Women should not be strong and independent.'
  'Men should not be tender and nurturant.'

- Your culture.
  (Asian) 'You must be very conscious of saving people's face.'
  (Anglo-Saxon) 'You should not express emotions too openly.'

- Your race.
  'Whites are better than blacks.'
  'Whites are less smart than Asians.'

- Your peer group.
  'You must conform to group norms.'
  'You must be popular.'

- Your age.
  'Children should be seen and not heard.'
  'Parents know better than children.'

- Your schooling.
  'Teachers know better than pupils.'
  'Older children are better than younger children.'

Probably everyone possesses some unrealistic personal rules that impede their capacity for assertion. These get reflected in 'mustabatory' demands on your self and your partner. Some of these are listed below

> I/my partner must be nice
> I/my partner must avoid conflict
> I/my partner must be liked
> I/my partner must be feminine
> I/my partner must be masculine
> I/my partner must not wear the pants
> I/my partner must not have wishes of my own
> I/my partner must never hurt each other
> I/my partner must not seem vulnerable
> I/my partner must not show anger
> I/my partner must not make a mistake
> I/my partner must not admit a mistake

The first step in overcoming unrealistic personal rules that hinder assertion is to become aware that you possess them. Then you can logically analyse how realistic they are and what their positive and negative consequences are for you. Additionally, you can reformulate them into flexible rules that work better for your relationship. Below is an example.

> *Inflexible rule:* 'I/my partner must never hurt each other.'
> *Flexible rule:* 'While we prefer not to hurt each other, we think it is important to our relationship to confront significant issues between us, even though this may sometimes cause pain.'

In addition to your each striving to possess realistic personal rules, it is important that partners subscribe to assertion rules supportive of their relationship. Below I suggest some beneficial assertion rules for a relationship.

> 'It is important to let each other know where we are.'
> 'Each of us cares sufficiently about the other to want to know their thoughts and feelings.'
> 'Each of us wants to meet the legitimate needs of the other.'
> 'Each of us cares enough about the other to be considerate in the way we assert ourselves and to allow time and attention to process together the implications of our assertions.'

Predicting gain and loss

Sometimes in the context of a loving relationship assertion can seem even more risky than in relationships where you have much less to lose. You may find that you are testing the limits of your partner's commitment to your relationship. On the bright side, you may find that you have a fuller awareness both of your partner's commitment to you and also of the extent of openness possible in your relationship.

Earlier I mentioned catastrophizing as a form of negative self-talk. In catastrophizing the consequences of assertion you greatly overestimate the probability of negative outcomes. Furthermore, you may minimize your resources for coping with negative consequences. However, many of you may fail to be assertive less because you *overestimate the negative consequences* but more because you *underestimate the positive consequences* of assertion. Minimization of the potential for reward rather than maximization of the potential for loss holds you back. Because you inadequately perceive the gain side of the loss/gain ledger balance, you are unwilling to take risks that might have a high chance of bringing genuine gains to your relationship.

Below are some of the general gains of being assertive in your relationships.

- You build more equal relationships.
- Each of you is able to be more open.
- Each of you has a greater knowledge of the other.
- You have a greater appreciation of the strengths and weaknesses of your relationship.
- You are able to show your concern for each other by taking action to correct unhelpful behaviours.
- You are able to clarify misperceptions.
- You are able to affirm the positives in your relationship as well as express the negatives.
- You have a clearer idea of the degree of commitment in your relationship.

Awareness of any tendency you may have either to overestimate the negative or to underestimate the positive consequences of assertion is the starting point for working on these thinking skills weaknesses. For each weakness, you have to challenge your existing thinking by making sure you achieve a realistic appraisal of both the potential gains and losses of your assertion. If you underestimate the gains you may have to work hard to generate and assess the realistic benefits of being more assertive.

EXERCISE
—33—

Assessing my strengths and weaknesses in thinking
· assertively

INSTRUCTIONS

Assess your skills strengths and weaknesses in each of the
following areas of thinking assertively in your relationships.

Thinking skill	My strengths	My weaknesses
Attributing cause accurately		
Using coping self-talk		
Choosing realistic rules		
Predicting gain and loss		

1. Summarize your strengths and weaknesses in thinking
   assertively.

2. To what extent do you consider that your strengths and
   weaknesses in thinking assertively reflect (a) your sex-role
   upbringing and (b) your cultural upbringing? If relevant,
   illustrate with specific examples.

3. Set yourself specific goals for overcoming any skills weaknesses in thinking assertively that you may possess.

BEHAVING ASSERTIVELY

Behaving assertively involves showing commitment to your relationship not only by trying to be a rewarding person for your partner but also by helping your partner to be more rewarding for you. In Chapter 8, I dealt with the role of caring in deepening relationships. With caring you assert yourself by *offering* rewards to your partner. In this chapter the emphasis is on initiating, making requests for behaviour change, handling power plays, ending a relationship, and encouraging each other's assertion.

Dimensions of assertive behaviour

Behaving assertively follows from thinking assertively. Furthermore, assertive behaviour is not just *what* you do but *how* you do it. Table 9.1 is a grid for looking at the choices involved in non-assertive, aggressive and assertive behaviour. In assertive behaviour your thinking is disciplined, realistic and goal-oriented; your basic feeling is that of adequacy and you keep in check any self-defeating feelings; your verbal message is clear; your voice and body messages back up your verbal message with an appropriate degree of muscle; and, if necessary, so do your actions. Non-assertive and aggressive behaviour is deficient, to a greater or lesser degree, on each of the above dimensions.

When being assertive, your voice and body messages can greatly add or detract from your overall message. For instance, a firm tone of voice may communicate to others that your verbal assertion is to be taken seriously, while a weak tone dilutes it. Assertion is not only a matter of *presence* or desirable verbal, voice and body messages, but also involves *absence* of undesirable messages. Above all, verbal, voice and body messages that are 'put-downs' of others are to be avoided.

- *Voice messages.* Some voice messages likely to support an assertive verbal message include the following.

Volume	– reasonably loud.
Tone	– firm, not putting on a 'little girl' or 'little boy' voice.
Inflection	– presence of positive inflections and absence of negative inflections that indicate aggression and are 'put-downs'.

Table 9.1 A grid for looking at the choices involved in non-assertive, aggressive and assertive behaviour.

	Your thoughts	Your feelings	Your verbal messages	Your voice messages	Your body messages	Your actions
Non-assertive behaviour						
Aggressive behaviour						
Assertive behaviour						

- *Body messages.* Some body messages likely to support an assertive verbal message include the following.

Eye contact	– looking another directly in the eye.
Facial expression	– being genuine, for instance not smiling when you are angry.
Body posture	– erect posture if standing or sitting, not slumping.
Gesture	– using hand and arm movements to help express yourself in a constructive fashion.
Proximity	– not avoiding another, not 'hitting and running'.
Absence of negative body communication	– head shaking, door slamming, fist shaking, finger pointing.
Absence of distracting body communication	– hair pulling, fiddling with fingers.

A *six-step framework for assertive behaviour*

Below is a six-step framework for behaving assertively in specific situations in your relationship.

1. *Awareness.* Become aware of where you may be acting either non-assertively or aggressively. Listen to feedback from your partner as well as to your own thoughts and feelings.
2. *Specify goals.* You may fail to be assertive through lack of clarity concerning your goals. Be specific as to what you want and assess whether it is in the best interests of your relationship. During this process you may generate and evaluate many goals prior to deciding which is best.
3. *Develop a plan.* Develop a plan to attain your goals. Your plan is likely to focus on how to change your thinking as well as your behaviour. Take into account appropriate voice, body and action messages.
4. *Rehearse and practise.* Especially if you anticipate finding your assertion difficult, rehearse and practise it in advance. You may role play with another how you want to behave. Alternatively you can use visualized rehearsal and practice.

Remember to anticipate set-backs and difficulties in your practice.
5. *Implement your assertion.* Pick an appropriate time to give your assertive message and go ahead and do it.
6. *Evaluate.* Evaluate how well you used assertion skills and their positive and negative consequences for yourself, your partner and your relationship. Learn both from your successes and mistakes.

When learning to be more assertive you may find it helpful to work on easier problems before moving on to more difficult ones. Hopefully your success in being assertive in the 'shallow end' will give you the confidence to move on to the 'deep end'. In loving relationships, your partner can be an invaluable resource in helping you to become more assertive. She or he can assist you with your assertion skills both in general and also in specific situations. Furthermore, you can gain confidence if you know your attempts at assertion are likely to be met with respect, if not always with agreement.

Initiating

In equal relationships, each partner feels free to initiate. Taking or suggesting an initiative means assuming responsibility for making things happen rather than waiting for your partner to make the first move. Butler (1981) considers that a couple's first date frequently sets up an unequal relationship between a man and a woman that may last for the whole of their married life. She considers that a woman 'waits for a phone call, waits to be asked out on a date, allows a man to initiate sexual contact, and yokes her expression of affection to his' (p. 16).

Many women feel that they are controlled by men in their relationships. Frequently, these women consider that they are expected to behave passively, wait for the male to take a lead, buttress the male ego and not have their own competence and authority fully acknowledged. However, the reverse is also true and some men feel controlled and dominated by women. This tends to be less so, for reasons such as men's larger physical size and their greater control over financial resources. In reality, both sexes allow themselves to be controlled by their role expectations not only of each other but of themselves.

There are certain areas where, traditionally, women expect and are expected to take the lead: for instance, cooking, looking after the house and being a harmonizer in family relations. There are certain areas where, traditionally, men expect and are expected to take a lead: for instance, being the breadwinner, looking after the car, and in bed. Traditional relationships are permeated with double standards for both sexes, with different permissions and prohibitions regarding taking and suggesting initiatives.

You can be non-assertive, aggressive and assertive in initiating.

Non-assertive: 'Do you want to go to the movies tonight?'
Aggressive: 'Come on. We're going to the movies
     tonight whether you like it or not.'
Assertive: 'I would like to go to the movies tonight. Do
     you want to come?'

Note that in the above example the assertive initiative is expressed as an 'I' message and invites discussion. This verbal message is accompanied by appropriate voice and body messages.

The following considerations about initiating seem important assuming that you do not want a relationship based on traditional sex-role expectations. First, both of you have to be strongly committed to relating on an equal basis. Second, listen carefully to your own wants and wishes and to help your partner do the same. Third, respect each other's right to suggest initiatives. Fourth, respect each other's right to say 'no'. Fifth, develop the skills of working through and negotiating differences.

EXPERIMENT
——10——

What happens when I initiate?

INSTRUCTIONS

Part A: assessment

Assess the degree to which you are prepared to initiate in each of the following areas of a male–female relationship.

Asking for a date
Making phone contact between dates
Ordering a meal
Paying the bill after eating out
Providing transportation
Driving
Bring up topics of conversation
Touching in an affectionate way
Initiating sexual activity
Taking responsibility for contraception
Initiating variations in lovemaking
Initiating recreational activities
Initiating caring
Requesting support
Showing affection
Initiating discussion of money matters

Any other areas that you consider important.

Part B: make an 'If . . . then . . .' statement

Choose an area in a specific relationship in which you wish to
initiate more. Make an 'If . . . then . . .' statement along the
lines of *'If* I implement my changed behaviour (specify), then
(a), (b), (c) etc. predictions are likely to come true'.

Part C: try out and evaluate your changed behaviour

Try out your changed behaviour. How well did you do it?
What were its positive and negative consequences for yourself,
the other person, and for your relationship? Have your predictions been confirmed or disconfirmed? Has this experiment
taught you something about how you can use initiating skills
more to attain your relationship goals? If so, what?

Requesting changes in behaviour

People in relationships build up patterns of behaviour. When
you request a change in your partner's behaviour you may have
one of three goals: getting them (1) to do something that they
are not already doing; (2) getting them to do something that
they are already doing either more and/or better; or (3)
lessening or stopping an unwanted behaviour. You may be

non-assertive, aggressive or assertive in each of these three areas. Below are some examples.

- *Requesting a new behaviour.* Doris wants Tim to bring her flowers on birthdays and anniversaries.

Non-assertive:	Keep commenting on how other people bring their partners flowers on birthdays and anniversaries.
Aggressive:	'You've got no imagination. Don't you know that a woman likes flowers on birthdays and anniversaries?'
Assertive:	'One thing that would give me a lot of pleasure is if you could bring me flowers on birthdays and anniversaries.'

- *Requesting more of an existing behaviour.* George wishes that Wanda would caress his body more in their lovemaking.

Non-assertive:	Say nothing, but feel bad.
Aggressive:	'You only seem interested in receiving pleasure. Why don't you take more interest in giving it to me?'
Assertive:	'I love it when you caress my body with your fingertips. I feel wonderful all over. Please keep doing it.'

- *Requesting less or the stopping of an existing behaviour.* You study for an exam and your partner plays the stereo very loud.

Non-assertive:	You thump the table and curse to yourself.
Aggressive:	'Turn that goddamn stereo down. Don't you realize that I have work to do?'
Assertive:	'I'm upset because I can't concentrate with the stereo so loud. Would you please turn it down?'

There are a number of considerations for making behaviour change requests in a relationship. These include the following.

- *Assume cooperative intentions.* Where possible assume that your partner is committed not only to their welfare but also to yours and to that of your relationship. This assumption may lessen unwanted inhibition and aggression.

• *Ask yourself 'Is it worth being assertive?'* Assertion can be overdone. Some behaviours may not be worth bothering about. In a primary relationship it is hard to get away from irritating behaviours. However, with other relationships you have more choice. Another issue is that of how realistic it is to be assertive where you know another person to be highly threatened and potentially destructive if challenged. It is naïve to expect that assertive messages, however well sent, always bring a happy outcome.

• *Watch out for your own defensiveness.* When your view of yourself is threatened you may be very tempted to strike back under the guise of being assertive. Especially when you feel strongly, you may label your behaviour as assertive when in reality it is aggresssive and destructive to your relationship.

• *Pay attention to timing.* If you want your partner to hear your assertion message, be sensitive to timing. Sometimes, as with the example of the loud stereo, you may not have much choice. On other occasions, you may need to wait until your feelings are more under control.

• *Make 'I' statements.* Locate the source of your requests directly in you. This allows them to remain requests rather than demands. Demands are much more likely to threaten and create resistance.

• *Be specific.* A golden rule of making requests is to be specific. Trite as it sounds, this rule is frequently violated. For instance, Gary sulks and plays the victim rather than tell Mary Beth that he prefers it if she does not wear hair curlers at breakfast.

• *Consider using honest positives.* It is very easy to initiate a cycle of negativity when requesting a behaviour change. You may soften your requests if you comment on some positive as well as on the negative aspects of your partner's behaviour (Kassorla, 1984).

- *Make requests positively.* Where possible, emphasize the positive by stating what you want rather than what you do not want. A simple example is to rephrase 'You look awful when you wear curlers at breakfast' to 'I like seeing your hair without curlers at breakfast'.

- *Pay great attention to voice and body messages.* This has already been stressed. Firmness need not be at the expense of consideration and kindness.

- *Use listening skills.* Listen carefully to the feedback generated by your assertive messages. Regard your assertive messages as invitations to discuss your requests rather than as demands. Also, it is important that your partner feels understood.

- *Use FER messages.* You can follow the FER (feeling, explanation, request) format when confronting negative behaviour, though not slavishly in that order. F is how you feel. E is your explanation of why you feel that way. This should specify the behaviour that you find negative. R is your request that either the negative behaviour be ended or, at the least, explained.

- *Use the minimum necessary muscle.* Basically, muscle entails taking into consideration how forceful to be (Butler, 1981). As a rule of thumb, assertive messages should use the minimum level of muscle to achieve their objectives. There are two main reasons for this. First, the greater the use of muscle the more chance there may be of eliciting resistance. Second, even if you get what you want, the more muscle you use the greater is the chance that you leave a residue of resentment. This unfinished business may later hinder your relationship.

- *Deal with defensiveness as best as possible.* There are *inner* and *outer* agendas when faced with defensiveness. The *inner* agenda concerns how you handle your own thoughts and feelings. Defensiveness is a common initial reaction to assertive messages. It does not necessarily indicate either that you have asserted yourself poorly or that you may not ultimately be successful. Even if unsuccessful, you can only be responsible for your own behaviour. The expectation that your partner will always do what you want is unrealistic. It can only contribute to your denigrating yourself when they do not.

The *outer* agenda concerns how you behave toward your partner. Assuming you decide to persist in the assertion, you have a number of options. First, you may pause after the negative response and then calmly yet firmly repeat your behaviour change request. Second, you may reflect your partner's feelings before repeating your request.

Partner A: 'I'm upset because I can't concentrate with the stereo so loud. Would you please turn it down.'

Partner B: 'Why the hell are you complaining?'

Partner A: 'I realize you're angry at my request, but I badly need to concentrate on my study and would be grateful if you could turn the stereo down.'

Partner B: (still not too pleased) 'OK'.

A third option is to use more muscle. For instance, you may both use a firmer voice and also strengthen your verbal message by saying 'I'm serious, please turn the stereo down'. A fourth option is to try to negotiate a mutually acceptable solution: for instance, negotiating times when your partner can play the stereo and times when you can study without it. The skills of managing conflict are covered later in the book.

- *Take cultural considerations into account.* When relating to someone from a non-Western culture, you must be especially careful to tailor your requests for behaviour change so that they can understand them and still be prepared to listen. You need be aware of cultural differences in assertion. For instance, in Indonesia submissiveness is valued more than assertiveness (Argyle, 1983), gaze is much more sparingly used in Japan than in Britain and in Asia great value is placed on not losing face.

EXERCISE
—34—

Writing assertive request for behaviour change scripts

INSTRUCTIONS

Using the FER (feeling, explanation, request) format, write assertive behaviour change request scripts to a real or imaginary partner in the following areas:

Not leaving the bathroom so dirty
Spending more time with you
Not coming home drunk
Expressing affection more openly
Not leaving all the initiating of sex to you
Listening to you more carefully
Initiating conversations more often

Any other areas that are relevant to your *current* relationships.

EXPERIMENT
—11—

What happens when I make an assertive request for a behaviour change?

Part A: assessment

1. Take a relationship that is important to you and assess your skills strengths and weaknesses in making requests for behaviour change in the following areas.

	Skills strengths	Skills weaknesses
Requesting a new behaviour		

Requesting more or better of an existing behaviour		
Requesting less of or trying to stop a behaviour		

Part B: make an 'If . . . then . . .' statement

Choose a specific area in which you wish to make an assertive request for a behaviour change in a relationship. Make an 'If . . . then . . .' statement along the lines of '*If* I implement my changed behaviour (specify) then, (a), (b), (c) etc. predictions are likely to come true'.

Part C: try out and evaluate your changed behaviour

Try out your changed behaviour. How well did you do it? What were its positive and negative consequences for yourself, the other person and for your relationship? Have your predictions been confirmed or disconfirmed? Has this experiment taught you something about how you can use assertive requests for behaviour change in your relationships? If so, what?

Handling power plays

Power plays are attempts by others to get you to do what they want rather than what you want (Berne, 1962; Steiner, 1981). Geoff uses his anger to get what he wants. Mike obscures the issue to avoid dealing with his partner directly. Vera finds that tears are very effective in getting her partner to bend to her wishes. Joan withdraws affection if her partner does not give her the feedback she wants. In all the above instances people use power plays – anger, mystification, tears and withdrawal of affection – to get what they want at their partner's expense. Sometimes a whole relationship has underlying assumptions that place one of the partners at a disadvantage. This may be the case where, on the basis of traditional sex-role assumptions, a man discourages a woman from pursuing her career.

Being aware of others' attempts to operate on your self-definition and to manipulate you is the first step in being able to handle their power plays. You then have a number of options. First, being submissive and at least tacitly acquiescing in their false definitions and manipulations. Second, being aggressive and perhaps escalating the tension and emotional temperature by counterattacking. Third, being assertive by quietly yet firmly persisting in your definition of yourself and/or the situation. This option may also include working on your own tendencies to either acquiescence or escalation. Additionally, you may confront your partner with how they behave and invite discussion of it. Fourth, if you find you are relating to a highly manipulative person, getting out of the relationship. This may also be viewed as an assertive option.

Ending a relationship

Ending a relationship can be achieved in non-assertive, aggressive or assertive ways. To start, you need to be clear that this is what you really want. For example, Jane asks Peter not to come round to her place any more. However, each time he does come she lets him in and has a long conversation with him. Here Jane is giving a very mixed message about ending the relationship.

Some of you may be non-assertive about ending a relationship because you take on responsibility for another person's life. For instance, Russell does not come right out and tell Eva that he thinks they have no future because he tells himself he is afraid that she will not be able to handle being on her own. In reality, Russell may be afraid of the confrontation. After a period of adjustment Eva might manage very well on her own. Many relationships end with hurtful rows after which the participants are not on speaking terms. Aggressive endings to relationships can add to the pain of parting for either or both of you. Furthermore, they can negate the good times that you may have had in the relationship.

There are several factors which may make it difficult to end a relationship assertively, especially if you are married and have children and shared property. Here the focus is on ending non-marital relationships assertively. Already you may have set some limits in the relationship: for instance, by restricting the intimacy level of your disclosures and by limiting the amount of physical contact. Many of the assertion considerations mentioned in requesting a behaviour change apply to ending a relationship. These include: the use of 'I' messages, the minimum necessary use of muscle, where possible stating honest positives, and accompanying your verbal message with firm yet kind voice and body messages.

Though sometimes relationships end abruptly, most often there is some prior indication that they are in trouble. If both of you are coordinated in your wish to end the relationship, this eases the ending. Where you are the person who intiates the ending of the relationship, it is generally better to come right out and say what you want rather than fudge the issue. You may either be asked or feel it appropriate to give an explanation of your decision. Alternatively, you may be the recipient of a tirade of abuse. In either event you may be able to show your strength by doing minimal damage to the self-esteem of the person with whom you have been involved. Ending a relationship assertively entails showing respect for yourself and the other person rather than being brutal and ruthless. Though you may well be contributing to another's pain, you have a responsibility for your own happiness and fulfilment. Provided you have not raised another's expectations dishonestly, part of the implicit contract in your relationship was probably that either of you could withdraw and seek your happiness elsewhere.

EXERCISE
—35—

Ending a relationship: saying goodbye assertively

INSTRUCTIONS

1. Write down what you think are the main considerations in ending a relationship assertively.

2. Do you experience or anticipate any special areas of difficulty in ending a relationship?

3. If relevant, pick a relationship that you have ended or would like to end. Take a sheet of paper and draw a line down the middle. At the top of the left-hand column write

PAST/PRESENT BEHAVIOUR; at the top of the right-hand column write PROPOSED ASSERTIVE ALTERNATIVE. Fill in both columns.

4. Do you think that you are influenced by any special sex-role or cultural considerations in how you might end a relationship? If so, please specify.

ENCOURAGING EACH OTHER'S ASSERTION

In a loving relationship based on assumptions of teamwork and equality, you feel responsible for the happiness and fulfilment of each other and not constantly absorbed with securing your own rights. Assertion for 'us', rather than just either for 'me' or for 'you', is motivated by your positive feelings for each other. This can involve both of you in demonstrating quiet strength, caring and vigilance on a daily basis.

Below are some of the many ways you can encourage each other's assertion for the sake of your relationship.

- *Possessing realistic relationship goals and rules.* You can openly discuss the goals of your relationship: for example, a commitment to honest and open communication on the basis of equality. You can also try to clarify the relationship rules most likely to attain them: for example, 'Each of us cares enough about the other to be considerate in the way we assert ourselves and to allow time and attention to process together the implications of our assertions'. In short, you give each other permission to be assertive.

- *Providing rewarding consequences.* The consequences you provide for each other's assertions can either encourage or discourage them. There are various ways you can provide rewards for assertive messages. Perhaps the main one is by treating them with respect and concern. This is demonstrated by the quality of your listening and understanding. At times you may even praise each other for having the courage to be assertive in difficult areas. Another way of providing rewarding consequences is to acknowledge caring assertions, for instance a compliment, with gratitude.

- *Demonstrating assertive thinking and behaviour.* Assertive thinking and behaviour can be contagious. If you are open and honest it generally makes it easier for your partner. This is a protection against getting into destructive cycles of mutual inhibition or aggression.

- *Providing openers and confrontations.* You can show that you care for each other's views by asking what they are. If you think that your partner holds back and requires encouragement to be assertive, you can offer this encouragement. If necessary, you can confront your partner with the need to keep being assertive.

- *Showing understanding.* If either of you thinks that you have a problem with assertion, the other can be there to offer assistance and support as you explore it. Sometimes this may involve working through painful past experiences that have contributed to present difficulties in being assertive.

- *Encouraging outside assertion.* If each of you adopts assertion as a way of life outside your relationship, this may make it easier to be assertive within it. You can support each other in your attempts to be assertive in your outside contacts.

Assertion for 'us' requires constant vigilance. It is easy to settle for less than the potential for happiness and fulfilment of your relationship. Working together as a team you are more likely to attain the potential than if each of you is bound up with your own assertion agendas.

CONCLUDING SELF-TALK

In a loving relationship, as well as being assertive for myself I can be assertive for my partner and for the well-being of our relationship. We are a team that helps each other both to develop and use assertion skills. We also strive to avoid being either non-assertive or aggressive.

Assertion involves both thinking and behaviour. Four important thinking skills I can use to support my assertive behaviour are: attributing cause accurately, using coping self-talk, choosing realistic personal and relationship rules, and predicting the consequences of my behaviour as accurately as possible. I can use my assertion skills in suggesting and taking initiatives in my relationships. I can also be tactful, yet firm in making requests for behaviour change. Additionally, I can handle power plays and end relationships assertively. I and my partner can work through the issues raised by our assertive messages in a spirit of mutual respect and caring.

Managing anger

The more violent the love, the more violent the anger.

Burmese proverb

Love's best habit is a soothing tongue.

William Shakespeare

*A*nger, a major manifestation of psychological pain, features prominently in virtually all close relationships. It is often intense, repetitive and violently expressed. Furthermore, it can be combined with high defensiveness in which you are unwilling to examine your behaviour. All of you carry psychological pain from hurtful events in your upbringing into your relationships. Additionally, you are subject to current stresses outside them. Thus, from both past and current sources you import the potential for anger. Then you have the further stresses of each other's negative behaviours.

The destructive consequences of anger scarcely require stating. Anger can be directed either at other people, anger *out*, or at yourself, anger *in* (Tavris, 1989). When directed outside, its two main negative forms are hostility and withdrawal. These behaviours can lead to alienation and distress in relationships to the point of total breakdown.

Anger can also have positive consequences. Possessing angry feelings does not in itself destroy relationships, but handling them poorly may do so. Anger can be a *signal* for yourself and your partner that something is wrong and requires attention. This should be a cue to examine your own behaviour and not just that of your partner. It can be an *energizer* leading to assertive requests for behaviour change and to confronting festering conflicts. Also anger can be a *purge* so that afterwards you may calm down and be more rational. In a loving relationship partners can work out rules that allow their anger to be used for constructive purposes such as the above rather than to tear each other apart.

Thinking and action skills

Since anger can be the mortal enemy of love it is important to develop the skills of both regulating and expressing it. Though they overlap, you need to focus both on your thinking and action skills. Some thinking and action skills for managing anger are listed in Table 10.1. In a loving relationship the best way to handle unnecessary anger is to prevent it. Your use of thinking skills may help you avoid 'laying your trips' on your partner. Furthermore, how you think can support your taking positive as well as avoiding negative actions when angry. This chapter reviews the skills listed in Table 10.1. Often you may use these skills in combination rather than singly.

Table 10.1 Some thinking and action skills for managing your anger

Thinking skills	Action skills
Owning responsibility for your anger	Assertion skills
Realistic personal rules	– expressing anger
Perceiving provocations differently	– requesting behaviour changes
Coping self-talk	Handling aggressive criticism
Using visualizing	Relaxing yourself
	Managing stress
	Helping each other

THINKING SKILLS

Paraphrasing Shakespeare: 'Love's best habit is a soothing mind.' A soothing *mind* is the precondition for a soothing *tongue*. There are many occasions when you can exhibit your love by disciplining your thinking so that you either prevent, or do not express, or dilute your expression of anger. On the one hand you can choose to think yourself into hatred, aggressive blaming, nursing resentments, wanting to cause psychological pain and acting violently. On the other hand you can choose to think yourself into a calmer and more problem-solving frame of mind.

Owning responsibility for your anger

Anger is a complex emotion. For instance, it gets combined with other emotions such as hurt, jealousy, anxiety, low self-esteem, powerlessness, frustration, irritability and depression. Owning responsibility for your angry feelings is a starting point for working on them.

There are many reasons why you may be reluctant to own your anger and its related feelings. For example, you may have learned that it is not feminine to be angry or that it is not masculine to admit to feeling hurt and vulnerable. Furthermore, people of both sexes, possibly especially males, may be reluctant to admit how they use anger to control others. You may have been brought up in a home where expression of anger was considered inappropriate. Furthermore, your angry feelings may have been of such strength that you found it easier to repress them rather than face the consequences of acknowledging and acting on them. Additionally, your religion and culture may have taught you that being angry was wrong.

Currently you may possess skills weaknesses that block you from fully being aware of and owning your anger. These include the following.

- *Deficient inner listening skills.* You may be poor at becoming aware that you are angry. Your angry feelings may go either unacknowledged or only partially acknowledged. Your body may experience anger through heightened blood pressure, tension, ulcers and insomnia. However, you may be deficient in understanding the meaning of these physical reactions.

- *Faulty use of language.* The way you use language may distance you from owning responsibility for 'angering' yourself (Glasser, 1984). For example, you may say 'He/she/you/it/they make(s) me angry'. The cause of your angry feelings is located outside of yourself. Additionally, you may use phrases like 'It's only natural to react with anger' or 'I had no choice but to be angry'.

- *Unrealistic personal rules.* You may have personal rules that make it difficult for you to acknowledge your anger: for example, 'Women should not get angry' or 'Christians should not get angry.'

- *Defensive processes.* You may have ways of handling your anxiety that avoid assuming responsibility for acknowledging and managing your angry feelings and being fully aware of their consequences. These defensive processes include the following.

  - *Denial.* For instance, either hating someone and not being prepared to acknowledge this or being unwilling to realize the consequences for someone of either your psychological or physical violence.
  - *Projection.* For instance, hating someone yet making out that they hate you.
  - *Reaction formation.* Forming reactions that are the opposite of what you really feel: for instance, love masking intense anger.
  - *Misattributing responsibility.* An overemphasis on making others responsible for how you feel. Blaming someone for making you angry is perhaps the prime example.
  - *Defensive lying.* Making up stories about yourself and others intended to have the outcome of making you seem in the right and the other person seem in the wrong. Giving way to the Nelson-Jones Reality Principle: 'If you can't accept reality, create it!' Defensive lying differs from deliberate lying in that you believe the distortions of reality entailed in your dishonesty.
  - *Attack.* Attacking another who provides unwelcome feedback concerning your anger and its consequences. Trying to control another's feedback by putting overt and/or subtle emotional pressure on them.
  - *Avoidance.* Avoiding issues where you are likely to be confronted with having to deal with your own angry feelings. Withdrawing emotionally and physically.

EXERCISE
—36—

Exploring how I handle my anger in my relationships

INSTRUCTIONS

Write out your answers to the following questions.

1. To what extent is managing your anger a problem for you in your relationships?

2. How good are you at tuning into your angry feelings?

3. To what extent do you get angry with yourself (anger in) rather than with other people (anger out)?

4. How confident a person are you and to what extent does this affect your proneness to anger?

5. To what extent do you consider that other people make you angry? Give reasons for your answer.

6. To what extent do you consider you are less of a person because you have angry feelings? If so, please explain.

7. Are you are aware of engaging in any of the following defensive processes to avoid assuming responsibility for your anger and its consequences?
   - denial
   - projection
   - reaction formation
   - misattributing responsibility
   - defensive lying
   - attack
   - avoidance

8. What are the other feelings, for instance hurt or anxiety, that you experience when you are angry?

9. What physical reactions, for instance tension, do you experience when angry?

10. List the kinds of thoughts you have when you are angry about the other person involved.

11. What verbal, voice, body and action messages do you send when you are angry?

12. Have you ever been or do you consider you have the potential to be physically violent when angry? If so, please elaborate.

13. When in a relationship do you and your partner take a teamwork approach to helping each other manage anger? If so, please explain.

14. What are the positive and negative consequences for yourself and your relationships stemming from how you currently handle your anger?

15. Assess the extent to which you are effective in owning responsibility for acknowledging and managing your anger in your relationships.

Choosing realistic personal rules

Like any feeling, anger can be viewed within the ABC framework:

A The activating event (provocation or trigger)
B Your thoughts
C Your feelings and actions.

Possessing unrealistic personal rules contributes to destructive anger (for example, Lopez and Thurman, 1986). You can set yourself up for feeling angry by mustabatory rules about how you, your partner and your relationship should be.

Mustabatory demands that you may place on *yourself* include the following.

I must never make mistakes.
I must always be right.
I must be rational and consistent all the time.
I must always get my revenge.
I must never make a fool of myself.

Mustabatory demands that you may place on *your partner* include the following:

My partner must never make me feel angry.
My partner must never disagree with me.
My partner must never criticize me.
My partner must always let me be right.
My partner must always let me have my way.
My partner must always be able to read my mind.
My partner must not in any way attempt to restrict my freedom.
My partner must always be feminine/masculine.
My partner must meet 100 per cent of my needs.
Where cultural differences exist, my partner must always adjust to my culture.

Mustabatory demands that you may place on *your relationship* include the following.

Our relationship must never have conflict in it.
Our relationship must seem conflict-free to outsiders.
We must compete rather than collaborate with each other.

When you find yourself getting angry, it helps if you do not act impulsively. Instead stop and think whether any of your unrealistic personal rules contribute to it. You can develop the skill of backtracking from your angry feelings to the thoughts that generate and sustain them. Then you evaluate how realistic these rules are and what their positive and negative consequences are for you and your relationship. Additionally, you can reformulate unrealistic anger-evoking personal rules into ones that are more self-supporting. As mentioned in Chapter 6, some of the main characteristics of self-supporting personal rules are the following: (a) expressing preferences rather than demands; (b) a coping emphasis rather than perfectionism; (c) being based on your own valuing process; (d) flexibility, being amenable to change in light of new information; and (e) leading to a functional rating of specific characteristics and to the absence of global self-rating of your personhood.

Here are some examples of reformulating anger-evoking personal rules into more realistic rules.

Unrealistic rule: 'I must always get my revenge.'
Realistic rule: 'My interests are not best served by

thinking in terms of revenge. I can work out more appropriate strategies for meeting my needs and keeping my relationship intact.'

Unrealistic rule: 'My partner must not criticize me.'

Realistic rule: 'Feedback is important in our relationship. I would prefer that my partner is tactful when giving feedback.'

EXERCISE
—37—

Managing anger: identifying and reformulating unrealistic personal rules

INSTRUCTIONS

Think of one or more recent situations in your relationships where you have felt angry. For each situation write out:

1. the activating event, trigger or provocation;

2. your thoughts: focus on identifying both realistic and unrealistic personal rules;

3. how you felt and how you acted;

4. a reformulation of each unrealistic into a more realistic personal rule; and

5. any changes in how you feel and act that might result from your more realistic personal rules.

It may help if you tape-record your reformulated rules and play them back to yourself at least once a day for the next week.

———————————————

Perceiving provocations differently

> *How strange it is to see with how much passion*
> *People see things only in their own fashion.*
>
> Molière

This section focuses on not being unnecessarily hard in the way you judge others' behaviour. This also can be a way of not being too hard on yourself.

Jimmy and Peggy had been going out for two months. Every time Peggy said that she found another man attractive, Jimmy felt jealous, put down and angry with her.

Cindy and Pete were newlyweds. When Pete started coming home from the office a little later than usual, Cindy concluded that he was becoming bored with her. She resented this.

Lisa and André had been living together for 6 months. Lisa was becoming extremely uptight because André was not more openly affectionate. She concluded that he did not love her any more.

In Chapter 6, I discussed how jumping to perceptual conclusions contributes to shyness. The same is true for anger (for example, Feindler, Marriott & Iwata, 1984). Let us assume that the explanations Jimmy, Cindy and Lisa chose to give themselves were erroneous. This may have been partly due to their own insecurities and partly because they have insufficiently developed skills of perceiving accurately. The outcome of each of their misperceptions was that they felt angry with their partner.

An obvious but often overlooked skill of trying to explain another's behaviour is to ask them what is going on. You check out their reasons before jumping to conclusions. Another skill is to generate alternative explanations and then choose the one that best fits the factual evidence. Here are some examples.

(a) Alternative explanations that Jimmy might have given himself for Peggy's behaviour.

   – I tell her how I find other women attractive so why shouldn't she tell me the same about men.

– Peggy would not make such comments to me if she did not feel safe with me.
– Our relationship is deteriorating and she does not try to be tactful any more.

(b) Alternative explanations that Cindy might have given herself for Pete's behaviour.

– He told me that they have a big job on at work. It's my own insecurity talking when I feel he is bored with me.
– Pete has a girlfriend at the office and our marriage is already on the rocks. He is being unfaithful.
– Pete is working extra hard to ensure that we are on a sound financial footing.

(c) Alternative explanations that Lisa might have given herself for André's behaviour.

– He never has been openly affectionate, but he has always been there for me when I want him.
– André is good at showing affection. It's just that I am very demanding.
– André came from a family where neither parent was openly affectionate and he needs help in becoming more expressive.

If you become aware that you have a tendency to become unnecessarily aggressive, a useful skill is that of trying to curb your 'knee-jerk' reactions to perceived provocations and to search for alternative and better ways of explaining them. Sometimes this process is called reframing or reappraising. As with combating shyness, this managing-anger skill involves you in the following kinds of self-talk.

'Stop . . . think . . . what are my perceptual choices?'
'Are my perceptions based on fact or inference?'
'If they are based on inference are there other ways of perceiving the situation that are more closely related to the factual evidence?'
'If necessary, what further information do I need to collect?'
'What is the perception I choose because it represents the best fit in relation to the factual evidence?'

EXERCISE
—38—

Managing anger: generating and evaluating different perceptions

INSTRUCTIONS

1. Choose one or more situations in your relationships in which you have felt angry, possibly without due cause.

2. For each situation make a worksheet in the following format.

Situation	Upsetting perception(s) (initial explanations(s))	Different perceptions (alternative explanations)

3. Write down the situation and, in the upsetting perception(s) column, any perceptions associated with your anger. Assess the realism of your upsetting perception(s) by logically analysing them.

4. In the different perceptions column, write down as many different perceptions of the situation as you can generate. Then evaluate which has the 'best fit' for explaining the situation.

5. Assess the ways in which the emotional and behavioural consequences of your 'best fit' perceptions would have been different from those of your initial perceptions.

Using coping self-talk

Those of you with a tendency to be impulsive when angry and 'shoot' your mouth might consider using coping self-talk.

Anger-evoking situations may be viewed as challenging you to respond in task-oriented rather than in impulsive and self-defeating ways. Simple self-instructions like 'calm down', 'cool it', 'count to ten' and 'take it easy' can often give you the time and space to get your feelings more under control (Goldstein and Keller, 1987). Once this takes place you have considerably more choice concerning both whether or not and how to express your anger.

> Beth is angry with Joe because he said he could collect her from work and has kept her waiting for half an hour. When he finally arrives looking tired and rushed she tells herself: 'Take it easy. Count to ten. He is obviously tired and this is no time for either of us to have a row.' Joe apologizes and says that he was delayed by having to change a flat tyre.

In many relationships provocations are relatively predictable. You know that your partner may tease you, leave their clothes around, not do a domestic chore or some other thing that you dislike. Here you can use coping self-talk to help achieve your goal of managing a specific provocation better. This entails making choices that increase your sense of mastery and lessen the likelihood of your anger being both unpleasant for yourself and counterproductive in your relationship (Novaco, 1977; Meichenbaum, 1983). Coping self-talk involves both *calming* self-instructions, for instance 'stay calm', and *coaching* self-instructions that help you stay focused on how you can perform best the task at hand.

Possible coping self-talk statements that you might tell yourself *before* a potentially anger-evoking provocation include:

> 'Keep calm and remember what I want to achieve in this situation.'
> 'Remember, stick to the issues and avoid put-downs.'
> 'I can handle this situation if I don't let my stupid pride get in the way.'

Possible coping self-talk statements that you might tell yourself *during* an anger-evoking provocation include:

> 'Stay cool. I'm not going to let him/her have the satisfaction of getting to me.'

'Relax. My anger is a signal telling me to calm down and keep my goal in mind.'
'Just because he/she is being competitive, there is no reason for me to get sucked in.'

Possible coping self-talk statements that you might tell yourself *after* an anger-evoking provocation include:

'I'm learning to cope better without being aggresssive.'
'Even though the situation is unresolved, I'm glad I didn't come on strong.'
'Using my coping self-talk prevents me from feeling powerless and overwhelmed.'

Along with using coping self-talk, you can diminish your physical reactions to an anger provocation by breathing slowly and regularly. Additionally, sometimes it pays to defer dealing with a provocation until you have your feelings more under control.

EXERCISE
—39—

Managing anger: using coping self-talk

INSTRUCTIONS

1. Make a list of your anger-evoking self statements. If you find difficulty doing this, keep a diary and record your anger-evoking self-talk.

2. Identify a specific situation in your relationships where you consider that your anger is harmful. Write down:
   (a) your goals in this situation; and
   (b) at least three coping self-talk statements for each of before, during and after the situation.

It may help if you write each statement on a 3 × 5 card for practice and use-in-emergency purposes.

EXPERIMENT

——12——

What happens when I use coping self-talk to manage anger?

Part A: assessment

Look back at your answer to Exercise 39 and use the situation for which you formulated coping self-talk statements.

Part B: make an 'If . . . then . . .' statement

1. The 'If . . .' part of your statement relates to rehearsing, practising and using your self-talk statements before, during and after an anger-evoking situation. Rehearsal and practice is important. Spend at least two separate periods rehearsing and practising your coping self-talk as you imagine yourself before, during and after your anger-evoking situation.

2. The 'then' part of the statement indicates the specific consequences you predict will follow from the changes in your behaviour. In brief: 'If I use coping self-talk, *then* these consequences (specify) will follow'.

Part C: try out and evaluate your changed behaviour

Try out your changed behaviour. How well did you use coping self-talk? Assess its positive and negative consequences for yourself and your relationship. Have your predictions been confirmed or disconfirmed? Has the experiment taught you something about how you can stay more in control of your feelings and behaviour by using coping self-talk? If so, please be specific.

Using visualizing

You do not only think in words, you think in pictures or images too. You can use visualizing, or consciously changing the images in your mind, to help you manage anger better. Ways that you can use visualizing include the following.

● *Visualized rehearsal.* When preparing how to handle an anger-evoking provocation you can visually go through the various steps in how you want to behave. Once you have worked this out you can repeatedly imagine yourself handling the provocation competently. When you play these 'movies in your mind' you may also have a sound-track of coping self-talk.

● *Visualized relaxation.* Visualization is best done by being in a quiet and comfortable place, shutting your eyes and getting relaxed. You may visualize restful scenes not only as a prelude to other forms of visualization, for example visualized rehearsal, but also as a way of calming yourself down when angry. Visualized relaxation may be used independently of, or in conjunction with, muscular relaxation, which is described later in this chapter. Each of you probably has one or more special scenes where you feel relaxed: for instance, looking at a valley with lush green meadows, or sitting in a favourite chair at home. The following is an example of a visual relaxation scene.

> I'm lying on an uncrowded beach on a pleasant, sunny day enjoying the sensations of warmth on my body. There is a gentle breeze. I can hear the peaceful noise of the sea lapping against the shore nearby. I haven't a care in the world and enjoy my feelings of peace, calm, relaxation and well-being.

● *Visualizing the opposite.* When you are in the grip of anger, hatred and resentment, switching from a verbal to a visual mode of thinking may help disrupt your negative ruminations. You can use visualizing to help you get in touch with your kinder feelings about the person with whom you are angry. When angry, it is very easy to allow yourself to erect negative stereotypes of others.

At their cancer clinic in Dallas, Texas, the Simontons have used an imagery process to help patients let go of resentments and forgive people who have hurt them (Simonton, Matthews-Simonton & Creighton, 1978). Patients are asked to get a clear picture in their minds of the person to whom they feel resentment. They are then instructed to:

> Picture good things happening to that person. See him or her receive love or attention or money,

whatever you believe that person would see as a good thing. (p. 152)

The Simontons report that as patients continue to use the process of visualizing good things happening they begin to get a different perspective on the person resented. Consequently, they begin to feel more relaxed, less resentful, and more forgiving. Some other ways of using visualizing to access more loving feelings are included in Exercise 40.

- *Visualizing another's viewpoint.* You can use visualizing to help you understand how the other person might view a situation in which you become angry. By taking their perspective you may gain insight into your own contribution to the conflict.

EXERCISE
—40—

Managing anger: using visualizing to become more forgiving

INSTRUCTIONS

Find a quiet place where you can be uninterrupted. Sit in a comfortable chair and after you read each instruction close your eyes.

1. Visualize a restful and relaxing scene. Evoke not only the sights, but the sounds, smells and other sensations that make this such a calm and peaceful scene for you. Stay in this scene for at least 2 minutes.

2. Visualize a clear picture of a person towards whom you feel anger. Then do each of the following visualizations. Spend at least 2 minutes on each and take note of your reactions.

   (a) Visualize good things happening to that person, the sort of things that make them happy.
   (b) Visualize one or more happy times in your relationship that you have both enjoyed.
   (c) Visualize yourself doing good things to that person.

(d) Visualize that person doing good things to you.
(e) Visualize characteristics of the other person that you like.
(f) Visualize your saying to the other person that you love them and value your relationship.

After doing the above visualizations, review which ones, if any, helped you to feel better about the other person and more relaxed. Which of them might help you to become more forgiving and behave more appropriately? You are likely to have to repeat these visualizations a number of times to gain the full benefit from them.

ACTION SKILLS

Being assertive

The previous chapter emphasized being assertive both in initiating and also in making requests for behaviour change. These can be skills of preventing anger as well as of managing it. Below are some examples where people's failure to be assertive contributes to their anger.

- *Not initiating and saying what you want.* There may be occasions when you are angry because you are too timid about sharing your thoughts and feelings.

   Paul and Barb usually do what Paul wants. Paul is very positive about initiating and stating his wants and wishes. Barb is very inhibited about stating what she wants. She resents Paul because she thinks he is too domineering and should know what she wants without having to be told.

- *Not making requests for behaviour change.* There may be instances when you disapprove of another's behaviour and either bottle up your anger or let it come out indirectly, for instance through cynicism and gossiping. Until you have made a genuine effort to change another's behaviour you may be colluding in situations that help you to feel resentful.

Rita and Vera are sisters. Rita does not like lending Vera money. Every time Vera asks, Rita grudgingly lets her have the money and then nags Vera until she gets repaid. Rita gets furious with Vera both because of her continual requests and also because Vera is poor at meeting repayment deadlines. Rita could prevent her anger if she made it clear to Vera that she wanted no more loan requests. If she backed up her words by not lending money, it is possible that, after a period of adjustment, Vera would stop asking her.

Chapter 9 reviewed non-assertive, aggressive and assertive ways of initiating and making requests for behaviour change. Please see that chapter for further details regarding how to be assertive in these areas.

Handling aggressive criticism

When you think someone criticizes you aggressively, you can react in a non-assertive manner, 'I'm sorry. It's all my fault. I won't do it again', in an aggressive manner, 'How dare you say that to me? You fool', or in an assertive manner. Though you may not always have time in the heat of the moment, examine your *thinking* choices. For example, your unrealistic personal rules may contribute to your perceiving accurate feedback as aggressive criticism. Also, you may have jumped to the conclusion that you are being unjustly criticized without having looked at the evidence and reviewed whether there are more accurate ways of perceiving it. Additionally, you may react impulsively without thinking through whether the criticism is worth bothering about. A reason for this is that you may not be using coping self-talk to stay calm and stick to the issues.

There are numerous *action* choices that you can make in dealing with aggressive criticism. Some of these are the skills of trying to stay calm. For instance, you can keep quiet and avoid an impulsive 'knee-jerk' reaction when your emotions are aroused by criticism. Instead you may give yourself time and space to compose your thoughts and feelings. Additionally, you may regulate your breathing. You may tell yourself to relax, calm down and breathe slowly and regularly until you feel more under control.

Below are five verbal strategies for dealing with aggressive criticism. You need to accompany your verbal messages with appropriate voice and body messages. The strategies may be used in combination as well as singly.

1. *Reflective strategy.* Here you allow the other person to vent their strong feelings and respond in a way that shows you have understood both their feelings and their reasons. For example, 'You feel mad at me because you think I am not pulling my weight in doing the household chores'. Often people stay stuck in their anger like broken records because they rightly or wrongly consider they are not being heard. Reflecting their anger gives them the message 'I hear your anger and criticism and I accept it as being your internal viewpoint'. Reflecting another's anger does not mean that you automatically agree with them.

2. *Deflective strategy.* The object here is to blunt the thrust of the aggressive criticism by agreeing with part of it. This is especially applicable where you actually do agree with part of the criticism. Examples of this are: 'You may have a point, I can be rather untidy at times', or 'I'm not always as considerate as I would like to be'. Having allowed the other person to establish the legitimacy of their area of criticism, you may find that he or she is more prepared to review with you whether criticism is justified in this specific case.

3. *Enquiry strategy.* Following on from either a reflective or a deflective response or from both responses, you may then use an enquiring response: 'Would you please be more specific about what I've done to upset you?' The enquiry response may further defuse the aggressiveness of the criticism since it shows you are willing to allow the other to elaborate their internal viewpoint. Furthermore, it may provide you with the information to clear up any misunderstandings that may have arisen. However, there may be instances where the enquiry response ignites rather than defuses anger. Some people become threatened when asked to specify the reasons for their anger.

4. *Feedback strategy.* After showing that you have heard another's criticism you may choose to give feedback both about the criticism and the manner in which it was given. For example: 'I feel very uncomfortable when you criticize me so harshly. The reason that I am so late in picking you up was that I had a flat tyre on the way over'. Sometimes when

another person attempts to talk you down, you may calmly and firmly repeat your position at the same time as acknowledging that they feel differently.

5. *Deferral strategy*. Often you have a choice as to whether to back off now and react to criticism at a later date. Backing off does not mean backing down. Rather you husband your resources for when you can be most effective. You may say something like: 'I've heard what you're saying (if necessary specify). I would like some time to think about it.' Alternatively, if it becomes clear that you disagree, you might say: 'It's obvious that we disagree. I think we both need some time to think about it. Could we fix a time to discuss it again?' Deferral strategies are not intended to avoid issues. Rather they should allow either or both parties time to cool down and later more rationally to deal with the emotions and issues raised by the criticism. The skills of managing conflict discussed in the next chapter can be highly relevant in this regard.

EXERCISE
—41—

Managing anger: dealing with aggressive criticism

INSTRUCTIONS

1. Write down how you see yourself feeling, thinking and acting when you are aggressively criticized. Give specific examples.

2. Below is a hypothetical situation in which you are being aggressively criticized. Other person (shouting and finger-pointing):

> Why don't you ever pull your weight with the household chores? Do you expect me to be your servant? You never keep your side of our agreements.

For each of the following strategies, write out a response to the above aggressive criticism of you.

- reflective strategy,
- deflective strategy,
- enquiry strategy,
- feedback strategy, and
- deferral strategy.

Which, if any, of the above strategies do you think might be effective if used by you either singly or in combination?

3. If appropriate, choose a situation from your current relationships where you are either being or at risk of being aggressively criticized. Write out:

   (a) how you are/might be criticized,
   (b) responses based on each of the five strategies, and
   (c) which, if any, of these strategies you think might be most effective, including stating your reasons.

Relaxing yourself

Mention has already been made of how you can try to counteract angry feelings by visualizing a restful scene. Progressive muscular relaxation is another method by which you can work to dissipate your anger. The term 'progressive relaxation' refers to the progressive cultivation of the relaxation response. You may use progressive muscular relaxation in conjunction both with visualized relaxation and also with other thinking skills, for example coping self-talk (Deffenbacher, Story, Brandon, Hogg & Hazaleus, 1988). Relaxation skills can help you to deal with unpleasant and counterproductive aspects of heightened emotional arousal. The desired consequences of this are that you think and act more rationally.

The first step in physically relaxing yourself is to find a quiet space where you will be uninterrupted. You may use a mattress, a recliner chair or a comfortable chair with a headrest. If possible wear loose-fitting, comfortable clothing and remove items such as glasses and shoes. Your arms should be either by your side if you are lying down or on the arms of your chair if seated. Your legs should be uncrossed and your eyes shut.

Progressive muscular relaxation involves you in tensing and relaxing various muscle groups. There is a five-step tension–relax cycle that you go through for each muscle group (Bernstein & Borkovec, 1973). These steps are: (1) *focus*, focus attention on a particular muscle group; (2) *tense*, tense the muscle group; (3) *hold*, maintain the tension for five to seven seconds; (4) *release*, release the tension in the muscle group; and (5) *relax*, spending 20 to 30 seconds focusing attention on the letting go of tension and further relaxing of the muscle group.

Table 10.2 lists the various muscle groupings and self-instructions for tensing them. You can make up a relaxation cassette for yourself that instructs you through the five steps for each muscular grouping. For example

(a) 'I'm *focusing* on my right hand and forearm.'
(b) 'Clench my right first and *tense* the muscles in my lower arm.'
(c) '*Hold* for 5 to 7 seconds.'
(d) '*Release*, let my body go back to its basic relaxed position.'
(e) '*Relax*. Focus on the sensations of tension leaving my right hand and forearm for 20 to 30 seconds.'

At the end of your progressive muscular relaxation instructions, also instruct yourself to imagine a restful scene for 3 to 5 minutes and to forget all your cares. Throughout making your relaxation cassette, speak in a slow, quiet, firm and relaxed voice.

Progressive muscular relaxation requires regular practice to gain the full benefit. When learning it you should practise daily for at least 15 minutes for a week. If you come back to it after a break, you should also practise until you are getting deeply relaxed again. However, there may be times when your anger is unexpected and immediate. At such times relaxing yourself, with or without the use of a cassette, may still help you to cope with your heightened arousal.

Table 10.2 Tensing self-instructions for progressive muscular relaxation.

Muscle group	Tensing self-instructions*
Right hand and forearm	Clench my right fist and tense the muscles in my lower arm.
Right biceps	Bend my right arm at the elbow and flex my biceps by tensing the muscles of my upper right arm.

Left hand and forearm	Clench my left fist and tense the muscles in my lower arm.
Left biceps	Bend my left arm at the elbow and flex my biceps by tensing the muscles of my upper left arm.
Forehead	Lift my eyebrows as high as possible.
Eyes, nose and upper cheeks	Squeeze my eyes tightly shut and wrinkle my nose.
Jaw and lower cheeks	Clench my teeth and pull the corners of my mouth firmly back.
Neck and throat	Pull my chin down hard towards my chest yet resist having it touch my chest.
Chest and shoulders	Pull my shoulder blades together and take a deep breath.
Stomach	Tighten the muscles in my stomach as though someone was about to hit me there.
Right thigh	Tense the muscles of my right upper leg by pressing the upper muscle down and the lower muscles up.
Right calf	Stretch my right leg and pull my toes towards my head.
Right foot	Point and curl the toes of my right foot and turn it inwards
Left thigh	Tense the muscles of my left upper leg by pressing the upper muscle down and the lower muscles up.
Left calf	Stretch my leg and pull my toes towards my head.
Left foot	Point and curl the toes of my left foot and turn it inwards.

* With left-handed people, tensing instructions for the left side of the body should come before those for the right.

EXERCISE
—42—

Managing anger: relaxing myself

INSTRUCTIONS

1. Make up a progressive muscular relaxation self-instruction cassette as described in the text.

2. Spend at least 15 minutes a day for the next week practising your muscular and visual relaxation skills.

3. If appropriate, when you feel angry in your daily life go to a quiet room with soft lighting and no distractions. Sit or lie in a comfortable position and practise your relaxation skills. Afterwards note any changes in how you feel.

Managing stress

Stress can come from both within and without. Both sources can contribute to anger. It is important that you develop your awareness regarding your signals of being stressed and how well you listen to them. Also, become more aware of what stresses you. This may help you not only to prevent and manage your anger but also to avoid taking it out on other people.

Each of you has an optimal level of stress or a particular level of stimulation at which you feel most comfortable. At this level you experience stress without distress (Selye, 1974). Beneath this level you may be insufficiently stimulated or bored. Above this level you are likely to experience physiological and psychological distress. Body reactions include hypertension and proneness to heart attacks and ulcers. Feelings of distress may include shock, depression, frustration, anger, disorientation and fears of insanity or nervous breakdown. If the heightened stress is prolonged or perceived as extremely severe, you may feel you are in a state of excessive stress or crisis.

Below are two examples of people whose stresses make them more prone to anger. Kim has allowed herself to develop an excessively stressful lifestyle. Leo is reacting to external pressures. However, in both examples there is an interaction between internal and external sources of stress.

Kim is a high-pressure stock and bond salesperson. She is always on the go both professionally and personally. She lives on her nerves and burns the candle at both ends and in the middle. When things go wrong, she gets tense and irritable. She is like a tightly stretched rubber band just waiting to break out in anger.

Leo has just received a promotion at work. He now has to supervise 15 people. While pleased at the promotion Leo still needs to develop the skills of being a good supervisor. He feels under pressure because of his promotion and is very irritable when he gets home. Leo does not sleep well and his appetite is poorer than usual.

Some of the skills of managing stress are peculiar to the specific situations in which people find themselves. For example, as Leo develops supervisory skills he is likely to feel less under stress. Other skills are more general. For instance, the more you can develop your relationship skills the less likely are you to generate stressful reactions from others. Additionally, by developing your thinking skills you can prevent stress. For example, people who set themselves perfectionist standards for achievement are excellent candidates for feelings of distress. They need to develop more realistic personal rules.

The following are further ways of managing stress so that you are less prone to anger.

- *Muscular and visual relaxation.* This has already been reviewed.

- *Developing adequate recreational outlets.* You may need to explore the extent to which you lead a balanced life based on meeting your needs as well as others' demands. How much time do you spend on rewarding leisure activities? Knowing when and how to take recreation is a most useful skill for preventing and managing anger.

- *Participating in your health.* Physical unfitness contributes to many people's feelings of being stressed. You may be: not exercising regularly; smoking a lot; drinking too much; engaging in drug abuse; and eating too much. If so, you need to change your attitude toward assuming responsibility for your health. Additionally, if you have physical symptoms attributable to stress, for instance hypertension, you should see a doctor.

- *Developing a support network.* If your support network is inadequate, you may wish to spend time developing it. Your support network is likely to consist of trusted friends, colleagues, relatives, neighbours and possibly people in the helping services. People without such networks are much more vulnerable to feeling isolated and powerless when things go wrong.

- *Developing managing-problems skills.* Life is full of hassles. The better you are able to deal with these, the less likely you are to be stressed. Your orientation to problems should be that they are an ordinary part of life. Where possible, break them down into their component parts so that they seem more manageable and you can define them accurately. Be creative about generating alternative solutions and realistic about evaluating the consequences of these. Then implement the 'best fit' solution and monitor and evaluate its consequences. Be prepared to modify or change plans that do not work for you.

The message of this section is that sometimes the most effective way to manage your anger is to analyse the broader context of the stresses in which it occurs. There may be choices that you can make and skills that you can develop for dealing with stresses outside a relationship that free you to be happier and more relaxed within it.

HELPING EACH OTHER TO MANAGE ANGER

In a loving relationship based on assumptions of teamwork and equality you can help each other to manage anger. A degree of anger is likely to be a fact of life in your relationship. You can each take responsibility for managing it constructively rather than destructively. Below are some ways in which you may work together as a team.

- *Possessing realistic relationship rules.* Together you can formulate realistic rules for the expression and management of anger in your relationship. The following rules may be helpful.

'Each of us tries to become aware of and openly locate our anger in ourselves.'

'Neither of us tries to control the other through the use of threats, anger or physical violence.'

'Each of us attempts to avoid hurting the other by aggressive put-downs and by shutting the other out through emotional withdrawal.'

'Expression of anger in our relationship is a signal to explore our own thoughts, feelings and actions and not just those of the other person.'

'If either of us has been destructively hurtful in anger, we openly acknowledge our negative behaviour when calmer.'

- *Developing accurate and caring models of each other.* Each of you attempts to move beyond a superficial personification of yourself and your partner to develop a more accurate understanding. You work to understand each other's fears and vulnerabilities, trigger points, stresses, burden of previous hurts, defences, and ways of showing and avoiding showing anger. Additionally, you strive to keep an awareness of each other's strengths and positive qualities.

- *Developing a soothing tongue.* You discipline yourself to watch your mouth. You express your anger assertively and show an awareness of what your partner is going through before, during and after your expression of anger. You give specific feedback that allows the other to understand the reasons for your anger rather than 'shoot your mouth'. Your expression of anger is an invitation for discussion rather than an end in itself.

- *Using listening and helpful responding skills.* Ways in which you can use listening and helpful responding skills include the following. First, you can tune into your partner and help them express angry feelings that they may either have difficulty acknowledging and/or getting out into the open. Second, you can show that you have clearly understood their feelings and reasons when they express anger. Third, you can help each other analyse and deal with the material underlying the anger. This may entail helping each other articulate *here and now* unmet needs and unstated requests in your relationship, work through hurtful *there-and-then* experiences prior to your relationship, and deal with current *there-and-now* stresses outside your relationship. Another way of looking at this is that you offer each other informal therapy. A risk here is that you focus exclusively on your partner when exploration of your contribution might also be fruitful.

● *Being prepared to admit to and change negative behaviours.* Defensiveness is probably more dangerous than anger in close relationships. If you are defensive you risk fanning the flames of each other's anger. However, if you are open, capable of acknowledging hurtful behaviours when pointed out, and willing to change them you not only defuse those situations but also make it easier for your partner to behave likewise. By your honesty and actions ill-will can get transformed into goodwill.

● *Developing a capacity for tolerance and forgiveness.* The German poet Schiller wrote: 'Happy is he who learns to bear what he cannot change!' One of the reasons for the increased divorce rate in Western countries is that expectations of marriage are higher than previously (Argyle and Henderson, 1985). You may need to examine your personal rules to see if your expectations are counterproductive to your own happiness and that of your partner. Additionally, you may need to work on the fears and insecurities that make it difficult for you to forgive and let go of past hurts. Martin Luther King (1963) observed that forgiveness does not entail ignoring what has happened, but means that you choose not to allow it to remain as a barrier to your relationship. This may be partly enlightened self-interest. Both understanding human frailty and valuing caring behaviour may also make it easier for you to forgive your partner. You may also need to learn to forgive yourself too!

As well as the teamwork skills mentioned above, you can help each other to manage anger by increasing your exchange of rewarding behaviours and by managing your conflicts collaboratively rather than in competition. These additional skills are the subject of the next chapter.

CONCLUDING SELF-TALK

I can use anger either constructively or destructively in my relationships. I need to develop my skills of tuning into my angry feelings and owning responsibility for them. Thinking skills that I can use to regulate angry feelings include: identifying and reformulating unrealistic personal rules; perceiving provocations differently; using coping self-talk; and developing relevant visualizing skills.

I can also use action skills to manage my anger. Assertion skills can help me both to prevent anger-evoking situations developing and to express anger constructively. There are a range of strategies, including reflection, that I can adopt to handle aggressive criticism. Also I can use muscular and visual relaxation skills to calm my heightened level of arousal. Additionally, by managing stresses better, I'm less likely to overreact to provocations.

In a close relationship we can use teamwork so that our anger does not become destructive. For instance, we can possess realistic relationship rules and formulate accurate and caring models of each other. Additionally, we can help each other express and understand the reasons for our anger. Also we can watch our tongues!

— 11 —

Preventing and managing conflict

So that's what Hell is. I'd never have believed it . . . . Do you remember, brimstone, the stake, the gridiron? . . . What a joke! No need of a gridiron, [when it comes to] Hell, it's other people.

Jean-Paul Sartre

The best part of married life is the fights. The rest is merely so-so.

Thornton Wilder

*T*he word conflict comes from the Latin roots *com-*, together and *fligere*, to strike. Dictionary definitions of conflict emphasize words like 'fight', 'struggle', 'antagonism' and 'sharp disagreement'. These dictionary definitions have three elements: first, a difference or disagreement; second, the disagreement is severe; and third, there is ill-will. This chapter focuses on managing differences in relationships. Though frequently otherwise, these differences need not be the cause of severe ill-will.

Conflicts are inevitable in ongoing relationships. Argyle (1983) observes: 'There is a very high level of conflict in marriage, and violence is quite common' (p. 155). Deutsch (1973) states that there are usually five basic types of issues in conflict: control over resources; preferences and nuisances; values; beliefs; and the nature of the relationship between the partners. People enter relationships with differences in: their socio-economic and, possibly, cultural backgrounds; sex-role expectations; levels of self-esteem; ability to tolerate stress; tastes and preferences; beliefs and values; interests; social and family networks; and capacity to change and grow. Add to this that many people are deficient in their loving skills, including those of managing conflict, and the inevitability of conflict becomes even more obvious.

Productive and destructive conflict

The negative effects of conflict scarcely need cataloguing. Conflicts can cause immense psychological pain which may last well after the relationship has ended. Relationships which offer promising opportunities for both partners can founder because conflicts have not been managed effectively. In Chapter 1, I provided statistics on the high level of marital breakdown and distress in marriages. Unhappy homes, where parents' energies are diverted both in fighting each other and also sometimes displacing their frustrations onto their children, can adversely affect those reared in them. Parental unhappiness or divorce can contribute to children's delinquency, aggression, disobedience, conduct problems, social withdrawal, depression, anxiety and bed-wetting. Additionally, children may learn poor skills of how to manage conflicts in their own lives. On a more subtle level conflicts can fester in a relationships and contribute to withdrawal and distance where previously there was happiness and closeness.

Work environments are also frequently characterized by destructive conflicts. Not only can these cause great stress and unhappiness, but they can also lower output; the extreme case being a strike. A degree of conflict is inevitable in work relationships just as in personal relationships. There may be scarce resources, your personal styles may grate, values and beliefs may differ, and you may have different expectations of each other and of the workplace. Additionally, you do not leave your loving skills weaknesses at home. You take them to work. This increases the likelihood of conflicts taking a destructive course both for the individual participants and for the attainment of group goals.

Conflict can be good as well as ill. The course of conflict may be productive rather than destructive. It is very easy to state the negative aspects of conflict. To redress the balance four positive aspects of conflict in relationships are stated here.

- *Greater trust.* Conflicts can build trust. People who can relate despite differences, as well as work through differences together, may feel that their relationship is much less fragile than those who have not had such experiences.

- *Increased intimacy.* An important aspect of intimacy is the ability to give and receive honest feedback. A fuller sharing of self can occur where partners can reveal and work through their differences rather than just inhibit their disagreements.

- *Increased self-esteem*. Partners who manage their conflicts effectively may gain in self-esteem. They know that their relationship is strong enough to withstand conflict. Each may feel better for being able to say what they think and feel. Problems may be identified, aired and solved rather than allowed to fester. Each may gain a firmer sense of their identity as well as greater knowledge of the other. Both may gain valuable practice in managing conflicts effectively.

- *Creative solutions*. The course of productive conflict can be viewed as a process of mutual problem-solving. Creative solutions which meet both parties' needs, sometimes called 'Win–Win' solutions, may be the outcome of this process. The opposite of a 'Win–Win' solution is a 'Lose–Lose' one where neither party gets their needs met. In a 'Win–Lose' solution only one party gets their needs met.

The remainder of this chapter presents some thinking and action skills for providing and managing conflicts.

THINKING SKILLS

Emotions can run very high in conflicts. You may get so aroused that, temporarily at least, you may lose your capacity to be rational. Causing pain, being right and ventilating your anger can take over as your main short-term objectives. The longer-term consequences of your behaviour may be obscured in the heat of the moment. In close relationships, partners can get stuck in repetitive patterns of conflict that undermine trust and mutual rewardingness. You may drag each other down in cycles of recrimination and bitterness. The lows in your relationship may get longer and deeper and the highs shorter and fewer.

Many thinking skills are relevant to both preventing avoidable conflicts and also managing unavoidable ones. These include the thinking skills covered in Chapter 10 to help you manage anger better: owning responsibility for your anger, choosing realistic personal rules, perceiving provocations differently, using coping self-talk and visualizing. In this chapter, I develop two interrelated areas of perceiving accurately: namely, owning personal responsibility for your choices and perceiving the other more accurately. Conflicts are frequently caused and sustained by misperceptions in these areas.

Owning personal responsibility for your choices

> *Seek not good from without: seek it within yourselves, or you will never find it.*
>
> Epictetus

Look at the ways in which people may describe their choices in conflicts.

> 'Until she stops being nasty to me, I'm not going to stop being nasty to her.'
> 'I had no choice but to tell him what I thought of him in no uncertain terms.'
> 'She makes me so mad that I can't help hitting her.'
> 'It's all your fault that our relationship is heading for the rocks.'
> 'You tell me how we can get out of this mess.'
> 'If you're not prepared to be reasonable, I don't give a damn what you think.'
> 'I'm so hurt by all that you've done to me that I find it impossible to forgive you.'

In each of the above instances the speaker is likely to stay stuck through inability to perceive and acknowledge responsibility for feeling, thinking and acting choices. Additionally, the speaker may worsen the conflict through aggressive voice and body messages.

There are numerous thinking errors in the above statements that indicate speakers inadequately own responsibility for their choices. These include the following.

- *Dependent thinking.* Allowing your feeling, thinking and actions to be controlled by another's behaviour.

- *Lack of alternatives thinking.* Saying that you have no choice rather than identifying where your choice points are.

- *Passive 'I'm the second to change' thinking.* Needing the other person to make the first move before you can alter your behaviour.

- *'Poor me' thinking.* Allowing yourself to wallow in self-pity and other negative emotions rather than acknowledging your strengths and coping capacities.

- *Misattributing cause.* Looking to blame another person rather than to assign cause accurately for what sustains the problem, including your own contribution to it.

- *Overemphasizing the past.* Dwelling on past hurts and resentments rather than trying to ensure that you relate better in the present and the future.

- *Insufficient consequential thinking.* Inadequately thinking through the consequences of your thinking and action choices for yourself and others.

- *Competitive thinking.* Thinking in terms of 'you' versus 'me' rather than collaborating to find solutions that work for 'you', 'me' and 'us'. The notion of replacing competition with collaboration is a recurring theme in this chapter.

- *Insufficient problem-management orientation.* Not seeing the difficulties and differences in your relationship as problems to be managed rather than excuses to give and receive pain.

Reversing the above errors provides a list of thinking skills that help you to own responsibility for your choices in relationship conflicts. These skills strengths are as follows:

- Independent thinking
- Flexible thinking that identifies alternatives
- Active 'I'm prepared to be the first to change' thinking
- 'Adequate me' thinking
- Realistically attributing cause

- Emphasizing the present and future much more than the past
- Consequential thinking
- Collaborative thinking
- Problem-management orientation

Exercises 43 and 44 are designed to raise your awareness that in conflicts you always have choices. Exercise 43 focuses on the thinking and action choices that others make that may hinder their effectiveness. Exercise 44 assumes that sometimes you can get insight into how you might approach a conflict if you view it in 180 degrees the opposite way to your current viewpoint.

EXERCISE
—43—

Exploring personal responsibility for managing conflict: some case studies

INSTRUCTIONS

For each of the following conflict case studies write down:

1. some of the main thinking skills weaknesses that may get in the way of the main character or characters acting effectively,

2. the specific ways in which the main character or characters act ineffectively,

3. how each of them might (a) think and (b) act differently to attain their goals.

Case studies

1. Steve is an 18-year-old who enjoys his girlfriend's company, but has frequent rows with her. During the rows he tends to make comments like: 'You women are all the same. You just can't make the effort to understand the male viewpoint'.

2. Mary and Eddie are 17-year-old twins who share the use of the second car in the family. Each is extremely touchy and

jealous over the other's use of the car. Each believes that the other is taking advantage of their weaknesses. They get very emotional and argue a lot. Their parents are getting fed up with their arguments and are threatening to stop both of them from having the use of the car.

3. Nancy is a 50-year-old widow who lives with her 18-year-old son, Eric, and 16-year-old daughter, Kate. Nancy is constantly nagging the children to help her more with the housework and be less messy. She makes remarks like: 'You are selfish children' and 'If your father were alive he would not let you behave this way'. Eric's reaction to Nancy's remarks is to get angry and sulky. Kate says that since Eric is not pulling his weight why should she.

4. Andy and Russ are junior executives both with very fixed ideas about how their unit should be run. They appear to be in a constant power struggle. When in meetings with their boss, both are trying to argue the strength of their case with him. Each presents his own point of view as though it were the only way and gets defensive when challenged by the other. Each is anxious for the approval of their boss and sees their meeting in 'Win–Lose' terms. Their boss regards both of them as rather immature and not yet ready for promotion.

5. Cherryl and Pete have been married ten years and feel they are drifting apart. They rarely go out together and each increasingly resents the other. They argue about how to bring up the children, how much to see their in-laws, what friends each other should have, how they should spend their money and so on. Pete's way of getting what he wants is to become emotional and angry. Often Cherryl gives in, but carries around a residue of resentment which shows up in snide remarks, deliberately not doing things which would please Pete, and telling Pete how difficult other people, like her friends and her mother, view him. Every now and then Cherryl explodes and they have a blazing row. During these rows they catalogue each other's deficiencies. Each has lost the desire to give real happiness to the other. The emotional atmosphere in their home is tense and bitter. Their children welcome the opportunity to play in their friends' homes.

EXERCISE
—44—

Choosing the reverse response in a conflict

INSTRUCTIONS

This exercise is designed to help you become more aware that you choose how you respond to others when in conflict. The idea is to get you thinking and responding in the opposite way to how you currently behave.

Think of someone with whom you either are or have recently been in conflict in a close personal or work relationship. Assume that you have been saying that they are wrong, disparaging them, and sending hostile voice, body, touch and action messages to them.

(a) Imagine going up to that person and acknowledging the rightness of their position. How might he/she react?

(b) Imagine paying a number of honest compliments to that person. How might he/she react?

(c) Imagine speaking in a kind and considerate tone of voice to that person. How might he/she react?

(d) Imagine going up to that person looking relaxed, smiling, open and friendly. How might he/she react?

(e) If appropriate, imagine either shaking hands with that person or giving him/her a hug and/or a kiss. How might he/she react?

(f) Imagine going out of your way to give something or do something for that person that they would really like. How might he/she react?

Perceiving the other more accurately

> *Two-thirds of what we see is behind our eyes.*
>
> Chinese proverb

Even when they are not in conflict, people in close relationships may have distorted pictures of each other. With the anxiety, threat and heightened emotionality generated in a conflict, these pictures may get even more distorted. Maslow

(1962) distinguishes between 'deficiency-motivated' and 'growth-motivated' perception. He writes: 'We may not be aware when *we* perceive in a need-determined way. But we certainly are aware when *we* ourselves are perceived this way . . . . We dislike being perceived as useful objects or as tools' (pp. 37–38). In deficiency-motivated perception your picture of me is likely to be distorted by your own needs and fears. You do not see me as I am. Instead you see me as you want me to be to fulfil your picture of yourself. For instance, if you need to see yourself as the victim, you need to see me as the persecutor.

Developing a more realistic, accurate and caring model of the other person is a skill for both preventing and managing conflicts. It helps prevent conflicts because you are less likely to jump to erroneous conclusions concerning their motivation. Similarly, during conflicts, you are more able to relate to them on the basis of balanced and accurate rather than distorted information.

How can you get greater accuracy into your perception of others? You may have to work hard to counteract your destructive negative perceptions that are not soundly based on reality. The first step is to become aware that your model of your partner may be inaccurate and that you may be perceiving them some of the time in a deficiency-motivated way.

The second step is to become aware of some of the specific ways in which you may distort your partner. These include the following.

- *Lack of information.* Many relationships get stuck at a level of self-disclosure that falls short of genuine intimacy. Since partners tend to reciprocate each other's behaviour this consolidates the stuckness. However, the less actual information partners provide about themselves, the more room there is for each other to provide 'make-believe' information to fill this vacuum. Thus your models of each other may not only contain information gaps but also your distorted pseudo-information to fill some of these gaps.

- *Perceptual errors.* There are numerous perceptual errors that may distort your vision of your partner, especially in the heat of conflict when you feel anxious and threatened. These errors include the following.

  - *Selective attention to negatives.* Focusing on your partner's negative behaviour and blocking out positive thoughts, feelings and reactions to them.

– *Exaggerating negative characteristics.* Trying to make a point through overstatement. For instance, 'You are never around to help in the house', where the word 'never' may be a gross exaggeration.
– *Rating personhood negatively.* Going beyond negative perceptions of specific behaviours to rate your partner negatively as a person. For instance, 'The reason that we keep having all these hassles in our relationship is because you have such a poor personality.'
– *Overgeneralizing,* drawing a broad conclusion from a specific observation. For instance, 'You did not remember our anniversary, therefore you do not love me any more.'
– *Black-and-white thinking,* thinking in either–or terms. For instance, 'You must either love me all the time or you do not love me at all.'
– *Misattributing cause,* giving inaccurate explanations for your partner's behaviour which lead to and sustain conflicts. For instance, 'You did not pick me up when you said you would because you wanted to take out your anger on me.'

The third step in trying to rid yourself of inaccurate and negative stereotypes of others is to work diligently to alter your thinking and behaviour. Some suggestions for this include the following.

• *Collect more information.* Both by using good listening and self-disclosing skills, you make it safer for your partner to reveal more of themselves. By taking more of an interest in your partner, including asking pertinent questions, you may amplify your model of them.

• *Understand the external contexts of their behaviour.* Get to know the past influences that have shaped your partner. What rules and directions were received from their family or origin and from other sources? Also, try to understand their current stresses outside your relationship, for instance at work.

• *Correct your specific perceptual errors.* Try to identify how you distort your perceptions when you are anxious, angry and in conflict. For instance, do you emphasize and exaggerate your partner's negative behaviours? If so, what are the consequences for you, your partner and your relationship? Where you catch yourself being unrealistically negative, consciously try to balance this out with more positive perceptions. Where you catch yourself over-generalizing, consciously try to draw more accurate inferences from the available facts.

- *Develop checking-out and clarifying skills.* Be willing to check out with your partner how they see themselves behaving and the reasons for this. If you are still unclear, you may request further clarification.

- *Develop perspective-taking skills.* Check tendencies you have towards egocentric thinking by trying to see how the other person views the conflict. How do they see you behaving? How do they see themselves behaving? What do they want for your relationship?

- *Behave differently.* Try altering your behaviour to see if your negative perceptions of your partner are as much a function of your behaviour as they are of theirs. Just as partners tend to reciprocate negative behaviours, they also tend to reciprocate positive behaviours. There may be realistic opportunities for you to behave differently and so lessen your negative perceptions of each other.

- *Work to eliminate a competitive attitude.* Where partners compete with each other on an 'I win, you lose' basis, each has a vested interest in perceiving the other negatively. You can develop a conciliatory and collaborative attitude to problems in your relationship. Where possible, your goal is to find solutions that are acceptable to both of you. Such solutions may be better than simple compromises in which each of you only gets part of what you want.

EXERCISE
—45—

Preventing and managing conflict by choosing to perceive another more accurately

INSTRUCTIONS

1. Regarding either your partner or some other person of your choice with whom you come into conflict, assess the extent to which you distort your picture of them through:

   (a) lack of information, and
   (b) specific perceptual errors,
       – selective attention to their negative characteristics,
       – exaggerating their negative characteristics,
       – rating their personhood negatively,
       – overgeneralizing,
       – black-and-white thinking, and
       – misattributing cause.

2. If you consider some of your perceptions either of your partner or some other person are inaccurate in ways that generate and sustain conflicts, assess the extent to which each of the following might help you to perceive him/her more accurately:

   (a) collecting more information,
   (b) understand the external contexts of their behaviour,
   (c) correcting specific perceptual errors (listed above),
   (d) developing checking-out and clarifying skills,
   (e) developing perspective-taking skills,
   (f) behaving differently yourself, and
   (g) adopting a more conciliatory and collaborative attitude.

3. Set yourself clear and realistic goals for perceiving either your partner or another person more realistically, then develop and implement a plan to achieve your goals.

ACTION SKILLS

As well as *thinking* less emotionally and more rationally, how can you *act* to prevent and manage conflicts? Here I focus on two important teamwork skills: increasing the exchange of rewarding behaviours and collaborating to'manage conflicts.

Increasing the exchange of rewarding behaviours

In Chapter 8, I introduced the notions of positive reciprocity, in which partners exchange rewarding behaviours, and negative reciprocity, in which they do the reverse. Most relationships are a mixture of the two. However, partners in distressed relationships reciprocate more unrewarding behaviours than those in happy relationships.

Exchanging a high number of rewarding behaviours both prevents and contains conflicts. It prevents conflicts because happy people are less likely to pick unnecessary fights. It contains conflicts because it creates an emotional climate of goodwill in which conflicts are more likely to be approached productively rather than destructively. However, increasing your exchange of rewarding behaviours is definitely not a substitute for developing the communication skills of managing conflicts collaboratively.

Partners in unhappy relationships may be well advised to take a systematic approach to increasing their exchange of rewarding behaviours. This can be viewed in six steps.

1. *Awareness* of the importance of exchanging rewarding behaviours
2. *Acknowledging* existing rewarding behaviours
3. *Making requests* for additional rewarding behaviours
4. *Agreeing* to exchange specific additional rewarding behaviours
5. *Implementing* your agreement
6. *Evaluating* progress and making further agreements

1. *Awareness of the importance of exchanging rewarding behaviours.* Though it may seem obvious, you may need to become more aware that people are more attractive to each other if they are rewarding rather than unrewarding. This

basic point can easily get lost in the heat of a conflict. Additionally, you may need to remind yourself that how you act influences how the other reacts. Stuart (1980) observes that a basic principle of social interaction is that: 'POSITIVE ACTIONS ARE LIKELY TO INDUCE POSITIVE REACTIONS, FIRST IN THE ATTITUDES OF OTHERS, AND THEN IN THEIR BEHAVIORS' (p. 194).

Humans may have a tendency to reciprocate negative behaviours more quickly than positive ones on a 'tit-for-tat' basis. Nevertheless, if you maintain it, there is a good chance that your rewarding behaviours may soften the attitude of your partner. In turn this may result in both an increase in their positive and a decrease in their negative behaviours towards you. Furthermore, if you both agree that insufficient exchange of rewarding behaviours is a problem in your relationship, the fact that each of you now makes an effort to please is likely to help rebuild trust.

2. *Acknowledging existing rewarding behaviours.* Partners in unhappy relationships tend to overemphasize each other's unrewarding behaviours. Conversely, they often misperceive, take for granted or fail to show appreciation for each other's rewarding behaviours. Both of you may need to become more aware of the rewards that already exist in your relationship. There are two main ways you can share your perceptions of existing rewarding behaviours. First, each of you can make a list of *your* behaviours that you perceive as rewarding for your partner. What do you do that pleases? What do you say that pleases? This can be a process in which people can find out for themselves not only the existing rewards they offer, but also how few of them there may be. Listing your own gaps in rewardingness may be less threatening than having them pointed out by your partner. These lists of 'Rewards that I give you' can be exchanged and discussed. Second, each partner can make a list of *the other's* behaviours that they perceive as rewarding. Here it is important not to spoil your positive feedback with negative 'hooks': for instance, 'I like it when you rub my back, but you could do it less clumsily'. These lists of 'Rewards that you give me' can be exchanged and discussed. During this discussion you should refrain from hostile criticism.

3. *Making requests for additional rewarding behaviours.* Each of you now answers the question: 'What rewarding

behaviours would I like you to do for me which you are not currently doing?' The behaviours you list must be specific and stated in the positive. For example, 'Not to be such a messy person' is neither specific nor stated in the positive. 'Not leaving your dirty socks on the bedroom floor' may be specific, but it is not stated in the positive. 'Put your dirty socks into the laundry basket' is both specific and stated in the positive. It is important that you include some small behaviours that are not necessarily in your areas of major conflict. This allows your partner to take some easy first steps. Additionally, try to make some of these behaviours the sort that can be performed almost daily: for example, 'Ask me how my day has been when I get home from work'. You may list the rewarding behaviours that you want in any area of your relationship: for example, companionship, sex, money, household chores and so on. Take time and care in making your lists. Keep in mind that your purpose is to influence the other person to become more rewarding for you and not to humiliate them, so be tactful. When both of you have had sufficient time to make your lists, exchange them.

4. *Agreeing to exchange specific additional rewarding behaviours.* Your goal here is to make an agreement in which you both state that you will perform some additional rewarding behaviours for the other for a specified time period, say the next two weeks. Each of you should feel free to choose which additional rewards you give. If necessary, clarify each other's requests. Sometimes both of you may make the same request: for example, 'Spend more time talking to me'. Much of the time each of you is likely to be agreeing to different requests.

A choice in making agreements or contracts is whether they should be *quid pro quo* – 'If you do this, I'll do that' – or based on good faith – 'My behaviour is independent of yours'. Good faith contracts are preferable in personal relationships since they make each of you responsible for your own behaviour. You can always review your partner's behaviour at the end of the agreement. An example of a simple good-faith contract made between a mother and her 17-year-old son Sam, both of whom wanted to improve their stormy relationship, was that:

For the next two weeks:

Mum agrees to:
Have a happy talk period for at least 10 minutes each evening when both of us are home;
Say 'I love you Sam' at least once.

Sam agrees to:
Have a happy talk period for at least 10 minutes each evening when both of us are at home;
Say 'I love you Mum' at least once;
Say 'Thank you' when Mum washes my clothes and gives me lifts;
Wash the dishes when asked;
Tidy my room at least once.

Each person should have a written copy of the 'agreement'. This can be signed and countersigned if you think it will help you to keep it. Each should post the agreement in a place where they are likely to be frequently reminded of its terms, for instance either on a bedroom door or notice board in the kitchen.

5. *Implementing your agreement.* Changing your pattern of behaviour from negative to positive may be difficult. If necessary, make a plan for how you are going to stick to your agreement. Remember that rewarding verbal messages need to be accompanied by rewarding voice and body messages if they are to have the desired effect. For example, you do not say 'I love you' when you are deep in reading the newspaper. Take a few risks in being more positive for the sake of your relationship. This may make it easier for the other person to reciprocate. If you wish to give further rewarding behaviours outside your agreement, feel free to do so.

A skill of implementing your agreement is to acknowledge and reward each other's attempts to be rewarding by saying 'Thank you', 'That's great', 'I like that', or 'I'm pleased'. A fundamental psychological principle is that behaviour that is rewarded is more likely to be maintained than behaviour which is not. Possibly each of you may have been less rewarded in the past because you insufficiently applied this principle.

6. *Evaluating progress and making further agreements.* Take note of your efforts to be rewarding. Also acknowledge what each of you has achieved. If you wish, make this a

stepping-stone for your next agreement in which you expand the scope of your rewarding behaviours. Even without agreements, you should develop the skills of monitoring your rewardingness for your partner and, if insufficient, taking appropriate action. Also, develop the skills of helping your partner to be more rewarding for you: for instance, by making specific, tactful requests for behaviour changes and by saying 'thank you'.

EXPERIMENT
——13——

What happens when we increase our exchange of rewarding behaviours?

INSTRUCTIONS

This experiment needs to be done with someone where both of you want to improve your relationship.

Part A: assessment

Work through the procedures described in the text for acknowledging existing rewarding behaviours and for making requests for additional rewarding behaviours.

Part B: make an 'If . . . then . . .' statement

Together make an 'If . . . then . . .' statement along the lines of '*If* we formulate and implement an agreement to increase the amount of rewarding behaviours exchanged in our relationship, *then* these consequences (specify) are likely to follow'.

Part C: try out and evaluate your changed behaviour

Try out your changed behaviour. Assess its positive and negative consequences for yourself, each other and for your relationship. Do you think that developing the skills of increasing the exchange of rewarding behaviours will help you to either prevent and/or manage conflicts better in future? If so, be specific in identifying how it will help.

Collaborating to manage conflicts

To jaw-jaw is better than to war-war.

Winston Churchill

An important way that partners can show their love and concern for each other is to work together on their differences, problems and conflicts. There are three main problem–management styles that you can adopt: the competitive, the compliant and the collaborative.

- **Competitive.** Here you view the problem as one in which there are scarce resources. Consequently, there has to be a winner and a loser. The loser is not going to be you. You adopt an 'I win–You lose' approach to the conflict and do all in your power to get your way. Your tactics may include manipulation, not telling the whole truth, not admitting mistakes, and sending aggressive verbal, voice and body messages. The risks of such an approach include not arriving at the best solution and your partner feeling violated. Though you may have won in the short term, you still may pay a high price for your victory.

- **Compliant.** Here either or both of you are unassertive. You may collude with each other in not confronting problems in your relationship. You may wish to keep the peace for fear of the psychological discomfort of confronting problems. Each of you may deceive yourselves as to your motivation for complying and not own your anxieties and fears. Compliant approaches to managing problems can involve either both partners avoiding issues or one partner giving way much of the time.

- **Collaborative.** Here you relate on a basis of mutual respect. You work as a team both to prevent unnecessary conflicts and also to arrive at mutually satisfactory solutions to real conflicts. Neither of you attempts to impose your wishes on the other. You seek so-called 'I win – You win too' solutions that maximize the gains and mini-mize the costs for each partner and your relationship. Additionally, each of you is prepared to work on your inner difficulties as well as with one another. Both of you strive to develop accurate models of each other and to avoid indulging in negative misperceptions.

Table 11.1 CUDSA: a five-step framework for managing conflicts

Task(s)	Illustrative skills
Step 1 Initiate the collaborative process	*CONFRONT the conflict* Owning the existence of the conflict, deciding whether or not to confront, being calm and keeping the threat level low, timing your confrontation, inviting the other to work on the conflict with you, choosing an appropriate time and place for further discussion.
Step 2 Clear up misunderstandings, clarify positions, defuse emotions	*UNDERSTAND each other's position* Sending 'I' messages, expressing feelings and stating wants and wishes assertively, giving specific feedback, stating honest positives, listening and responding helpfully, checking-out and clarifying, taking the other's perspective, admitting to and changing misperceptions.
Step 3 Arrive at mutually acceptable definition(s) of problem(s)	*DEFINE the problem(s)* Avoiding unfair fight tactics, identifying and acknowledging areas of common ground, admitting your own mistakes and hurtful behaviours, identifying actions of the other that sustain the conflict, identifying hidden agendas, acknowledging and communicating changes in your positions, stating the problem(s) clearly and simply.

Task(s)	Illustrative skills
Step 4 Generate and assess alternative solutions	*SEARCH for and evaluate alternative solutions* Generating solutions, evaluating the consequences of solutions, expressing reactions to solutions clearly, asking for the other's reactions, clarifying, making trade-offs and compromises.
Step 5 Reach a clear agreement that can be renegotiated if necessary	*AGREE upon, implement and evaluate the best solution(s)* Stating agreements clearly, checking out that they are clearly understood, planning, implementing and evaluating consequences, making requests to renegotiate rather than break agreements, modifying and changing agreements.

I now present CUDSA, a systematic five-step framework for managing conflicts in collaboration. Implementing it involves using almost all of the sender and receiver skills described in this book. The five steps of CUDSA are:

Step one:	*Confront* the conflict.
Step two:	*Understand* each other's position.
Step three:	*Define* the problem(s).
Step four:	*Search* for and evaluate alternative solutions.
Step five:	*Agree* upon, implement and evaluate the best solution(s).

The five steps of this confront–understand–define–search–agree framework frequently overlap. Table 11.1 gives an overview of the central task and illustrative skills involved in each step of the framework. Though not indicated in the table, participants in conflicts need to discipline themselves to avoid aggressive voice and body messages that are perceived as put-downs. This injunction is relevant to all steps in the framework.

CUDSA provides an easily comprehensible and memorized framework for you and your partner to use in managing your conflicts. Sometimes conflicts can be handled in a more informal way. However, on other occasions, you may need to work together more systematically. Even where only one of you is prepared to adhere to the framework, it may help that person influence the conflict management process constructively. Unfortunately, some people are so prone to defensive thinking in conflicts that there are limits to the applicability of a framework that assumes some capacity to be rational in both of you.

Step one: confront the conflict

Phil and Debbie had been dating for two months and thought each other special. However, both were aware of tensions in their relationship. They avoided talking directly about these difficulties for fear of hurting and then losing each other.

Natalie was getting increasingly steamed up because Bob was not doing his share of the washing up. She kept her resentment to herself until one evening she blew her stack and said a whole lot of things she later regretted.

Some of you, like Phil and Debbie, may find it easier to avoid confronting conflicts. Other, like Natalie, may collect trading stamps and one day cash them in by going for someone's jugular vein. There are many skills of confronting conflicts in ways that are likely to initiate a rational rather than a destructive process.

When you are aware of and own a conflict you may still have a choice as to whether you confront it openly. There are many considerations involved here, including whether there is anything to be gained and whether the conflict is important enough to either or both of you to bring it out into the open. Assuming that the conflict is not so obvious that your partner cannot ignore it and also that you decide to bring it into the open, the following skills may help.

- *Keep calm.* While you want the other person to take notice of you, you wish to avoid being unnecessarily threatening. Shouting and screaming is likely to alienate them and may consolidate their unwanted behaviours.

- *Pay attention to timing.* You have to choose the best time for raising the issue that there is a problem between you. Poor times are likely to be when either of you is rushing off to work, when you have visitors, or when you have both arrived home tired after a hard day. A good time may be after a meal when both of you have more energy.

- *Assert yourself.* Confronting a conflict involves assertion. You need to avoid the twin dangers of non-assertiveness and aggression. Furthermore, if the other person still resists owning that there is a problem in your relationship, you need to persist in your assertion to the point where they recognize that there is a problem for them as well as for you.

- *Invite the other to work.* Some conflicts may be resolved quickly and amicably once they are out in the open and discussed. If this is not the case, you attempt to enlist the other in taking a collaborative approach to managing the conflict. In essence you say: 'We have a problem in our relationship. Let's see if we can collaborate together to solve it for our mutual benefit'. Both of you then need to set aside sufficient time and energy for dealing with it. Also, ideally you need a quiet and comfortable location free from interruptions and distractions.

Step two: understand each other's position

Jack and Sophie are unhappy in their marriage. When they argue, neither of them closely listens to the other. Instead they shout, finger point and make comments like 'You *never* think of anyone but yourself' and 'You have *always* been selfish'.

Make an agreement that, at the start of discussing a conflict, each of you takes turns in having *uninterrupted* 'air time' to state your position. During your air time the only talking that your partner can do is to reflect and ask you to clarify your internal viewpoint. Partners are likely to be more prepared to listen once they are safe in the knowledge that they will have their turn. If your partner interrupts, you have a number of choices, including: pausing; saying something like 'Please let me finish, you have had (will have) your turn'; and putting out your arm with your palm facing them – a standard body message requesting silence.

There are a number of reasons why making the effort to try to understand each other's position is critical to managing conflicts effectively. First, you may discover that your so-called conflict is based on misunderstandings and misperceptions. It need not exist in future. Second, it indicates that each of you has a commitment to a collaborative approach to managing your conflict. You show respect for each other. Third, it may take some of the emotional steam out of the conflict. Often when people feel they have been heard and understood they calm down and become less aggressive. This helps them to think more rationally. Fourth, it enables both of you to start identifying the real rather than the imaginary issues in the conflict.

Below are some of the sender and receiver skills of understanding each other's position.

- *Send 'I' messages.* You own your perceptions by sending 'I' messages rather than a competitive series of 'You-blame' messages. Do not communicate as though you have a monopoly of the truth and wish to impose your definition of the conflict on your partner.

- *Express feelings and wishes assertively.* You share your feelings in an open, yet tactful, way. Where you have wants and wishes you state these clearly. You do not expect your partner to read your mind.

- *Stick to the issues.* You focus on the current issues and avoid both verbal personal attacks and putting your partner down by means of hurtful voice and body messages. You also avoid dragging in irrelevant past history.

- *Give specific feedback.* Avoid sending general negative messages that lead nowhere. Give specific feedback so that your partner knows the behaviour you would like changed. Also, be willing to intermingle honest positives. You are more likely to be listened to if you do since you lessen the risk of being perceived as doing a 'hatchet job'.

- *Use listening and helpful responding skills.* Use good attending behaviour. Listen to and observe voice and body as well as verbal messages. Help your partner to share their perceptions of the conflict. Use restatements and reflections to show that you have understood. Pay particular attention to tuning in accurately to your partner's feelings. This, above all, may help them to feel understood by you.

- *Use checking-out and clarifying skills.* At the end of your partner's initial statement of their position, it may help if you make a summary restatement of it to check out the accuracy of your understanding. Where something your partner says is unclear, tactfully request clarification: for instance, 'I think I hear you saying . . ., but I'm not altogether certain?' Endeavour to make your understanding of the other's internal viewpoint as accurate as possible rather than make unwarranted assumptions and inferences.

- *Admit to and alter misperceptions.* Where you have misunderstood your partner's actions and intentions, be prepared to let them know this. Also, update your model of your partner in light of any significant new information.

Step three: define the problem(s)

Tim and Ginger were both in their early twenties and had been seeing each other for over a year. The moment they became engaged their previously happy relationship became full of conflict. Whereas previously they made decisions easily, now they argued over practically everything: which restaurants to go to, what films to see, and so on. One evening when they were trying to become reconciled, Ginger redefined the conflict. She admitted that getting engaged symbolized the loss of her autonomy. She was panicking because she felt trapped. Once she identified her hidden agenda she and Tim were able to work through her underlying fears. They are now happily married with two children.

In step two each of you may have been offering your own definitions of the problem. Conflicts get extremely destructive when each partner competes to define the problem on their terms. Both of you risk repetitively stating your positions and getting increasingly frustrated and resentful. The task of step three is to try to arrive at a mutually acceptable definition of your problem(s).

Some of the skills of defining problems include the following.

- *Avoid unfair fight tactics.* Unfair fight tactics are competitive put-downs that show a lack of respect for your partner. They may be viewed as power plays designed to influence another's definition of you, themselves and the problems between you. They include the following.
  - Mindreading and ascribing negative motives.
  - Unnecessarily attacking psychologically vulnerable spots.
  - Engaging in overkill and coming on far too strong.
  - Monologuing and dominating the conversation.
  - Using threats that engender insecurity.
  - Sending threatening body messages: for instance, finger pointing, eyes blazing, punching, scratching.
  - Sending threatening voice messages: for instance, shouting and screaming.
  - Unnecessarily dragging in third parties' opinions to support your own.
  - Using passive aggressive tactics, such as attacking while making yourself out to be the victim.
  - Using tears to engender guilt.
  - Sulking and emotional withdrawal.
  - Playing games, such as feigning collaboration yet always frustrating the finding of mutually acceptable definitions to your problem(s).

- *Identify areas of common ground.* Even in a real conflict not based on misunderstanding, you may still have considerable common ground. Often people polarize conflicts into a simple 'Good guy–bad guy' format that obscures their areas of agreement. Identify and acknowledge any common ground. An important way you can both acknowledge common ground and defuse emotions is to acknowledge your own mistakes and hurtful behaviours. This may make it easier for your partner to be less defensive too.

- *Identify hidden agendas.* Try to deal with the real rather than the surface agendas. For instance, if a spouse suspects his or her partner is having an affair, picking on him or her in a whole range of other issues is not the best way of trying to define and solve the problem. Ideally, both of you should be able to communicate your needs, including those that are unmet, simply and clearly. Being allowed to say 'I want' and 'I need' without recrimination can contribute to identifying the real agendas in a conflict.

- *Identify specific actions that sustain the problem(s)*. Focus on the specific actions of yourself and your partner that maintain the conflict. In short, focus more on *how* it is sustained rather than on *who* started it or *why* it happened.

- *State the problem(s) clearly and simply*. The end product of step three is a simple statement of the problem.

  Having raised 3 children, Monique wanted to return to the workforce. Her husband Henry was unhappy about this because he was already under terrific job pressure and did not want any extra work at home. Once they became calmer they both agreed to define the problem as how to get the housework done. Henry admitted he had changed his position from not wanting Monique to have a job once they defined the problem in a way that allowed both of their needs to be met.

Step four: search for and evaluate alternative solutions

Take the above example of Monique and Henry. Having now defined the problem they can join in the collaborative search for mutually acceptable solutions. These might include: getting a smaller house, paying someone to clean the house, eating out more, getting more take-away meals and so on. Searching for alternative solutions is often best done with two distinct stages: first, *generating* and, second, *evaluating* solutions. Generating solutions is a creative process that may be inhibited by premature evaluation of emerging solutions. Some of the skills of step four include the following.

- *Generate solutions*. Generating solutions is a creative process. The objective is to generate a range of options amongst which may be effective ones. Sometimes it helps to brainstorm. The object of brainstorming is 'idea finding'. The rules for a brainstorming period include: criticism and evaluation of ideas is ruled out and quantity is wanted.

- *Evaluate solutions.* You evaluate solutions on the basis of what is best for both of us. You agree on which solutions seem 'goers' and assess the possible consequences of each of them. Each of you needs to state your reactions to the possible solutions as clearly as possible.

- *Use checking-out and clarifying skills.* Be prepared to ask the other person for their reactions to a proposed solution. Also, if necessary, further clarify their reactions.

- *Make trade-offs and compromises.* As you evaluate alternative solutions, you may be faced with choices as to whether or not you modify your position. A useful skill is that of being able to make realistic trade-offs and compromises. Acknowledge and show appreciation of any concessions made by the other person. Also, if necessary, be prepared to remind them of any concessions that you make.

Step five: agree upon, implement and evaluate the best solution(s)

Ben and Fiona thought they had an agreement as to who would do the dishes on what evening. On Tuesday, the dishes remained unwashed and each said they did not do them because it was the other's turn.

Having evaluated the better of your possible solutions, you then make an agreement or contract. Agreements need to be implement, evaluated and, if necessary, renegotiated. Some of the skills of step five are as follows.

- *State agreements clearly.* If agreements are unclear they are more likely to be broken, if only through misunderstanding. This risks rekindling your conflict. Agreements vary according to the nature of the conflict. For instance, if your conflict has been about household chores, the contract will concern *who* is to do *what* and *when*. It is generally desirable to put agreements in writing. This acts as a check on whether they are clearly understood and avoids future conflicts over the terms of the agreement. Also, written agreements can be placed where they serve as reminders to implement them.

- *Make a plan where necessary.* Some agreements involve planning. For instance, Eleanor and Andy have been in considerable conflict over how to spend their vacation. Having now agreed to spend three weeks motoring in France, they now need to plan how best to go about this. Possibly, their agreement should include who plans which aspects of the vacation by when.

- *Renegotiate rather than break agreements.* If for whatever reason you cannot live within an agreement it is much preferable to renegotiate it than to break it. Breaking your agreement is a breach of trust. Furthermore, your partner may consider this gives them similar rights. This may further damage your relationship.

- *Modify and change agreements where necessary.* Some solutions may turn out to be deficient on implementation. Frequently, this entails only minor modifications to the initial agreement. However, on other occasions, either or both of you may discover that the 'best' solution has major weaknesses. Possibly, you have another reasonable solution available from your earlier search for alternatives. Otherwise you need to generate and evaluate further solutions.

A final point about CUDSA is that partners in a conflict may wish to monitor and evaluate the success of their managing-conflict procedures and modify them if necessary. The framework suggested here is not meant to be a strait-jacket. You may need to adjust it to suit your personal style. Nevertheless, if the CUDSA framework has been helpful, this may motivate you to use it in managing future conflicts.

EXPERIMENT
──14──

What happens when we collaborate to manage a conflict within the CUDSA framework?

INSTRUCTIONS

This experiment needs to be done with someone where both of you want to work through a specific conflict.

Part A: assessment

What have been your attempted solutions to the conflict to date? What have been the consequences of your attempted solutions? What so far have been your skills strengths and weaknesses in trying to manage the conflict?

Part B: make an 'If . . . then . . .' statement

Together make an 'If . . . then . . .' statement along the lines of 'If we collaborate in a sincere attempt to manage our conflict (specify) within the CUDSA framework, *then* these consequences (specify) are likely to follow'.

Part C: try out and evaluate your changed behaviour

Try out your changed behaviour. How well did you implement it? Assess its positive and negative consequences for yourself, each other and your relationship. Do you think that developing the skills of collaboratively managing your conflicts within a systematic framework will help you in future? What parts of the CUDSA framework, if any, did you find particularly helpful?

CONCLUDING SELF-TALK

Conflicts are inevitable in my close relationships. They may help as well as harm them. What is important is that I develop the skills both of preventing and also of managing conflicts as effectively as possible. This involves me in working on both thinking and action skills.

All the thinking skills that help me manage anger better are relevant to preventing and managing conflicts. When in conflict it is easy to avoid responsibility for my choices, for instance both by blaming and also by waiting for the other to make the first move at reconciliation. I need to discipline myself not to do this. Additionally, I need accurately to perceive those to whom I relate rather than see them in terms of my own needs and fears. Two teamwork skills that my partner and I can use to prevent and manage conflicts are increasing our exchange of rewarding behaviours and collaborating to manage our problems in a systematic fashion. Increasing our exchange of rewarding behaviours involves awareness of its importance, making requests, and implementing and evaluating agreements to be more positive. Together we can approach areas of difference within the CUDSA framework for managing conflicts. Its five steps are: (1) *confront* the conflict, (2) *understand* each other's position, (3) *define* the problem(s), (4) *search* for and evaluate alternative solutions, and (5) *agree* upon, implement and evaluate the best solution(s). This framework challenges each of us to use a range of loving skills when the going gets rough.

Maintaining and developing your loving skills

Yes! to this thought I hold with firm persistence;
The last resort of wisdom stamps it true;
He only earns his freedom and existence;
Who daily conquers them anew.

J.W. von Goethe

*T*his chapter focuses on how you can maintain and develop your loving skills. For the remainder of your life you are faced with the possibility of making good or poor loving skills choices: choices that help you achieve your goals or choices that end you in trouble. Thus you need to maintain your loving skills daily. Additionally, for the sakes of others and yourself, you are responsible for developing them.

REASSESSING YOUR SKILLS

In Exercise 1 you were asked to give an initial assessment of your loving skills. Exercise 46 asks you to reassess your loving skills in light of reading this book. Also, I hope, you have completed some, if not all, of the exercises and experiments. Additionally, you will probably have tried to develop many of the skills by practising them in your daily life. Take your time over the exercise. Accurate assessment is vital in pinpointing weaknesses. Once weaknesses are clearly identified, you have made considerable progress in doing something about them. You may wish to use Exercise 46 periodically in future to maintain and reassess your skills.

EXERCISE
—46—

Reassessing my loving skills strengths and weaknesses

INSTRUCTIONS

Using the format below make a worksheet for reassessing your loving skills strengths and weaknesses. For more detail about a skills area, see the relevant chapter.

Skills area	My strengths	My weaknesses
Understanding what I bring to relationships		
Disclosing myself		
Being a rewarding listener		
Responding helpfully		
Making initial contact		
Choosing relationships		
Deepening relationships		
Asserting myself		
Managing anger		
Preventing and managing conflict		

Make a list of the specific skills weaknesses upon which you most need to work.

MAINTAINING AND DEVELOPING YOUR SKILLS

Once you have acquired some loving skills strengths, how can you keep them going? There are numerous pressures on you not to maintain your loving skills. Some of these pressures come from yourself. For instance, you may feel the pull of long-established weaknesses when skills strengths have recently been learned. Some of you may give up too easily because you have insufficiently learned that maintaining your loving skills, for instance in times of conflict, involves inner strength and toughness. Some of you may play the comparison game whereby, because someone else fails to use good skills, this legitimizes you in relinquishing them too.

Some of the pressures not to maintain your skills come from outside. Relatives, friends and colleagues may reward some of your weaknesses rather than your strengths; for instance you may be more comfortable for them if you are non-assertive. The media constantly bombard you with messages conducive to superficial relationships. Additionally, the notion of people working hard in their relationship skills has still to gain widespread acceptance. This kind of personal excellence tends to get left to individuals to develop as best they can.

Whether the pressures come from yourself, others or both, it is easy to backslide and translate some of your loving skills strengths into weaknesses. However, where possible, you should be going in the other direction. Below are some suggestions for maintaining and developing your loving skills.

- *Remembering to view relating in skills terms*. In Chapter 1, I stressed the importance of viewing relationships in skills terms. Furthermore, that these skills represented choices which might be well or poorly made. Because many of you have not been brought up to see your relationships in skills terms, you may lose not only this perspective but also the benefits that derive from it. Viewing relationships in skills terms gives you a set of skills 'handles' with which to work on relating better. Furthermore, this perspective assumes that you are personally responsible for making the skills choices that are most conducive to your happiness and fulfilment. It keeps relationships out of the realm of magic and places them firmly into the realm of practicality.

● *Clarifying your values.* Some people approach their relationships as though the others involved are objects to be manipulated or conquered rather than as persons worthy of respect. Others treat themselves like objects and scarcely allow themselves enough time and energy to relate well. Neither group places sufficient value on affirming others and themselves through the quality of their relationships. Both groups need to confront themselves with the consequences of their choices. You are more likely to commit yourself to developing your loving skills if you set a high value on the personal growth of yourself and others. If you value other goals more, such as making money or sexual conquests, this is likely to interfere with the actualizing of your full humanity. If so, you need to reassess and clarify your values. It is a contemporary tragedy that large numbers of people are not fully committed to their own development, nor to that of their partners, nor to that of their children. A realization of more fundamental values, sometimes with the aid of religion, can release many people to become more caring and compassionate.

● *Remaining open to inner and outer feedback.* Being an effective human animal involves both inner and outer listening. You require inner responsiveness to your significant feelings and physical reactions. Additionally, you are faced with a constant struggle to avoid misperceiving yourself, others and the outer feedback you receive. One important way of motivating yourself to maintain and develop your loving skills is to be mindful of positive consequences from using them. You are more likely to repeat behaviours that you perceive as bringing rewards than those you perceive otherwise.

> William was a married man with three teenaged girls. As he worked on his tendencies to be violent in getting his way in his family he felt he was losing some of his power. However, when he thought of the positive consequences of treating his wife and family in a more democratic and considerate way, he realized the importance of continuing to curb his temper and to use his managing anger and conflict skills.

● *Having a contract.* Commitment and motivation are

crucial to maintaining and improving loving skills. Loving skills contracts can be created for individuals, couples or families. A loving skills contract establishes a written commitment amongst those participating both to use, maintain and develop and also to help each other to use, maintain and develop your loving skills. Table 12.1 contains an example of an individual contract. This can be amended where others are involved. Also you could reword the contract into your own language.

Table 12.1 An individual loving skills contract

---

1. I am ultimately responsible for my feelings, thoughts and actions in my relationships.
2. I commit myself to using, maintaining and developing my loving skills.
3. Where appropriate, I commit myself to helping others to whom I relate to use, maintain and develop their loving skills.
4. The loving skills that I commit myself to using, maintaining and developing include:
   – being in touch with my feelings
   – starting relationships, where appropriate
   – being prepared to develop relationships through openness and honesty
   – listening to and helping others to feel understood
   – responding helpfully to others
   – managing my feelings of anger constructively
   – managing conflict constructively.
5. Though I may make mistakes and have shortcomings, I commit myself to persist in trying to honour this contract.

Signed _____
Date _____

This contract should be posted in an obvious place as a reminder.

● *Working together with a partner.* A number of times I have emphasized the importance of partners working together in various loving skills areas, for instance managing anger. When each of you uses your loving skills strengths you encourage your partner to do likewise. By relating in a more open and direct way, you make it easier for your partner to reciprocate. By helping each other work through specific difficulties either in your individual lives or in your relationship, you demonstrate your active concern for each other's welfare. By having an implicit or explicit loving skills contract and by endeavouring to implement it in your daily life, you increase your chances of maintaining a high level of mutual rewardingness in your relationship. Your joint use of loving skills is likely to increase the good times and lessen the bad times. Furthermore, you help each other stay out of destructive negative spirals.

- *Co-counselling.* Co-counselling is an approach to working together. You may choose to co-counsel either with your partner or with someone else. The latter has risks if your partner disapproves of sensitive material being discussed with third parties. In co-counselling you have joint counselling sessions on a regular basis. You decide who starts as 'counsellor' and 'client'. The 'counsellor' gives the 'client' air time to examine his/her relationship concerns and skills and supports this exploration by responding helpfully. This may last for 10 or 15 minutes, longer if necessary. Afterwards you reverse roles. This may be followed by a sharing and discussion session. Co-counselling with a spouse or partner has much to recommend it. It can help maintain communication as well as allow you to work together to improve your own and each other's loving skills.

- *Practising your skills daily.* The old saying 'practice makes perfect' is relevant to loving skills, even though perfection in relationships is more myth than reality. By practising your skills conscientiously, not just in crises but all the time, you are likely to improve them. You may become both more confident and also more flexible in applying your skills. There can be a very important gap between learning a skill and putting it into practice. Psychologists call overcoming the gap 'transfer of training'. However, transfer of training can go beyond maintaining a skill to improving it with continued practice.

● *Improving your support network*. People exist in support networks of varying degrees of adequacy. In reality, an individual's network comprises participation in many different networks: family, friends, work colleagues, clubs, church, etc., as well as access to voluntary or professional helpers. With luck, your support network contains people who model and reward the skills you wish to maintain and develop. You may possess an adequate support network, but not use it to best effect. Alternatively, you may need to develop you skills of giving as well as receiving support. Additionally, your support network may be either insufficient or inadequate. In such instances, you may actively have to seek out more rewarding contacts.

● *Participating in a peer support group*. You may choose to meet on a regular basis with a group of other people to work on your loving skills. Being in a support group has the advantage of your being able to practise the skills, observe others' skills, and obtain feedback. Peer support groups can be specifically focused on discussing relationships and helping each other with problems in them. Alternatively, within the context of another focus, for instance either a women's or men's group or a bereavement group, you can work on the relationship skills pertinent to that group's main task.

● *Participating in workshops and training courses*. There are no hard and fast distinctions between training courses and workshops. However, if anything, training courses are spread over a longer period, say a month or more, whereas workshops are relatively intense experiences lasting from a day to a week. Means of finding out about loving skills workshops and training courses include: contact with a counselling service or personnel office; getting in touch with professional associations in psychology, counselling and social work; and keeping an eye on relevant journals and newsletters. In all instances look before you leap. Since acquiring good loving skills requires much work and practice, courses and workshops offering miracle cures should be avoided. Table 12.2 provides a check-list for assessing training courses and workshops.

Table 12.2 Check-list for assessing training courses and workshops

---

1. What are the goals?
2. What are the methods that may be employed during its life?
3. What is the pertinent training and experience of the trainer or trainers?
4. What is the size of the training course or workshop and is there a screening process prior to entry?
5. When does the course or workshop start? How long is each session? Over what period will the course or workshop continue? Where will it be held? Are the facilities adequate?
6. What, if any, is the fee for the course or workshop and are there any additional expenses that may be incurred?

- *Seeing a professional counsellor.* Some of you may consider that you need the services of a professional counsellor to help you improve your skills. On a training course or workshop there may be little chance for the trainer to spend much time on individuals' problems. Also some people are so under-confident that they require a safer environment. Group counselling may be desirable for some of you either instead of, concurrently with, or after individual counselling. Counselling groups tend to comprise a leader and around six to ten members. They provide a more sheltered environment for working on emotional and relationship issues than that found in many training groups and workshops. All the items on the Table 12.2 check-list are relevant to assessing counselling groups.

    Choosing a counsellor can be a difficult process. Counsellors differ greatly in their personalities, knowledge, skills and theoretical orientations. The kind of counsellor who reflects the theoretical orientation of this book would be one combining an existential–humanistic with a cognitive–behavioural perspective. Put in layperson's language somebody who: believes in the concept of loving skills; focuses on thinking and action skills as well as on feelings; and consistently encourages personal responsibility and self-help. Look for a counsellor with whom you feel comfortable and who both supports and challenges you to attain more of your potential. If dissatisfied, be prepared to change your counsellor.

You may not be immediately aware of a suitable counsellor. You may find the name of someone appropriate by asking a helping service professional: for instance, a psychologist, social worker, doctor or priest. You could look up the relevant occupational listings in the phone book. You could also contact a citizen's advice bureau. Additionally, you could make enquiries to relevant local, regional and national professional associations. Table 12.3 provides a listing of some national associations.

Table 12.3 Names and addresses of national professional associations for counselling and for psychology in Australia, Britain and New Zealand

Area	Names and addresses
Australia	
Counselling	The Australian Guidance and Counselling Association, PO Box 214, Pymble, NSW 2073
Psychology	The Australian Psychological Society, National Science Centre, 191 Royal Parade, Parkville, Victoria 3502
Britain	
Counselling	British Association for Counselling, 37A Sheep Street, Rugby CV21 3BX
Psychology	The British Psychological Society, St Andrews House, 48 Princess Road East, Leicester LE1 7DR
New Zealand	
Counselling	New Zealand Counselling and Guidance Association, c/o Dr H. Everts, Department of Education, University of Auckland, Private Bag, Auckland
Psychology	New Zealand Psychological Society, PO Box 4092, Wellington

- *Avoiding burnout.* People who have a combination of difficult environments and of poor skills in looking after themselves and managing relationships tend to be excellent candidates for *burnout*, if not *breakdown*.

Freudenberger (1980) defines burnout as follows: 'To deplete oneself. To exhaust one's physical and mental resources. To wear oneself out by excessively striving to reach some unrealistic expectation imposed by one's self or by the values of society' (p. 17). The better your loving skills, the less likely you are to create unnecessary problems in your relationships. Poor relationships are exhausting. They can lower your energy level so that your effectiveness gets diminished and you find it harder to use your skills.

There are many other skills weaknesses that may contribute to your feeling burned out. These include the following:

– Perfectionistic personal rules in any area of your life.
– Undue need for external approval.
– Poor skills at listening to how stressed your body is.
– Inability to set limits on others to say no to unreasonable requests.
– Inability to set limits on yourself and avoid needing to be 'superwoman' or 'superman'.
– Assuming too much responsibility for others' lives and too little for your own.
– Poor skills at leading a balanced life and having adequate recreational outlets.
– Poor skills at looking after your health and physical fitness.
– Poor time-management skills.
– Poor skills at managing problems and making decisions.

People who are punch-drunk with exhaustion often lack the energy to use good loving skills. They are cranky, irritable and can get highly abusive. Their perceptions of others gets coloured by their own distress and they are more likely to be disappointed in them. In Chapter 10, I mentioned some skills of managing stress: for instance, mental and visual relaxation, developing adequate recreational outlets and developing managing-problems skills. Feelings of exhaustion, being excessively stressed, and having no resilience can have numerous causes both within and outside your relationships. Consequently, you may need to use a wide variety of skills to deal with them adequately. When you are thoroughly run down, you do not feel at your most skilled. Consequently, where possible, preventing burnout is far preferable to trying to cure it.

● *Relevant reading.* Though requiring supplementing by practice, reading relevant books and articles is a further way to develop your loving skills. In the bibliography at the end I have marked with an asterisk books and articles likely to be of interest to the self-help reader. A further suggestion is to view this book as an ongoing resource. One approach is to go through the whole book every now and then as a refresher. Another approach is to focus on specific chapters, exercises and experiments when you consider you require further work to maintain and develop a skill.

EXERCISE
—47—

Maintaining and developing my loving skills

INSTRUCTIONS

Below are listed a number of different methods by which you can maintain and develop your loving skills. Using the worksheet below, assess whether and how you might use each method.

Method	My assessment of whether and how I can use each method
Viewing relating in skills terms	
Clarifying my values	
Remaining open to inner and outer feedback	
Having a contract	
Working together with a partner	

Co-counselling	
Practising my skills daily	
Improving my support network	
Participating in a peer support group	
Participating in workshops and training courses	
Seeing a professional counsellor	
Avoiding burnout	
Relevant reading	
Other methods not mentioned above	

Develop a plan for maintaining and improving your loving skills.

THE CHALLENGE OF LOVING RELATIONSHIPS

The stark truth is that many, if not most, close relationships end up in hatred, pain, mutual recrimination and often in hurting innocent parties, such as children. Also, many work settings are characterized by considerable hostility. Each person possesses their past and present pain and their skills weaknesses. However, the challenge of loving relationships is to affirm yourself and others despite these adverse factors. The answer to the challenge is to strive to use, maintain and develop your loving skills. Whatever progress you make, however slight, is a triumph. Thereby you choose to increase your own, other people's and the world's store of happiness.

CONCLUDING SELF-TALK

I am responsible for maintaining and developing my loving skills. I am constantly being challenged to make good choices in my relationships. Pressures not to do so can come both from within and outside me. Reassessing my skills can help me to pinpoint weaknesses and to do something about them.

There are many methods by which I can both maintain and develop my loving skills. These methods include: viewing relating in skills terms; clarifying my values; remaining open to inner and outer feedback; having a contract; working together with a partner; co-counselling; practising my skills daily; improving my support network; participating in a peer support group; participating in workshops and training courses; seeing a professional counsellor; avoiding burnout; and relevant reading.

Maintaining and developing my loving skills involves me in affirming my strengths despite adverse circumstances. This is hard work and I need to hang in there. I CAN AND WILL DEVELOP THE STRENGTH AND SKILLS TO BE A MORE LOVING PERSON.

BIBLIOGRAPHY

References likely to be of special interest to the self-help reader are indicated with an asterisk.

* Alberti, R.E. & Emmons, M.L. (1986) *Your Perfect Right: A Guide to Assertive Living* (5th edn.). San Luis Obispo, CA: Impact Publishers.

Altman, I. & Taylor, D.A. (1965) Interpersonal exchange in isolation. *Sociometry*, 28, 411–426.

Argyle, M. (1983) *The Psychology of Interpersonal Behaviour* (4th edn.). Harmondsworth: Penguin.

Argyle, M. (1984) Some new developments in social skills training. *Bulletin of the British Psychological Society*, 37(12), 405–410.

*Argyle, M. & Henderson, M. (1985) *The Anatomy of Relationships*. Harmondsworth: Penguin.

Australian Department of Immigration, Local Government and Ethnic Affairs (1988) *Australia's Population Trends and Prospects 1988*. Canberra: Australian Government Publishing Service.

Australian Institute of Family Studies (1985) *Families and Australia's Economic Future*. Melbourne: Australian Institute of Family Affairs.

Azrin, N.H., Besalel, V.A., Michalicek, A., Mancera, M., Carroll, D., Shuford, D. & Cox, J. (1980) Comparison of reciprocity and discussion-type counseling for marital problems. *American Journal of Family Therapy*, 8, 21–28.

Azrin, N.H., Naster, B.J. & Jones, R. (1973) Reciprocity counseling: A rapid learning-based procedure for marital counseling. *Behaviour Research and Therapy*, 11, 365–382.

*Bach, G.R. and Torbet, L. (1983) *The Inner Enemy*. New York: Berkley Books.

*Bach, G.R. & Wyden, P. (1968) *The Intimate Enemy*. New York: Avon.

Bandura, A. (1977) *Social Learning Theory*. Englewood Cliffs, NJ: Prentice-Hall.

Baucom, D.H. & Lester, G.W. (1986) The usefulness of cognitive restructuring as an adjunct to behavioral marital therapy. *Behavior Therapy*, 17, 385–403.

Beck, A.T. (1976) *Cognitive Therapy and the Emotional Disorders*. New York: New American Library.

Bem, S.L. (1974) The measurement of psychological androgyny. *Journal of Consulting and Clinical Psychology*, 42(2), 155–162.

Bem, S.L. (1981) Gender schema theory: A cognitive account of sex typing. *Psychological Review*, 88(4), 354–364.

Berensen, B.G., Mitchell, K.M. & Laney, R.C. (1968) Level of therapist functioning, types of confrontation and type of patient. *Journal of Clinical Psychology*, 24, 111–113.

* Berne, E. (1964) *Games People Play*. New York: Grove Press.

Bernstein, D.A. & Borkovec, T.D. (1973) *Progressive Relaxation Training: A Manual for the Helping Professions*. Champaign, IL: Research Press.

Besalel, V.A. & Azrin, N.H. (1981) The reduction of parent–youth problems by reciprocity counseling. *Behaviour Research and Therapy*, 19, 297–301.

* Bianchi, S.M. (1984) Wives who earn more than their husbands. *American Demographics*, 6(7), 19–23 & 44.

* Bianchi, S.M. & Seltzer, J.A. (1986) Life without father. *American Demographics*, 8(12), 43–47.

* Bloom, D.E. (1986) Women and work. *American Demographics*, 8(9), 25–30.

* Bolton, R. (1979) *People Skills: How to Assert Yourself, Listen to Others, and Resolve Conflicts*. Englewood Cliffs, NJ: Prentice-Hall.

* Bower, S.H. & Bower, G.H. (1976) *Asserting Your Self: A Practical Guide for Positive Change*. Reading, MA: Addison-Wesley.

* Brown, P. & Faulder, C. (1977) *Treat Yourself to Sex*. Harmondsworth: Penguin.

* Burley-Allen, M. (1982) *Listening: The Forgotten Skill*. New York: John Wiley.

Butler, G. & Mathews, A. (1987) Anticipatory anxiety and risk perception. *Cognitive Therapy and Research*, 11(5), 551–565.

* Butler, P.E. (1981) *Self-assertion for Women* (rev. edn.). San Francisco: Harper & Row.

Camper, P.M., Jacobson, N.S., Holtzworth-Munroe, A. & Schmaling, K.B. (1988) Causal attributions for interactional behavior in married couples. *Cognitive Therapy and Research*, 12(2), 195–209.

* Carkhuff, R.R. (1983) *The Art of Helping* (5th edn.). Amherst, MA: Human Resource Development Press.

Carmichael, G.A. (1985) Remarriage among divorced persons

in New Zealand. *Australian Journal of Social Issues*, **20**, 87–104.

Chelune, G.J. (1976) Reactions to male and female disclosure at two levels. *Journal of Personality and Social Psychology*, **34**(5), 1000–1003.

* Comfort, A. (1972) *The Joy of Sex: A Gourmet Guide to Lovemaking*. New York: Quartet.

* Comfort, A. (1973) *More Joy of Sex: A Lovemaker's Companion*. New York: Quartet.

Cozby, P. (1973) Self disclosure: a literature review. *Psychological Bulletin*, **79**, 73–91.

Cunningham, J.D. & Antill, J.K. (1981) Love in developing romantic relationships. In Duck, S. & Gilmour, R. (eds), *Personal Relationships. 2: Developing Personal Relationships*, pp. 27–51. New York: Academic Press.

Deffenbacher, J.L., Story, D.A., Brandon, A.D., Hogg, J.A. & Hazaleus, S.L. (1988) Cognitive and cognitive-relaxation treatments of anger. *Cognitive Therapy and Research*, **12**(2), 167–184.

Deffenbacher, J.L., Story, D.A., Stark, R.A., Hogg, J.A. & Brandon, A.D. (1987) Cognitive-relaxation and social skills interventions in the treatment of general anger. *Journal of Counseling Psychology*, **34**(2), 171–176.

* Derlega, V.J. & Chaikin, A.L., (1975) *Sharing Intimacy: What We Reveal to Others and Why*. Englewood Cliffs, NJ: Prentice-Hall.

Deutsch, M. (1973) *The Resolution of Conflict*. New Haven: Yale University Press.

Duck, S. (1983) *Friends for Life: The Psychology of Close Relationships*. Brighton: The Harvester Press.

Duck, S. (1986) *Human Relationships: An Introduction to Social Psychology*. Beverly Hills, CA: Sage Publications.

Eakins, B.W. & Eakins, R.G. (1978) *Sex Differences in Human Communication*. Boston: Houghton Mifflin.

* Egan, G. (1977) *You and Me: The Skills of Communicating and Relating to Others*. Monterey, CA: Brooks/Cole.

Egan, G. (1986) *The Skilled Helper: A Systematic Approach to Effective Helping* (3rd edn.). Monterey, CA: Brooks/Cole.

Eichler, M. (1983) *Families in Canada Today: Recent Changes and Their Policy Consequences*. Toronto: Gage Publishing.

Eidelson, R.J. & Epstein, N. (1982) Cognition and relationship maladjustment: development of a measure of dysfunctional relationship beliefs. *Journal of Consulting and Clinical Psychology*, 50, 721–726.

* Ekman, P., Friesen, W.V. & Bear, J. (1984) The international language of gestures. *Psychology Today*, May, 64–69.

Ekman, P., Friesen, W.V. & Ellsworth, P. (1972) *Emotions in the Human Face*. New York: Pergamon.

Ellis, A. (1980) Overview of the clinical theory of rational–emotive therapy. In R. Grieger and J. Boyd (eds), *Rational–emotive Therapy: A Skills Based Approach*, pp. 1–31. New York: Van Nostrand Reinhold.

Epstein, N., Pretzer, J.L. & Fleming, B. (1987) The role of cognitive appraisal in self-reports of marital communication. *Behavior Therapy*, 18, 51–69.

Feindler, E.L., Marriott, S.A. & Iwata, M. (1984) Group anger control training for junior high school delinquents. *Cognitive Therapy and Research*, 8(3), 299–311.

Fincham, F.D. (1985) Attribution processes in distressed and nondistressed couples. 2. Responsibility for marital problems. *Journal of Abnormal Psychology*, 94(2), 183–190.

Fincham, F.D., Beach, S.R. & Baucom, D.H. (1987) Attribution processes in distressed and nondistressed couples. 4. Self-partner attribution differences. *Journal of Personality and Social Psychology*, 52(4), 739–748.

Fincham, F.D., Beach, S. & Nelson, G. (1987) Attribution processes in distressed and nondistressed couples. 3. Causal and responsibility attributions for spouse behavior. *Cognitive Therapy and Research*, 11(1), 71–86.

* Freudenberger, H.J. (1980) *Burnout: The High Cost of High Achievement*. London: Arrow Books.

Frisch, M.B. & Froberg, W. (1987) Social validation of assertion strategies for handling aggressive criticism: evidence for consistency across situations. *Behavior Therapy*, 2, 181–191.

* Fromm, E. (1956) *The Art of Loving*. New York: Bantam Books.

Glasser, W. (1984) *Control Theory*. New York: Harper & Row.

* Glick, P.C. (1984) How American families are changing. *American Demographics*, 6(1), 20–25.

Goldstein, A.P. & Keller, H. (1987) *Aggressive Behavior: Assessment and Intervention*. New York: Pergamon Press.

* Gordon, T. (1970) *Parent Effectiveness Training*. New York: Wyden.

Grebe, S.C. (1986) Mediation in separation and divorce. *Journal of Counseling and Development*, 64(2), 379–382.

Haase, R.F. & Tepper, D. (1972) Nonverbal components of empathic communication. *Journal of Counseling Psychology*, 19, 417–424.

Hall, E.T. (1966) *The Hidden Dimension*. New York: Doubleday.

Haskey, J. (1986) One-parent families in Great Britain. *Population Trends*, 45, 5–13.

Haskey, J. (1988) Mid-1985 based population projections by marital status. *Population Trends*, 52, 30–32.

Hazaleus, S.L. & Deffenbacher, J.L. (1986) Relaxation and cognitive treatments of anger. *Journal of Consulting and Clinical Psychology*, 54(2), 222–226.

Henley, N.M. (1977) *Body Politics: Power, Sex and Nonverbal Communication*. Englewood Cliffs, NJ: Prentice-Hall.

Hutson, T.L., Surra, C.A., Fitzgerald, N.M. & Cate, R.M. (1981) From courtship to marriage: mate selection as an interpersonal process. In Duck, S. & Gilmour, R. (eds), *Personal Relationships. 2: Developing Personal Relationships*, pp. 53–88. New York: Academic Press.

Ivey, A.E. (1971) *Microcounseling: Innovations in Interviewing Training*. Springfield, IL: Charles C. Thomas.

Jacobson, N.S., Follette, V.M., Follette, W.C., Holtzworth-Munroe, A., Katt, J.L. & Schmaling, K.B. (1985) A component analysis of behavioral marital therapy: 1-year follow-up. *Behaviour Research and Therapy*, 23(5), 549–555.

Jacobson, N.S. & Margolin, G. (1979) *Marital Therapy: Strategies Based on Social Learning and Behavior Exchange Principles*. New York: Brunner/Mazel.

Jacobson, N.S., McDonald, D.W., Follette, W.C. & Berley, R.A. (1985) Attributional processes in distressed and non-distressed married couples. *Cognitive Therapy and Research*, 9(1), 35–50.

* James, J. & Schlesinger, I. (1987) *Are You the Right One for Me? How to Choose the Right Partner*. Reading: MA: Addison-Wesley.

James, W.A. (1983) Decline in coital rates with spouses' ages and duration of marriage. *Journal of Biosocial Science*, 15, 83–87.

* Johnson, D.W. (1986) *Reaching Out: Interpersonal Effectiveness and Self-actualization* (3rd edn.). Englewood Cliffs, NJ: Prentice-Hall.

* Jourard, S.M. (1964) *The Transparent Self*. New York: Van Nostrand Reinhold.
* Jourard, S.M. (1971a) *The Transparent Self* (rev. edn.). New York: Van Nostrand Reinhold.
Jourard, S.M. (1971b) *Self-disclosure: An Experimental Analysis of the Transparent Self*. New York: John Wiley.
Kagan, N. (1984) Interpersonal process recall: basic methods and recent research. In Larsen, D. *Teaching Psychological Skills*, pp. 261–269. Monterey, CA: Brooks/Cole.
Kaplan, H.S. (1974) *The New Sex Therapy: Active Treatment of Sexual Dysfunctions*. New York: Brunner/Mazel.
*Kassorla, I.C. (1980) *Nice Girls Do*. New York: Berkley Books.
* Kassorla, I.C. (1984) *Go for It: How to Win at Love, Work and Play*. New York: Dell.
* King, M.L. (1963) *Strength to Love*. New York: Harper & Row.
Kinsey, A.C., Pomeroy, W.B. & Martin, C.E. (1948) *Sexual Behavior in the Human Male*. Philadelphia: W.B. Saunders.
Kinsey, A.C., Pomeroy, W.B., Martin, C.E. & Gebhard, P.H. (1953) *Sexual Behavior in the Human Female*. Philadelphia: W.B. Saunders.
* Kohn, A. (1987) Shattered innocence. *Psychology Today*, February, 54–58.
* Lewinsohn, P.M., Munoz, R.F., Youngren, M.A. & Zeiss, A.M. (1986) *Control Your Depression* (rev. edn.). New York: Prentice Hall Press.
Lopez, F.G. & Thurman, C.W. (1986) A cognitive-behavioral investigation of anger among college students. *Cognitive Therapy and Research*, 10(2) 245–256.
Maslow, A.H. (1962) *Toward a Psychology of Being*. Princeton: Van Nostrand.
Maslow, A.H. (1970) *Motivation and Personality* (2nd edn.). New York: Harper & Row.
* Masters, W.H. & Johnson, V.C. (1975) *The Pleasure Bond*. New York: Bantam.
McDonald, P. (1988) Families in the future: The pursuit of personal autonomy. *Family Matters*, 22, 40–47.
McKie, D.C., Prentice, B. & Reed, P. (1983) *Divorce: Law and the Family in Canada*. Ottawa: Statistics Canada.
* Meichenbaum, D. (1983) *Coping with Stress*. London: Century Publishing.
Meichenbaum, D. (1985) *Stress Inoculation Training*. New York: Pergamon Press.

Moon, J.R. & Eisler, R.R. (1983) Anger control: an experimental comparison of three behavioral treatments. *Behavior Therapy*, 14, 493–505.

MORI (1983) *Survey*. London: Market Opinion Research International.

Nelson-Jones, R. (1984) *Personal Responsibility Counseling and Therapy*. Milton Keynes: Open University Press.

Nelson-Jones, R. (1988) *Practical Counselling and Helping Skills* (2nd edn.). London: Cassell.

* Nelson-Jones, R. (1989) *Effective Thinking Skills: Preventing and Managing Personal Problems*. London: Cassell.

Nelson-Jones, R. & Coxhead, P. (1980) Neuroticism, social desirability and anticipations and attributions affecting self-disclosure. *British Journal of Medical Psychology*, 53, 164–180.

Nelson-Jones, R. & Dryden, W. (1979) Anticipated risk and gain from negative and positive self-disclosures. *British Journal of Social and Clinical Psychology*, 18, 79–80.

Nelson-Jones, R. & Strong, S.R., (1976) Positive and negative self-disclosure, timing and personal attraction. *British Journal of Social and Clinical Psychology*, 15, 323–325.

Nelson-Jones, R. & Strong, S.R. (1977) British students' positive and negative evaluations of personal characteristics. *Journal of College Student Personnel*, 18(1), 32–37.

Novaco, R.W. (1977) Stress inoculation: a cognitive therapy for anger and its applications to a case of depression. *Journal of Consulting and Clinical Psychology*, 45, 600–608.

Oakley, A. (1972) *Sex, Gender, & Society*. London: Temple Smith.

Office of Population Census and Surveys (1987) Editorial: A review of 1986. *Population Trends*, 50, 1–12.

Office of Population Census and Surveys (1988) Tables: Table 12. *Population Trends*, 53, 56.

* Pease, A. (1981) *Body Language: How to Read Others' Thoughts by Their Gestures*. Sydney: Camel.

Pietromonaco, P.R. & Rook, K.S. (1987) Decision style in depression: The contribution of perceived risks versus benefits. *Journal of Personality and Social Psychology*, 52(2), 399–408.

Platt, J.J., Pout, M.F. & Metzger, D.S. (1986) Inter-personal cognitive problem-solving therapy (ICPS). In W. Dryden & W. Golden (eds), *Cognitive–Behavioural Approaches to Psychotherapy*, pp. 261–269. London: Harper & Row.

* Powell, J. (1969) *Why Am I Afraid to Love?* London: Fontana.
* Pryor, E. & Norris, D. (1983) Canada in the eighties. *American Demographics*, 5(12), 25–29 & 44.
* Robey, B. & Russell, C. (1984) Trends: All Americans. *American Demographics*, 6(2), 32–35.
Rogers, C.R. (1959) A theory of therapy, personality and inter-personal relationships as developed in the client-centred framework. In S. Koch (ed.). *Psychology: A Study of Science* (Study 1, Volume 3), pp. 184–256. New York: McGraw-Hill.
* Rogers, C.R. (1961) *On Becoming a Person.* Boston: Houghton Mifflin.
* Rogers, C.R. (1973) *Becoming Partners: Marriage and Its Alternatives.* London: Constable.
* Rogers, C.R. (1980) *A Way of Being.* Boston: Houghton Mifflin.
Rubin, Z. (1970) Measurement of romantic love. *Journal of Personality and Social Psychology*, 16(2), 265–273.
* Russell, C. & Exter, T. G. (1986) America at mid-decade. *American Demographics*, 8(1), 22–29.
Rutter, M. (1972) *Maternal Deprivation Reassessed.* Harmondsworth: Penguin Books.
* Satir, V. (1972) *Peoplemaking.* Palo Alto, CA: Science and Behavior Books.
* Selye, H. (1974) *Stress without Distress.* Sevenoaks: Hodder and Stoughton.
Shaw, C. (1988) Latest estimates of ethnic minority populations. *Population Trends*, 51, 5–8.
* Simonton, O.C., Matthews-Simonton, S. & Creighton, J.L. (1978) *Getting Well Again.* New York: Bantam Books.
* Solomon, M.R. (1986) Dress for effect. *Psychology Today*, April, 20–28.
* Spain, D. & Bianchi, S.M. (1983) How women have changed. *American Demographics*, 5(5), 19–25.
Steck, L., Levitan, D., McLane, D. & Kelley, H.H. (1982) Care, need, and conceptions of love. *Journal of Personality and Social Psychology*, 43(3), 481–491.
* Steiner, C.M. (1981) *The Other Side of Power.* New York: Grove Press.
Stuart, R.B. (1980) *Helping Couples Change: A Social Learning Approach to Marital Therapy.* New York: Guilford Press.

* Tavris, C. (1989) *Anger: The Misunderstood Emotion* (rev. edn). New York: Simon and Schuster.

Taylor, D.A. & Altman, I. (1966) *Intimacy-scaled Stimuli for Use in Studies of Interpersonal Relationships*. Bethesda, MD: Naval Medical Research Institute.

* Timnick, L. (1983) When women rape men. *Psychology Today*, September, 74–75.

* Trotter, R.J. (1986) The three faces of love. *Psychology Today*, September, 46–50 & 54.

Warren, N. & Gilner, F.H. (1978) Measurement of positive assertive behaviors: the behavioral test of tenderness expression. *Behavior Therapy*, 9, 178–184.

Watson, O.M. (1972) *Proxemic Behavior: A Cross Cultural Study*. The Hague: Mowton.

White, K.M., Speisman, J.C., Jackson, D., Bartis, S. & Costos, D. (1986) Intimacy maturity and its correlates in young married couples. *Journal of Personality and Social Psychology*, 50(1), 157–162.

Willison, B.G. & Masson, R.L. (1986) The role of touch in therapy: An adjunct to communication. *Journal of Counseling and Development*, 64(4), 497–500.

* Wilson, B.F. (1984) Marriage's melting pot. *American Demographics*, 6(7), 34–37 & 45.

* Wilson, B.F. & London, K.A. (1987) Going to the chapel. *American Demographics*, 9(12), 26–31.

Wolf, S.S. & Etzel, B.C. (1982) Reciprocity and marital counseling: a replication and analysis. *Behaviour Research and Therapy*, 20, 407–410.

* Zimbardo, P.G. (1977). *Shyness*. Reading, MA: Addison-Wesley.

Subject Index

Name Index